An Introduction to Computers for Paralegals

An Introduction to Computers for Paralegals

Second Edition

Kristen L. Battaile
University of San Diego

ASPEN LAW & BUSINESS
A Division of Aspen Publishers, Inc.

Printed in the United States of America

ISBN 1-56706-483-3

Permissions
Aspen Law & Business
A Division of Aspen Publishers, Inc.
1185 Avenue of the Americas
New York, NY 10036

1 2 3 4 5

To my mom and dad

Summary of Contents

Contents			*ix*
Preface			*xvii*
Acknowledgments			*xix*
Part I	**Overview**		1
	Chapter 1	Computers and the Law	3
	Chapter 2	Computer Hardware	17
	Chapter 3	Computer Software	41
Part II	**Operating Systems and Environments**		67
	Chapter 4	DOS	69
	Chapter 5	Windows	93
	Chapter 6	Windows 95	115
Part III	**Applications**		133
	Chapter 7	Word Processing	135
	Chapter 8	Electronic Spreadsheets	153
	Chapter 9	Databases	175
	Chapter 10	Office Automation	195
	Chapter 11	On-Line Services and the Internet	213
Glossary			*235*
Index			*247*

Contents

Preface *xvii*
Acknowledgments *xix*

Part I Overview **1**

Chapter 1 Computers and the Law 3
A. An Overview of Computers **3**
1. Categories of Computers 4
a. Microcomputer 4
b. Minicomputer 5
c. Mainframe 5
2. Hardware and Software 6
B. The First Uses of Computers in the Law **6**
1. Legal Research 7
a. LEXIS 8
b. WESTLAW 8
2. Legislative Drafting 9
3. Decision Prediction 9
4. Office Automation and Litigation Support 9
a. Law Office Automation 10
i. Service Bureaus 10
ii. Data Processing Machines 10
iii. Time-Sharing Computer Systems 10
b. Court Automation 10
i. Data Processing Machines 11
ii. Computers 11
c. Litigation Support 11
C. Modern Uses of Computers in the Practice of Law **12**
1. Office Automation and Litigation Support 12
2. Court Automation 13
3. Legal Research 13
D. Summary **14**
Key Terms *14*
Questions *15*
Discussion Questions *15*

Chapter 2 Computer Hardware 17
A. Hardware **17**
B. The System Unit **17**

1. The Central Processing Unit 18
a. The Arithmetic/Logic Unit 18
b. The Control Unit 18
c. The Main Memory Unit 19
2. ROM and RAM 19
3. Bits and Bytes 20
4. Microprocessors 21
C. Secondary Memory Storage **21**
1. Magnetic Disks 21
a. Hard Disks 23
b. Diskettes 24
i. Diskette Density 25
ii. Diskette Write Protection 25
iii. Diskette Care 26
2. Magnetic Tape 26
3. Optical Disks 27
a. CD-ROM Disks 27
b. Digital Video Disks (DVD) 28
c. Other Optical Disks 29
D. Input Devices **30**
1. The Keyboard 30
2. Punched Cards 31
3. Scanners 32
4. The Mouse 32
5. Track Balls, Integrated Pointing Devices, and Touch Pads 33
6. Bar Code Readers 34
7. Touch Screens 34
8. Speech Recognition 35
9. Handwriting Recognition 35
E. Output Devices **35**
1. Monitors 36
2. Printers 36
a. Impact Printers 36
b. Nonimpact Printers 36
3. Plotters 37
4. Speakers 37
F. Communications **37**
1. Modems 37
2. Local Area Networks (LANs) 38
3. Wide Area Networks (WANs) 38
4. Electronic Mail 38
G. Summary **39**
Key Terms *39*
Questions *40*
Discussion Questions *40*

Chapter 3 Computer Software 41
A. Software Defined **41**

B. Software Categories 42
1. Computer Languages 42
2. Operating Systems 43
a. DOS 43
b. Windows 95 45
c. Macintosh 45
d. OS/2 46
e. UNIX 46
3. Utility Programs 47
4. Application Programs 47
C. Law Office Software 47
1. Accounting and Time and Billing Software 47
2. Word Processing Software 51
3. Document Generation 51
4. Electronic Spreadsheet Software 52
a. Estate Planning 53
b. Tax Planning 53
c. Family Law 53
5. Damage Calculation Software 53
6. Document Management Software 55
7. Case Management Software 56
8. Calendaring Software 57
9. Forms Software 57
10. Deposition Summarization Software 59
11. Document Imaging 59
12. Database Management Systems 60
a. Summary Databases 60
b. Full-Text Databases 61
13. Communications Software 63
a. Modem and Fax Communications 63
b. Network Communications 64
D. Computer Software Copyrights and Ethical Considerations 64
E. Summary 65
Key Terms 65
Questions 66
Discussion Questions 66

Part II Operating Systems and Environments 67

Chapter 4 DOS 69
A. Introduction 69
1. Disk Organization 70
a. Drive Labels 70
b. Moving Between Drives 70
c. Directories 70
2. Files 72
B. DOS Commands 73
1. Formatting Disks—FORMAT 73

2. Displaying a List of Directories and Files 74
   a. *DIR* 74
   b. *Displaying a List of Files in a Directory* 75
   c. *Displaying a List of Files on Another Drive* 76
   d. *Displaying a List of Specific Files* 77
   e. *DIR/P* 77
   f. *DIR/W* 78
3. Making Directories—MD or MKDIR 79
4. Changing Directories—CD or CHDIR 82
5. Removing Directories—RD 84
6. Copying Files—COPY 85
7. Renaming Files—REN or RENAME 85
8. Erasing and Deleting Files—ERASE and DEL 86
9. Copying Disks—DISKCOPY 87

C. Global (Wild Card) Characters 87
D. Running an Application 88
E. Summary 89

Key Terms 89
DOS Commands List 89
Questions 91
Discussion Questions 91

Chapter 5 Windows 93

A. Using the Mouse 93
B. The Desktop, Windows, Dialog Boxes, and Icons 94
1. The Desktop 94
2. Windows 94
3. Dialog Boxes 95
4. Icons 96

C. Program Groups 96
1. Creating New Program Groups 96
2. Adding New Application Icons 97
3. Deleting Application Icons and Program Groups 97

D. The Pull-Down Menus 97
1. Keyboard Access to Menus 98
2. Keystroke Access to Dialog Boxes 98
3. Running an Application from the File Menu 98
4. Saving the Screen Settings 98

E. Windows Help 99
F. The File Manager 99
1. Drive Labels 99
2. Selecting a Drive 99
3. Directories 100
4. Files 101
5. Managing Files and Directories 102
   a. *Acting on Files* 102
   b. *Acting on Directories* 103

6. Disk Options 104
a. Formatting a Disk 104
b. Copying a Disk 104
G. A Case Example **105**
1. Creating a Directory Folder 105
2. Entering a Program 105
a. Saving a File 105
b. Exiting the Word Processor 106
3. Creating a Subdirectory 106
4. Moving a File 107
5. Copying a File or Folder to a Diskette 108
6. Deleting a File 109
7. Deleting a Directory Folder 109
H. Switching Between Applications **110**
I. Using the DOS Prompt **110**
J. Exiting Windows **111**
K. Summary **112**
Key Terms *112*
Questions *112*
Discussion Questions *113*

Chapter 6 Windows 95 115
A. Using the Mouse **115**
B. Windows 95 Basics **116**
1. The Desktop 116
2. Windows 116
3. Dialog Boxes 117
4. Icons 118
5. Shortcuts 118
6. Properties 119
C. The Start Menu **119**
1. Start Menu Options 120
2. The Programs Option 121
3. Adding and Deleting Program Folders 121
4. Adding and Deleting Shortcuts from a Program Folder 122
D. Running a Program **122**
1. Starting a Program 122
2. Pull-Down Menus 123
3. File Names 123
4. Specifying a Path When Opening and Saving Files 123
5. Opening a File 124
6. Saving a File 124
7. Exiting a Program 124
E. The My Computer Window **124**
1. Managing Folders and Files 125
a. Adding a New Folder 126
b. Changing the Name of a Folder or File 126

c. Moving a Folder or File 126
d. Copying a Folder or File 127
e. Acting on Multiple Folders and Files 127
f. Copying to a Diskette 127
g. Deleting Folders and Files 127
2. Formatting a Diskette 127
3. Creating Shortcuts 128
F. The Windows Explorer 128
1. Viewing the Tree 129
2. Managing Folders and Files 129
3. Creating Shortcuts 129
G. Exiting Windows 95 129
H. Summary 129
Key Terms 130
Questions 130
Discussion Questions 131

Part III Applications 133

Chapter 7 Word Processing 135
A. Word Processing 135
B. How the Legal Professional Uses a Word Processor 136
C. Common Word Processor Terms and Functions 136
1. Word Wrapping 136
2. Cursor 137
3. Insert and Typeover 137
4. Highlighting Text 137
5. Deleting Characters, Words, and Blocks of Text 138
6. Moving and Copying Text 138
7. Boldfacing, Underlining, and Italicizing Text 138
a. Boldfacing 139
b. Underlining 139
c. Italicizing 139
8. Justification 139
9. Centering 139
10. Tabbing and Indenting 140
11. Page Breaks 140
12. Spell Checking 142
13. Thesauruses 142
14. Fonts 142
D. Saving and Opening Documents 143
1. Saving a Document 143
2. Back-up Options 144
3. Opening a Document 144
E. Columns 144
F. Tables 145

G. **Merging** **146**
H. **Macros** **147**
I. **Printing** **150**
J. **Summary** **150**
Key Terms *151*
Questions *151*
Discussion Questions *151*
Exercise *152*

Chapter 8 Electronic Spreadsheets 153
A. **What Are Electronic Spreadsheets?** **153**
B. **Common Electronic Spreadsheet Terms** **154**
1. Columns and Rows 154
2. Cells 155
3. Cell Addresses 155
4. Cell Pointer 155
5. Ranges of Cells 156
6. Cell Entries 156
7. Input Line 157
C. **Electronic Spreadsheet Features** **157**
1. Adjustment of Columns and Rows 157
2. Automatic Recalculation 158
3. Relative and Absolute Cell Addresses 159
4. Moving and Copying Cells 160
5. Printing 161
D. **Spreadsheet Analysis and the "What If" Scenario** **161**
E. **The "What If" Scenario and Particular Areas of the Law** **163**
1. Estate Planning 163
2. Tax Planning 165
3. Family Law 165
F. **Summary** **169**
Key Terms *170*
Questions *170*
Discussion Questions *171*
Exercise *171*

Chapter 9 Databases 175
A. **Databases in the Law Office** **175**
B. **Summary Databases** **176**
1. Relational Operators 177
2. Connectors 178
a. NOT 178
b. AND 179
c. OR 179

3. Setting Up a Summary Database 180
4. Searching a Summary Database 183

C. Full-Text Databases 185

1. Full-Text Research Databases 185
   - *a. Computer-Assisted Legal Research (LEXIS and WESTLAW)* 185
   - *b. CD-ROM* 186
2. Full-Text Litigation Support Databases 187
3. Searching the Full-Text Database 187
   - *a. Key Words* 188
   - *b. Connectors* 188
   - *c. Proximity Operators* 189
   - *d. Root Expanders and Wild Card Characters* 189
   - *e. The Search Query* 189

D. Summary 190

Key Terms 191
Questions 192
Discussion Questions 192
Exercise 192

Chapter 10 Office Automation 195

A. The Computer Purchase 196

1. Assessing the Individual's or the Firm's Needs 196
2. Weighing the Costs 197
3. Projecting Future Growth 199
4. Shopping for the Computer System 199
5. Making the Purchase 200
6. Signing the Contract 201

B. Computer Organization 201

1. Disk Organization 201
2. Naming Files 205
3. System Backup 207
4. Archiving 208
5. The Contingency Plan 208
6. Passwords 209

C. Summary 209

Key Terms 211
Questions 211
Discussion Questions 211

Chapter 11 On-Line Services and the Internet 213

A. On-Line Etiquette 213

1. Message Boards and Newsgroups 214
2. E-Mail 214
3. FTP Sites 214
4. Chats 215
5. Tone of Message 215

B. Bulletin Board Systems **215**
1. Accessing a BBS 216
2. Downloading Files 217
3. Leaving the BBS 218
4. Law-Related BBSs 218

C. Commercial On-Line Services **218**
1. Accessing the Commercial On-Line Services 218
2. Sending E-Mail 219
3. Downloading Files 220
4. Internet Gateways 221
5. Posting and Reading Messages on Message Boards 221
6. Chats 221

D. The Internet **221**
1. Accessing the Internet 222
2. Internet Domains 222
3. UNIX 223
4. E-Mail 225
5. Mailing Lists 225
6. Usenet 226
7. Telnet 227
8. FTP 228
9. Gopher and WAIS 229
10. The World Wide Web 231

E. Summary **233**

Key Terms *233*
Questions *234*
Discussion Questions *234*

Glossary *235*
Index *247*

Preface

This book is written for the paralegal student and for practicing paralegals and other legal professionals. It provides essential background about computers and computing, and includes questions and exercises to test the student's knowledge and provide practical experience.

My intent in writing this book is to provide the paralegal student with a basic knowledge of the hardware and software found in the law office, while including advanced and little-known features for the student who already has a computer background. The text follows a logical order for teaching computers, beginning with a discussion of hardware and software and then moving on to specific software packages and computer systems used in the practice of law.

Due to the variety of computer systems and software used in training the paralegal student and used by the practicing legal professional, the text includes chapters on different operating systems, word processing programs, electronic spreadsheets, databases, and the Internet and on-line services. Students can study the chapters that apply to their computer system. Although no text can keep up with the rapidly changing computer technology, I have tried to provide the reader with fundamental current information, leaving it up to the instructor to discuss the most recent technological advances.

Today, a knowledge of computers is essential for paralegals and other legal professionals. Computers are on the desk of nearly every secretary, paralegal, and attorney. Paralegals are using computers to create documents, manage evidence, analyze alternatives, manage case information, and perform legal research. The law office tasks that can be performed on a computer are virtually endless. Learning about computers *can* be fun and interesting as new ways are discovered to computerize everyday tasks.

I hope that this book will provide the reader with a solid introduction to computers and with the confidence to master new computers and software.

Acknowledgments

I would like to thank the many people whose efforts and contributions helped to create this book: Susan Sullivan of the University of San Diego Lawyer's Assistant Program for giving me the opportunity to teach computers to paralegals, and without whom this book could never have been written; the staff and faculty of the University of San Diego; the Academic Computing Department, specifically Dr. Jack Pope, John Paul, and Hannah Kinney, for assisting me in locating specific software packages and for providing answers to my difficult questions; and the many hardware and software companies that provided me with information about and photographs of their products and services.

My admiration and thanks go to the editors and staff at Little, Brown and Company for their tireless efforts and professionalism in creating this book. Special thanks to Carol McGeehan, Elizabeth Kenny, Joan Horan, and my text editor, Richard Audet.

Thanks to my parents for giving me support, opportunities, and encouragement throughout my life.

And special thanks to my wonderful husband, Bill, and my daughters, Katie and Kimberly, for enduring my long hours and occasional irritability, while encouraging my endeavors.

I am grateful to those companies whose products I frequently mentioned in this text for their generous permission to reprint information about and examples of their products:

Figures 2.4 and 2.8 courtesy of Toshiba American Information Systems, Inc.
Figure 2.5 courtesy of Memtek Products, Inc.
Figure 2.6 by permission of Imation Enterprises Corp., Oakdale, MN.
Figure 2.9 courtesy of International Business Machines Corporation. Unauthorized use not permitted.
Figures 2.10, 2.11, and 2.12 courtesy of Logitech, Inc.
Figures 3.1-3.3, 5.1-5.9, 6.1-6.7, and 10.1-10.4 copyright © Microsoft Corporation. Screen shots reprinted by permission from Microsoft Corporation.
Figure 3.4, System 7.1 screen, copyright © 1983-1992, Apple Computer, Inc., Used with permission. Apple® and the Apple logo are registered trademarks of Apple Computer, Inc. All rights reserved.
Figure 3.11 courtesy of Advocate Software.
Figures 3.12, 3.13, and 3.14 courtesy of Abacus Data Systems, Inc.
Figures 7.2, 7.5, 7.6, and 7.8, copyright © 1991-1996 Corel Corporation Limited. All rights reserved. Reprinted with permission from Corel Corporation Limited.
Figure 9.3 reprinted with the permission of LEXIS-NEXIS, a division of Reed Elsevier Inc. LEXIS® is a registered trademark of Reed Elsevier Properties Inc.
Figure 9.3 (screen contents) reprinted with permission of Bancroft-Whitney, a division of Thomson Legal Publishing.
Figure 11.1 courtesy of Paul Bernstein, Alfred Roth, Barry Lowe, and Ron Kritzman, Co SysOps, Law MUG BBS.
Figures 11.2 and 11.3 copyright 1995-1996 America Online, Inc. All Rights Reserved.

An Introduction to Computers for Paralegals

PART I

Overview

CHAPTER

1

Computers and the Law

Computers have become a part of our daily lives. In the community, they handle our bank transactions, direct our telephone calls, and calculate our purchases. In our homes, they help us to write letters, manage our money, explore the Internet, send and receive electronic mail, and play games. At work, they help us to prepare documents, communicate with others, analyze alternatives, and obtain information.

As a paralegal, you will use computers to draft letters, pleadings, and memoranda. You will also use computers to manage client accounts and cases, perform legal research, calendar hearings and due dates, and organize evidence and case information.

To begin learning about computers and how you will use them as a paralegal, this chapter will cover

- the definition of a computer
- the three categories of computers
- the definitions of hardware and software
- the first uses of computers in the practice of law
- the ways computers are used today in the practice of law

If you are an experienced computer user, this chapter will provide you with a little legal computing history to add to your knowledge. If you are a computer novice, you will learn, in addition to the history, some basics about the computer and how it operates.

A. AN OVERVIEW OF COMPUTERS

A computer is an electronic machine that can be instructed to perform many tasks quickly and accurately. Legal professionals use computers to

- prepare letters and documents
- prepare billing statements and accounting reports
- organize evidence and case information
- maintain an office calendar
- perform legal research
- analyze alternative scenarios
- develop graphs and drawings
- send electronic mail

To operate a computer the person using the computer—the **user**—selects a set of instructions called a **"program."** Once this selection has been made, the user enters information with a keyboard or other device. Information entered into the computer is called **"input."** The program receives the input and processes it according to the instructions. The processed information, called **"output,"** is directed to a **monitor** (display screen), **printer,** or other output device.

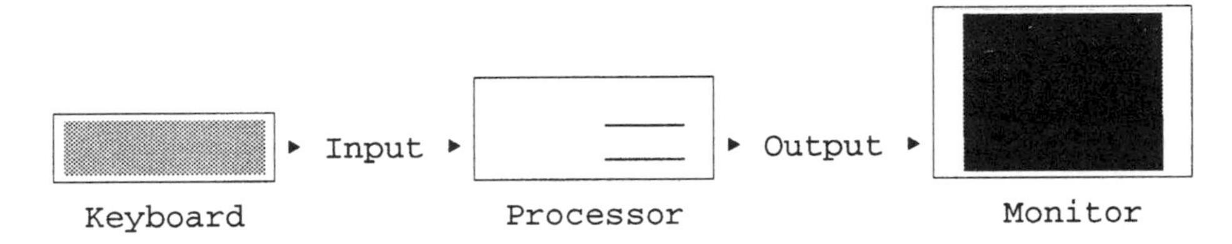

1. Categories of Computers

The computers you see and use fall into categories according to their ability to store and process information. There are three main categories of computers: microcomputers, minicomputers, and mainframes.

a. Microcomputer

Microcomputers are the smallest type of computer and are commonly called **"personal computers"** or **"PCs."** This category includes desktop computers such as laptops, notebooks, subnotebooks, and palmtops. Many law offices use microcomputers as their primary type of office computer. They are the least expensive of the three categories and are easy to use.

Microcomputers can operate alone or can be connected with other computers to form a configuration called a **"local area network"** or **"LAN."** A local area network allows all of the computers in the network to access the same bank of information and to share **peripheral devices** such as printers.

In law offices, local area networks are popular because of their ability to share software, printers, modems, scanners, and other devices. The individual microcomputers in the LAN are called **"workstations."** All of the workstations are cabled together in a LAN formation that allows them to access information from the other workstations or a main workstation called a **"file server."** A big advantage of a LAN is that in the event of a failure of the computer operating the LAN, the individual microcomputers of the network are able to work as independent computers.

b. Minicomputer

Minicomputers are midsized computers that operate at a faster speed than microcomputers and can store more information. The minicomputer is built for multiple users, like a LAN, allowing them to share the same information and peripheral devices. The individual workstation of a minicomputer system can be either a microcomputer or only a keyboard and a monitor. A keyboard and a monitor without a processor is called a **"terminal"** and is dependent on the minicomputer. While a microcomputer workstation would be able to continue on its own in the event of a failure of the minicomputer, a terminal would be inoperable until the minicomputer was brought back on line.

c. Mainframe

Mainframes are the largest computers and have the greatest capabilities in terms of speed and information storage. These computers are found in law firms whose size and information storage requirements warrant the use and cost of such a large system. The mainframe is a multiple-user machine like the minicomputer. An individual workstation for a mainframe may consist of a microcomputer or a terminal, depending on how the office uses the mainframe.

The term **"supercomputer"** is used to describe the world's fastest computing mainframes. Supercomputers of the past were built with very large central processing units (CPUs). These CPUs can process vast amounts of information quickly but generate a lot of heat and require sufficient air conditioning to allow them to operate. Today's supercomputers use a revolutionary method for processing their information called **"massively parallel processing."** Massively parallel processing was invented as an alternative to the large CPUs. With massively parallel processing, the CPUs of microcomputers, called **"microprocessors,"** are placed side by side within the computer. The parallel processors work together, each handling part of the task that needs to be computed. The first teraflops supercomputer will be built by Intel and Sandia National Laboratories and should be completed in late 1996. "Flops" is short for "floating point operations per second." "Tera" means trillion. Prior to this supercomputer, the fastest computers in the world were measured in gigaflops (billions of floating point operations per second). The processing unit of the Intel/Sandia teraflops will consist of thousands of Intel's Pentium Pro microprocessors. The computer will be located at Sandia National Laboratories in New Mexico, one of the United States' three nuclear weapons laboratories. Its primary function will be to simulate nuclear weapons tests in the laboratory.

2. Hardware and Software

Hardware and software are the main components of a computer system. Hardware and software are discussed in depth in Chapters 2 and 3, respectively.

Hardware consists of the tangible parts of a computer. These tangible parts include

- **The system unit,** which contains the computer's main memory, information processors, circuits, and disk drives;
- **Input devices,** such as a keyboard, which allow a user to input information into the computer; and
- **Output devices,** such as a monitor or printer, which allow a user to see the results of processed information.

Software is the coded program of instructions that directs the computer's hardware in the processing of information. Software can be written by the user or purchased from a software programmer or vendor. Software is sold on one or more magnetic disks or compact disks (CDs). The disks are then inserted into one of the computer's disk drives to be used or to be transferred to the computer's internal magnetic disk.

WordPerfect®, DOS, Lotus® 1-2-3®, and Microsoft® Windows® are all examples of software.

B. THE FIRST USES OF COMPUTERS IN THE LAW

> . . . [R]eliance on computers or on similar devices will, assuredly, blunt a lawyer's professional skills, just as undue reliance on laboratory reports detracts from the accuracy of a doctor's clinical diagnoses. . . .
>
> . . . [M]embers of the Bar will be well advised to stay very far away from computers if they want to remain—or become—lawyers rather than simply attorneys at law. Computers are fine for inertial guidance problems—but the law is neither a missile nor an atomic submarine.
>
> —Frederick Bernays Wiener, Decision Prediction by Computers: Nonsense Cubed—and Worse, 48 A.B.A.J. 1023, 1026, 1028 (Nov. 1962)

In the late 1950s and early 1960s, the use of computers to assist in the practice of law began to be explored. As shown by the quotation above, some attorneys considered the use of computers as contrary to the traditional practice of law. Ignoring the naysayers, computer and legal professionals joined forces to evaluate the practice of law and determine how computers could enhance the field. The first experiments in computerizing legal tasks focused on legal research, legislative drafting, and decision prediction.

1. Legal Research

Legal research was a logical area for the computer to assist in the practice of law. The aim of legal research is to find some similar or pertinent precedent in order to respond to a question or to support or rebut an issue. A computer that could search the entire text of codes and case reporters for specific words or phrases could save the legal professional hours of manual research.

The first public demonstration of computerized legal research occurred at the 83rd Annual Meeting of the American Bar Association in 1960. The demonstration was jointly sponsored by IBM, the Health Law Center of the University of Pittsburgh, the United States Patent Office, and the American Bar Association's Electronic Data Retrieval Committee. An IBM 650 mainframe computer was used for the demonstration.

To create a database of laws regarding hospitals, every state's statutes dealing with hospitals were keypunched onto punch cards and fed into a card reader in the IBM computer. The information from the cards was stored on reels of magnetic tape. Key words relating to an issue were then selected for searching within the database. This process is very similar to the way the LEXIS® and WESTLAW® computer-assisted legal research databases are searched today. The issue for which authority is being sought is broken down into key words that would likely be found in authorities regarding the issue. For example, to locate statutes regarding the permission required from a parent or guardian to perform surgery on a minor, you would search for the key words *minor, permission, hospital* or *physician,* and *parent* or *guardian.*

In the 1960 demonstration, a search was performed by punching the selected key words onto punched cards and reading the cards into the computer. The computer then identified those statutes that contained the key words. The time required to process a search for this demonstration was approximately 26 minutes. This time was consistent for any search run on this bank of statutes due to the use of magnetic tape storage. Magnetic tape uses a sequential access data storage and retrieval method rather than the direct access method of a magnetic disk. This means that the computer must read the entire tape to complete its processing. The processing time increased when more statutes were added to the tape.

The average law office could not afford to implement this type of computer-assisted legal research. The keypunching of all statutes and cases onto punched cards involved incredible labor costs. The IBM computer itself sold for approximately $600,000 or rented for approximately $12,000 per month.

Though the use of this computer-assisted legal research was not practical in the early 1960s, these demonstrations did foster some ideas that were later used in the advanced legal research computer systems of LEXIS and WESTLAW. These ideas included

- a centrally located main computer with law office access through an in-house computer or terminal
- the searching of words within a certain proximity of other words
- the use of a scanner to scan the printed documents into the computer

a. LEXIS

In 1967 the Ohio State Bar Association in conjunction with Data Corporation, which would later become part of Mead Data Central, entered into a contract to form a full-text legal research computer system. This system, named O.B.A.R. (Ohio Bar Automated Research), distinguished itself from previous computer-assisted legal research systems in three ways:

1. The system contained the entire unaltered text of documents, such as statutes, cases, and regulations;
2. the system operated with a centrally located main computer allowing subscribing agencies and attorneys to access the system through the telephone lines and a terminal in their own office; and
3. the system allowed a continuing dialogue with the computer; after an initial search was completed, an attorney could adjust his or her search to more accurately meet research needs.

Using the experience gained in working with the Ohio Bar, Mead Data Central developed LEXIS. LEXIS became commercially available by subscription in May 1973. The original system contained the following databases:

- General Federal Law
- Federal Securities Law
- Federal Tax Law
- New York Law
- Ohio Law
- Missouri Law
- Texas Law
- Illinois Law

b. WESTLAW

WESTLAW, West Publishing Company's computer-assisted legal research system, became available to the legal community in 1975. At that time it differed from LEXIS in that it did not provide the full text of cases and statutes. Instead, WESTLAW contained just the headnotes of decisions, accompanied by West's "key numbering system." An example of a West headnote and key number is shown in Figure 1.1. With the key numbering system, once a desirable headnote is found, its corresponding key number can be entered to search for other cases with headnotes on the same subject.

In early searches of WESTLAW, headnotes that met the search request would be displayed on the terminal screen. WESTLAW organized the applicable headnotes by assigning a relevance factor to each. The more relevant headnotes were displayed first. A search could be refined using the key number corresponding to a particularly relevant headnote.

Like LEXIS, the WESTLAW database was contained within a large central

1. Negligence 🔑103
To prevail on complaint of negligence, plaintiff must show duty, breach of that duty, injury, and that breach of duty was proximate cause of injury.

FIGURE 1.1 A West headnote and corresponding key number.

computer. Access to the WESTLAW database was made through a local terminal or computer using the telephone lines. In the late 1970s WESTLAW added the full text of statutes and opinions to its database.

2. Legislative Drafting

Another early use for computers in the law was in the drafting of new legislation. When proposing new legislation, a legislator in most cases would like it to remain consistent with the current body of law. This involves locating any current statutes within the same jurisdiction that will be affected by the new legislation.

To accomplish a search for related legislation, a database of the desired statutes is selected. Key words relevant to the proposed legislation are then submitted to the computer for processing. Statutes containing the key words are found and listed for the user. The list of statutes is then reviewed by the legislator in order to create compatible legislation. New York was one of the first states to provide a computer tape database of its state statutes.

3. Decision Prediction

The most controversial proposal for the use of computers in the practice of law was the use of a computer to predict judicial decisions. This idea was threatening to attorneys and judges alike. The question arose, "Could the entire practice of law be reduced to attorneys submitting arguments on punched cards to the computer judge for processing?" Justice, it turns out, is not that simple. The inherent problem with computerized decision prediction is that the computer is based on logic. Judicial decisions, however, do not always follow a logical pattern. Emotion, bias, and reasoning all factor into a human judge's decisions, and even computers that utilize artificial intelligence do not emulate all of these human traits well enough to be used to predict decisions.

4. Office Automation and Litigation Support

In the 1960s computers and data processing machines began to be used to automate law offices and courts. Data processing machines—the precursors of computers—

count, organize, and compare data. They cannot run the many different types of programs available for computers.

a. Law Office Automation

Only a few law firms in the 1960s could actually afford to have a computer in their offices. Early automation of law office functions, therefore, involved the use of service bureaus, data processing machines, and time-sharing computer systems.

i. Service Bureaus

Service bureaus are companies that use their own computers to process information for others. The first service bureaus were used to automate accounting functions. A law office would supply time and billing information, and the service bureau would prepare the desired monthly reports. The service bureau's fees were often less than the cost of adding an extra bookkeeper to the firm's payroll.

ii. Data Processing Machines

Data processing machines, along with their card punches, readers, and sorters, were used within the law office to organize data for many in-house items. These items included the office's list of employees, clients, equipment, supplies, and cases.

iii. Time-Sharing Computer Systems

As time went on, many firms moved from service bureaus to time-sharing computer systems. With time sharing, the law office purchased processing time and storage space on an off-site computer. The computer was accessed through the telephone lines with a terminal located in the law office.

Time-sharing computers that provided accounting services allowed firms to input and access their billing information immediately from their own offices. This access to up-to-the-minute billings was preferable to the monthly reports provided by the service bureaus.

b. Court Automation

The system of courts in the United States is ideally suited for computerization. In an increasingly litigious society, the organization of case information is essential if cases are to proceed efficiently through the court system.

i. Data Processing Machines

The first court to attempt to substantially automate its data processing and calendar was the Court of Common Pleas in Allegheny County, Pennsylvania, in 1963. The court did not use a computer but an IBM punched-card data processing machine. Information was filled out on a punched card when an attorney filed a complaint. The card was then sent to the data processing department for punching. The court's cards could be sorted in any manner desired, and information on a particular case was easily available.

ii. Computers

Computers first found their way into the courthouse for use by the traffic courts and for selecting potential jurors. Traffic courts used computers to track the issuance of citations and to issue notices, summonses, and warrants. Those courts using the technology were able to increase the rate of the collections on their citations, thereby increasing the jurisdiction's revenue.

Computer storage of voter registration information enabled courts to streamline the juror selection process. Computers were used to select potential jurors from the voter rolls, issue the summonses for jury duty, and compute the jurors' compensation.

c. Litigation Support

Computers were first used as litigation support tools in the areas of antitrust law, health law, and patent law. Computers were also used for specific cases involving estate planning, medical malpractice, automobile accidents, taxation, and interstate commerce.

Law firms that handled estate planning, for example, were able to subscribe to a service bureau that would analyze and compute estate planning alternatives. Estate planning involves a number of computations and the analysis of alternatives to optimize the value of an estate. An office that subscribed to the estate planning service bureau would complete questionnaires regarding the estate and the services desired. This information was then fed into the service bureau's computer for processing. Upon the attorney's request, the computer could be asked to perform tax calculations or conduct hypothetical probate situations for analysis by the attorney (e.g., the effect on family income if the husband predeceased the wife, or vice versa).

Service bureaus and time-sharing computers were the main forms of computerized litigation support until computers became affordable to individual law firms.

C. MODERN USES OF COMPUTERS IN THE PRACTICE OF LAW

Computers are used today in almost every facet of legal practice and by almost every legal professional in a law office. Law offices, courts, and law libraries are all exploring new ways to use computers to produce documents and to organize and retrieve information. The paralegal can expect to use a computer to draft documents, manage databases, perform research, and maintain calendar and case information.

1. Office Automation and Litigation Support

In the law office, computers are primarily used to perform accounting functions, create documents, conduct legal research, manage case information, maintain the firm's calendar, and manage evidence.

Time and billing software is normally one of the first software purchases for a law firm. For a service business such as law, the accounting department must bill effectively in order to maintain a steady stream of income into the firm. Another important software purchase in a law firm is a word processing package. The creation of letters and documents is the main focus of the legal service.

Computerized legal research can be conducted by searching legal databases on-line or on CD-ROM disks. A CD-ROM disk, which is similar to a music CD, can store hundreds of thousands of pages of text. A few of these disks can hold entire state codes or case reporters.

Case management software is used to keep a record of each case's name, number, parties, counsel, pleadings, calendar, and other information. With this software, information such as the telephone number of opposing counsel can be accessed in a few seconds on the computer screen. Firms that do not have case management software may decide to purchase a calendaring software package.

In order to avoid sanctions, malpractice, and embarrassment, a firm must keep an accurate calendar. Traditional calendaring methods involve the submission of calendar (tickler) slips to a person in charge of the firm's calendar. These slips are organized by date in a file box or are posted on a wall calendar. Warnings of upcoming dates are given by word of mouth, memo, or tickler sheet. A computerized calendar stores the dates within the computer, warns the user of upcoming calendar items, and can produce and print the entire calendar or a particular portion relating to specific dates or cases.

Managing evidence in litigation requires a degree of organization that is not always attainable with manual document indexing. A database management system can keep track of documents by storing a short summary of each piece of evidence or the entire text or image of the document. When certain documents need to be located (e.g., all documents written by John Smith), a search can be conducted looking for the words "John Smith" within the summary or within the full text of the document.

2. Court Automation

Courts continue to automate their operations and offer access to their computer information through the telephone lines. For example, in some jurisdictions, law offices are able to file their pleadings by computer or by fax machine; judges in some jurisdictions request jury instructions on diskette; and other jurisdictions allow access to the court's calendars and slip opinions with a computer. This automation streamlines the litigation process, saving the court time and allowing cases to proceed to trial at a faster rate.

In the courtroom, computers are used to display evidence documents to the judge, jury, and counsel. Rather than hauling boxes of paper evidence into the courtroom, attorneys can scan their documents onto optical disks. A few optical disks can store hundreds of boxes of documents. The optical disks are loaded into a computer, and selected documents are displayed on monitors throughout the courtroom.

Computers are also used to provide an instant transcript of the court proceedings. The court reporter uses a shorthand reporting machine to type out sound combinations as people speak in the courtroom. Instead of translating the tape personally, computer software is available that will instantly translate the code created by the machine into text and display it on computer monitors. The judge and counsel can then read pertinent portions of the proceedings themselves without asking the court reporter to look through her paper tape and read back testimony or waiting for the typed transcript.

3. Legal Research

Legal research can be performed on computers using on-line services, the Internet, and CD-ROM disks. The two primary on-line services used by legal researchers are LEXIS and WESTLAW. There are other on-line services that provide access to nonlegal information such as medical materials, newspapers, business journals, business records, and intellectual property records. These nonlegal on-line services are used by attorneys whose area of practice requries the specific type of information provided by the service.

The Internet contains many legal reference areas. To find them you need to browse through the World Wide Web and locate the specific sites that contain legal information. At some of these sites you can find guides that will help you to locate other sites that contain legal information. You can download these guides and print them on your printer to use for reference purposes. There are some potential pitfalls to using legal reference materials that you find on the Internet. First, the information is not always current. Second, you do not know if the information posted is accurate. Third, a Web site that is here today may be gone tomorrow, and, fourth, the searching methods used at many of these sites are primitive. A benefit to using the Internet is that the cost to you is only the cost of the time on your Internet service provider. Many of these services have a very low monthly charge when compared to the costs of LEXIS or WESTLAW.

CD-ROM disks are fast becoming the legal researcher's tool of choice. CD-ROM disks contain materials from all different areas of law and many areas of the country, enabling a legal professional to pick the specific information that is needed for research in his or her practice. A legal professional who practices primarily California law, for example, could purchase CD-ROM disks that contain California cases, statues, digests, and ALR. Many offices that use CD-ROM disks as research tools have purchased external CD-ROM stack drives that allow for many of these CDs to be loaded together for easy access through the office computer network. Although these CD-ROM disks are expensive, you are not charged for the time that you spend using them as you would with an on-line service.

D. SUMMARY

Computers fall into three categories: microcomputers, minicomputers, and mainframes. Microcomputers (often referred to as PCs) are the primary computer choice of law firms due to their low price and ability to work alone or with other computers.

Computers were first proposed for use by attorneys to perform legal research, draft legislation, and predict judicial decisions. The early computer automation of law offices involved service bureaus that process information for others, and time-sharing computer systems that rent a portion of their computer's processing time and storage space.

The courts first found computers useful in managing traffic court proceedings and establishing juror lists. Modern court automation includes the ability to file pleadings and to access court information by computer. In the courtroom, computers are used to display evidence and to provide an instant translation of the court reporter's transcript.

Modern law offices use computers for accounting, word processing, legal research, managing cases and evidence, and calendaring. Legal and nonlegal research databases, available through on-line services, on the Internet, and on CD-ROM disks, put libraries of data as close as the computer's keyboard.

Computers have made significant changes in how law is practiced. Almost all legal professionals now use computers in some area of their practice. They find that computers make their jobs easier, help to keep them organized, and in many cases improve the legal services provided to the client.

KEY TERMS

file server, 4
hardware, 6
input, 4
input devices, 6

local area network (LAN), 4
mainframe, 5
massively parallel processing, 5
microcomputer, 4
microprocessors, 5
minicomputer, 5
monitor, 4
output, 4
output devices, 6
peripheral device, 4
personal computer (PC), 4
printer, 4
program, 4
service bureaus, 10
software, 6
supercomputer, 5
system unit, 6
terminal, 5
user, 4
workstation, 4

QUESTIONS

1. What are the three categories of computers?
2. A personal computer falls into which category of computers?
3. Define the terms "hardware" and "software."
4. Name three tasks that a computer can perform in a law office.
5. How can you use a computer to perform legal research?

DISCUSSION QUESTIONS

1. Why would a microcomputer local area network (LAN) be preferable to a minicomputer with terminals (just a keyboard and monitor) in the law office environment?
2. Given the cost of computer-assisted legal research services such as LEXIS and WESTLAW, is it more cost-effective simply to do the research manually in the bound volumes?

CHAPTER

2

Computer Hardware

A. HARDWARE

Hardware is the term used to describe the physical components of the computer system. This chapter will explain the following types of computer hardware:

- the main computer unit
- devices for storing information
- devices for sending information into the computer
- devices for displaying the results of the computer's processing
- communications devices
- networks

Examples of computer hardware are pictured in Figure 2.1.

B. THE SYSTEM UNIT

The **system unit** of a computer is the piece of hardware that houses the computer's central processing unit (CPU), main memory, expansion slots, control circuits, hard disk, and diskette drives. This is the main unit of the computer. The **expansion slots** in the system unit allow you to expand the features of your computer by adding circuit boards for devices such as a modem or speakers. The expansion slots, at the rear of the system unit, are shown in Figure 2.2.

This section will discuss the central processing unit, main memory (ROM and RAM), bits and bytes, and microprocessors.

FIGURE 2.1 An IBM-compatible microcomputer's system unit, monitor, keyboard, and mouse.

1. The Central Processing Unit

The computer's **central processing unit (CPU)** is its brain. A CPU is housed within the system unit and is made up of an arithmetic/logic unit, a control unit, and a main memory unit.

a. The Arithmetic/Logic Unit

The **arithmetic/logic unit** performs calculations and other functions on data entered into the computer. This unit can add, subtract, multiply, and divide numbers. It can also compare two numbers to determine which is larger or if they are equal.

b. The Control Unit

The **control unit** directs the operation of the various parts of the computer. It receives and interprets program instructions, directs their processing, and sends the processed information to memory or to an output device. The control unit is like the traffic cop of the computer.

FIGURE 2.2 The expansion slots at the rear of the system unit (on the right) allow you to add more features to your computer.

c. *The Main Memory Unit*

The **main memory unit** is where data is stored when not being acted on by the other two units. The main memory unit

- contains permanent instructions for the operation of the computer;
- receives and stores software programs selected for use;
- stores the data input by the user before and after its use by the arithmetic/logic unit and control unit;
- stores the final results of the programmed data until the control unit sends it to a printer or other output device; and
- continues to store the software program and any data results until directed by the control unit to remove these items from memory.

2. ROM and RAM

There are two types of memory within the computer's main memory: ROM (Read Only Memory) and RAM (Random Access Memory). This main memory is stored on silicon chips in the computer's system unit.

ROM (Read Only Memory) is permanent memory that can be read but cannot be written to, or altered, during normal computer operations. It is always present in the computer and is not erased when the computer is turned off. The computer's manufacturer stores information and instructions in this memory to make communication possible between the CPU and other hardware components of the computer.

RAM (Random Access Memory) is temporary memory that is utilized while the computer is operating. Unlike ROM, this memory is erased when the computer is turned off. Data can be written to, and can be accessed from, RAM. RAM is your work space. When you select a program to use, such as WordPerfect, the program is brought into RAM. As you type, the characters are also being stored in RAM. In order to save the document being created, the information that has been placed in RAM must be saved on a secondary memory storage device such as a magnetic disk. If the computer is turned off, or if a power outage occurs prior to saving the document, the RAM will be erased and the document will be lost. When you exit a program, the program is erased from the RAM chips but remains intact on the secondary memory storage device (usually the hard disk).

With multitasking environments like Windows, software programs can be open in RAM concurrently. The number of programs that can be open concurrently depends on the amount of RAM present within the computer. The more RAM available, the bigger the work space.

3. Bits and Bytes

A computer's memory is made up of electronic components that have the ability to store letters, numbers, and characters. An individual unit of memory is called a **"bit."** A bit is either turned on or off like a light switch. Computers use a series of bits to represent a single letter, number, or character. The storage unit for a single letter, number, or character is called a **"byte."** In most computers a byte is made up of eight bits that are turned on or off according to the code for the letter, number, or character the byte is to represent. The bit configuration below, with 0 indicating "off" and 1 indicating "on," represents a byte for the letter *A*.

0	1	0	0	0	0	0	1

You may also see a 1 and 0 on the on/off switches of your computer and coffee maker. 1 indicates "on," 0 indicates "off."

The amount of RAM and secondary memory storage that you have available on your computer is measured in bytes. The terms "kilobyte," "megabyte," "gigabyte," and "terabyte" are used to refer to approximate quantities of bytes.

kilobyte(KB): one thousand bytes
megabyte (MB): one million bytes
gigabyte (GB): one billion bytes
terabyte (TB): one trillion bytes

A 1.6 gigabyte hard disk, therefore, would be capable of storing approximately 1.6 billion bytes of data.

4. Microprocessors

The CPU in a microcomputer is referred to as a **"microprocessor."** Microprocessors are measured by their speed and processing ability. The microprocessor's speed is determined by the number of electronic pulses emitted per second by the computer's master clock. This speed, referred to as "clock speed," is measured in megahertz (MHz). An increase in clock speed increases the rate of the electronic pulses and processes information at a faster speed. Therefore, a 133 megahertz microprocessor will process instructions faster than a 33 megahertz microprocessor.

Microprocessors are also measured by the number of bits they are able to process simultaneously. A microprocessor that simultaneously processes 32 bits (4 bytes) is faster than one that processes 16 bits (2 bytes) at a time. To compare a microprocessor to a highway, the megahertz would be the speed at which the vehicles (bytes) are traveling. For every 8 bits (1 byte), there would be one lane on the highway. A 32-bit microprocessor would have four lanes; a 16-bit microprocessor would have two lanes. A 32-bit microprocessor will therefore allow more vehicles (bytes) through the CPU at a time than the 16-bit microprocessor.

Intel Corporation introduced the first microprocessor in 1971. The IBM compatible microcomputer, sometimes referred to as a "personal computer," has evolved as new microprocessors have been developed. Figure 2.3 charts the evolution of the personal computer and the Intel microprocessor.

C. SECONDARY MEMORY STORAGE

Secondary memory storage (also referred to as "auxiliary memory storage") is where software files are stored. Secondary memory storage includes magnetic disks, magnetic tape, and optical disks. When a document, spreadsheet, database, or other type of file is created in a software program, the data must be stored somewhere in order to use it again. Data cannot be stored in ROM because ROM can only be read. Data cannot be permanently stored in RAM because RAM is erased when the computer is turned off. Therefore, data is stored in secondary memory storage. The various types of secondary memory storage are explained below.

1. Magnetic Disks

Magnetic disks are the secondary memory storage devices most often used by microcomputers. Data may be stored to and retrieved from magnetic disks.

There are two types of magnetic disks—hard disks and diskettes (also called

Personal Computer	8088 processor. The first processor used in the IBM personal computer, it utilized 16-bit internal registers and an 8-bit data bus. The computer contained two diskette drives for accessing and storing software files.
PC XT	8088 processor. This computer used the same processor as the original personal computer, but added a hard disk for the internal storage of software files.
286	80286 processor. This processor was built upon the 8088 technology. It incorporated memory management for limited software multitasking, and expanded the data bus to 16 bits.
386	Intel386 processor. The first of the 32-bit processors developed by Intel. This processor allowed more complex multitasking.
486	Intel486 processor. Built upon the Intel386 technology. This processor added an on-chip math coprocessor, an enhanced bus interface unit, and a unified data/instruction cache.
Pentium	Pentium processor. A 32-bit processor with an external 64-bit bus to allow more efficient communication between the processor and system memory. This processor incorporated superscalar technology, branch prediction, and separate internal data and code write-back caches.
Pentium Pro	Pentium Pro processor. A 32-bit processor with the same external 64-bit bus as the Pentium. This processor uses "Dynamic Execution" to predict the instructions that will need to be processed and organizes the processing in a logical order.

FIGURE 2.3 The evolution of the personal computer and the Intel microprocessor.

"floppy disks"). Hard disks are normally fixed within the system unit and cannot be removed. Diskettes are portable.

Magnetic disks can be purchased blank or preformatted. Formatting places numbered concentric circles, called "tracks," on the disk. Each track is divided into sectors. This creates a circular grid on the disk. The number of tracks and sectors placed on the surface of a disk determines the amount of data the disk can store. Blank disks must be formatted by the computer's operating system before they can be used to store data.

An index called a "file allocation table" (FAT) is created on each disk when it is formatted. This index, on the outermost track of the disk, keeps a record of each file placed on the disk and its location (tracks and sectors) on the grid. When you retrieve a file from a disk, the operating system reads the FAT and moves the disk drive's read/write head to the location of the file's data. The FAT also enables the operating system to locate free storage space on a disk where new files may be stored.

A **disk drive** houses magnetic disks so that data can be read from, and written to, them. Most hard disks are permanently contained in their disk drives. There are some hard disks that are removable and utilize a special type of disk drive.

Diskettes are inserted and removed from disk drives. A disk drive spins the disk at a very high speed, reading and writing data with a **read/write head** similar to the needle of a record player. Data is recorded when the read/write head places a magnetized spot (bit) representing a 1 or a 0 ("on" or "off") on the disk. Eight of these spots, or bits of data, represent a single character (byte).

a. Hard Disks

Hard disks are magnetic storage disks that are rigid. A hard disk is either enclosed in a disk drive in the computer's system unit or within an external hard disk drive. Hard disk drives can contain a single disk or several disks stacked on top of one another. The stacked disks will have read/write heads above and below each disk. The operating system will recognize the stacked disks as a single disk. A stack of hard disks representing a single disk is shown in Figure 2.4.

A hard disk can range in storage capacity from a small 40 megabyte disk up to a disk capable of storing several hundred gigabytes. You will store on a hard disk those files that you use frequently. For example, your applications like WordPerfect, and your operating system, DOS or Windows, will be stored on the hard

FIGURE 2.4 A hard disk removed from its disk drive.

disk. Files that you create with any of these programs can also be stored on the hard disk. It is a good idea for you to keep a copy of your hard disk's files on diskettes or magnetic tape in case the hard disk becomes damaged.

b. Diskettes

A **diskette,** or **floppy disk,** is a portable magnetic disk on which files are stored. Diskettes are used to store files you do not want to keep on the hard disk, to keep copies of the files stored on the hard disk, or to transport a file to another computer.

The common sizes of these disks are 5¼-inch and 3½-inch, both of which are shown in Figure 2.5. The 5¼-inch diskettes are called "floppy disks" because they are flexible. The 3½-inch diskettes have a more rigid cover but are still referred to as "floppy disks." The 3½-inch diskettes can take more abuse than their larger counterparts.

The 5¼-inch and 3½-inch diskettes are inserted into the disk drives, label side up, with the write protection notch or hole on the left-hand side of the disk. The 5¼-inch disk drive has a latch or "gate" that must be shut to allow the computer to access the disk.

FIGURE 2.5 3½-inch and 5¼-inch diskettes.

i. Diskette Density

Diskettes can be purchased in varying densities. The density of the disk refers to the amount of data, or bytes, it can store.

5¼-inch double (low) density diskettes can be formatted to store approximately 360 kilobytes (360,000 characters)
5¼-inch high density diskettes can be formatted at "low density" to store 360 kilobytes, or at high density to store approximately 1.2 megabytes (1.2 million characters)
3½-inch double (low) density diskettes can be formatted to store approximately 720 kilobytes (720,000 characters)
3½-inch high density diskettes can be formatted at low density to store 720 kilobytes, or at high density to store a range from 1.4 megabytes (1.4 million characters) to many more megabytes, depending on the diskette you purchase

The size, storage capabilities, and durability of the 3½-inch diskettes make them more attractive than the 5¼-inch diskettes. The 5¼-inch diskettes continue to be used, however, because not all computers are equipped with 3½-inch diskette drives. To give you an idea of how much text diskettes can store, this book required 400 kilobytes of storage space. I stored a copy on my hard disk and a back-up copy on a high density 3½-inch diskette.

If a diskette's density is not labeled, you can determine the density by looking at the diskette itself. A low density 5¼-inch diskette is distinguished from its high density counterpart by a distinct ring around its center hole. A high density 3½-inch diskette is distinguished from a low density 3½-inch diskette by the two square holes punched in its cover. The low density diskette will have only one. You can see the difference between the two 3½-inch diskettes in Figure 2.5.

The disk drives for 5¼-inch and 3½-inch diskettes will have low or high density capabilities. Low density disk drives are found on older computers and can only read and write to double (low) density diskettes or high density diskettes formatted at low density. High density disk drives can read and write to both low and high density diskettes.

ii. Diskette Write Protection

To prevent the accidental alteration of data stored on a diskette, you may place a **write protect tab** over a notch in the disk (5¼-inch) or lock the disk (3½-inch). Data stored on a write-protected diskette can be read but not written to.

The write protect notch on a 5¼-inch diskette is literally a notch cut into the plastic covering of the disk. Write protection is established by placing a write protect tab (a piece of tape supplied by the diskette manufacturer) over the notch.

A 3½-inch diskette has a square hole with a sliding piece of plastic on the back of the diskette that enables the user to "lock" the disk. When the plastic piece is closed over the hole, data can be written to the disk. When it is open, data on the disk may not be altered.

iii. Diskette Care

It is important to take proper care of diskettes so as not to lose the data stored on them.

5¼-inch Diskettes

- Store in protective envelope when not in use.
- Hold the disk by its corners.
- Only use felt tip pens to write on labels on the disk.
- Do not paper clip disks together or paper clip a message to the disk.
- Do not place a rubber band around a group of disks.
- Do not bend the disk.

Any contact between the disk jacket and the disk may make a mark on the disk. This mark can damage stored data or parts of the disk. It is a good practice to store magnetic disks in the box in which they were purchased or in some other type of protective container.

5¼-inch and *3½-inch Diskettes*

- Do not touch the disk itself.
- Do not leave the disk in the sun.
- Do not try to clean the disk.
- Do not place the disk near a magnet.

The last point is very important. Placing the disk near a magnet will remove data from the diskette. Data has been known to "disappear" from disks left on top of magnetic paper clip holders.

2. Magnetic Tape

Magnetic tape cartridges are commonly used in law offices to "back up" the computer's hard disk. "Backing up" is the making of a copy of data stored on the disk as a backup in case of disk damage or accidental erasure. Magnetic tape drives for microcomputers and minicomputers are similar to diskette drives and can be placed in the system unit where a diskette drive would be located.

Data is stored on **magnetic tape** in a different way than on magnetic disks. Magnetic disk drives store and retrieve data by **direct access.** The operating system reads the disk's FAT and directs the read/write head directly to the data. Magnetic tape drives store and retrieve data on magnetic tapes by **sequential access.** This means that the computer must run sequentially through a magnetic tape until it reaches the data to be retrieved. Similarly, to store data, the computer must run through the tape until a blank space is found to store the data. Hence, the storage and retrieval of data with magnetic tape requires considerably more time than a magnetic disk.

The advantage of magnetic tape is that a single cartridge has much more data storage capacity than a diskette. A single magnetic tape cartridge can often store the entire contents of a hard disk; the cartridges can be purchased with storage capacities from a few megabytes to over a gigabyte. A magnetic tape cartridge is shown in Figure 2.6.

3. Optical Disks

Optical disks are disks that store data, sound, and pictures. Legal books and information as well as software can be purchased on optical disks, or the disks can be used to store documents and photographs. Data, sound, and images are stored on optical disks with a laser. Optical disks have their own type of disk drive, which may be placed within the system unit or may be an external piece of hardware. Most optical disks are read-only CD-ROM disks. Optical disks that can be erased and used to store new data and images require a special disk drive.

a. CD-ROM Disks

CD-ROM disks are optical disks that will eventually replace the volumes of legal reference books in our law libraries. CD-ROM (Compact Disk-Read Only

FIGURE 2.6 A magnetic tape cartridge.

FIGURE 2.7 A CD-ROM disk from West's CD-ROM Libraries.

Memory) technology involves the use of compact disks,* like those used to record music, to store volumes of text, sound, and images. A single compact disk can hold approximately 600 megabytes of data, or 250,000 to 500,000 pages of text. An example of a CD-ROM disk is shown in Figure 2.7.

Many firms have external CD-ROM disk drives that can hold several disks. This allows the user to access a variety of different source materials without having to insert new disks. Figure 2.8 shows both an internal and an external CD-ROM disk drive.

b. Digital Video Disks (DVD)

Digital video disks, commonly referred to as DVD disks, are similar to CD-ROMs in size and appearance. Due to their construction, the DVD-ROM disks are capable of storing between four and seventeen gigabytes of information. One DVD disk can hold a theater-quality feature-length film, interactive movie, or computer game with full-motion video and high quality sound. The DVD disk

*Optical disks such as CDs and DVDs frequently appear with the variant spelling "disc." For the sake of consistency in this text, the word will be spelled "disk" throughout.

FIGURE 2.8 An internal and an external CD-ROM disk drive.

is constructed using two bonded 0.6mm substrates, as opposed to the single-thickness 1.2mm plastic disk of the CD. This reduces the distance between the disk's surface and the physical pits on the disk that hold the information. Since the laser does not have to penetrate as much plastic, it can be focused on a smaller area. Therefore, the pits can be made smaller and placed closer together, increasing disk capacity. There are also DVD write-once disks and DVD rewritables. All DVD disks require a special drive. The DVD-ROM drive has two different lens apertures so that it can read both DVD and CD-ROM disks. This allows the use of the newer DVD technology without rendering your CDs obsolete.

c. *Other Optical Disks*

There are optical disks other than CD-ROM and DVD disks that can be written to once, or that allow repetitive writing and erasing like a magnetic diskette. Optical disks that can be written to once are called **WORM** disks (Write Once Read Many). Optical disk storage is beneficial for cases with large numbers of evidentiary documents because the entire case file can be carried on a few optical disks, giving the user the ability to view a picture of any document on the computer's monitor in a matter of seconds. Also, a hard copy of a document can be printed by a laser printer.

Rewritable optical disks allow for data storage and removal. These disks require a special disk drive that is capable of erasing and writing data on the optical disk. These disks provide many megabytes of storage capacity.

D. INPUT DEVICES

Input devices are those pieces of computer hardware that are used to input data to the computer. This section will discuss the many types of input devices.

1. The Keyboard

A **keyboard** is the primary input device used by law offices. Experiment with the keys on your own computer or one in an office or computer lab. A picture of a microcomputer keyboard is shown in Figure 2.9.

Main Keyboard. The main part of the keyboard contains the keys found on an ordinary typewriter. There are also special control keys, [Ctrl] and [Alt], that are always used in combination with another key. These key combinations perform different functions depending on the computer system and the software being used.

The Escape Key. In the upper left-hand corner of the keyboard is the [Esc] ("escape") key. With most DOS software packages, this key will allow the user to "escape" from or back out of a screen or command.

The Function Keys. The 12 keys along the top of the keyboard, labeled "F1" to "F12," are called the **"function keys."** (Some keyboards have the function keys on the left side of the keyboard.) Software packages assign various tasks to these keys. For instance, in Lotus 1-2-3, the [F1] key is the "Help" key. Pressing this key while in Lotus will bring up a screen that will help the user with

FIGURE 2.9 A microcomputer keyboard.

the program. In WordPerfect 5.1 for DOS, however, the [F1] key is the "Cancel" key and performs functions similar to the [Esc] key. The users' manual for each program will explain the uses of the function keys and in most cases will supply a template. A **template** is a piece of plastic or other material that lies above or around the function keys and indicates each key's function.

Print Screen, Scroll Lock, and Pause. The [Print Screen], [Scroll Lock], and [Pause] keys are normally located along the top row of the keyboard at the right side. Pressing the [Print Screen] key, or [Shift] + [Print Screen], will print the display currently on the monitor. In Windows, [Print Screen] will capture the screen onto the Clipboard. It can then be pasted into the Paintbrush application.

The [Scroll Lock] key is used to prevent the screen from "scrolling" (moving upwards with the top lines disappearing and new lines coming onto the screen from the bottom).

The [Pause] key will stop the computer's actions until the user chooses to continue by pressing the [Space Bar] or another key.

Special Keys. The group of six keys ([Insert], [Home], etc.) directly to the right of the main keys are special keys that also perform functions according to the software program in use. Their uses may be found in the software program's users' manual.

Cursor Movement (Arrow) Keys. The "arrow" keys to the right of the keyboard are called cursor movement keys. The **cursor** is the flashing horizontal or vertical line character that shows where data will be entered when a key is pressed. The cursor movement keys move the cursor in the direction indicated by the arrow on the key pressed.

Number Keypad. The last grouping of keys, at the far right of the keyboard, is the number keypad. These keys are repeats of keys found in other places on the keyboard. They are placed together in the keypad to make it easier to enter numbers into programs. The number and decimal keys of the keypad each have two functions. The key in the upper left of the keypad, the [Num Lock] key, turns the numbers on and off. With the [Num Lock] key on, numbers can be entered into the computer. With the [Num Lock] key off, the keypad performs operations similar to the special keys and cursor movement keys.

2. Punched Cards

Punched cards and punched card readers were the input device of early computers. They continue to be used in situations involving large computer systems, most notably vote counting in elections. Holes are punched into the cards to represent data or instructions. Later the cards are placed into a card reader and moved past a sensing device to translate the punched holes into electrical impulses understood by the CPU.

3. Scanners

Scanners are input devices that read printed pages or images into the computer. Scanners range from those that look like small copy machines to those that are hand held. As a printed page or picture is inserted into a scanner, or a hand-held scanner is run down a page, a light is focused onto the page. A reflection of the text falls onto a light-sensitive eye, which translates the document into digital signals recognized by the computer. The software used with the scanner will dictate whether an image (picture of the document or photograph) is stored on an optical disk or whether the text (the actual characters) of a document is stored on a magnetic disk. The computer's ability to recognize text from a scanned document is called **"optical character recognition"**; the storage of images is called **"imaging."**

Law offices use scanners to input documents into word processing programs for editing, into full-text databases for organization and fast retrieval, and onto optical disks for image storage.

4. The Mouse

A **mouse** is an input device that rolls on a ball located on its bottom surface. The movement of the ball corresponds with the movement of a pointer on the screen. A mouse is so called because of its size and the resemblance of its cord to a mouse's tail. Figures 2.10 and 2.11 show top and bottom views of a mouse.

FIGURE 2.10 A mouse with cord.

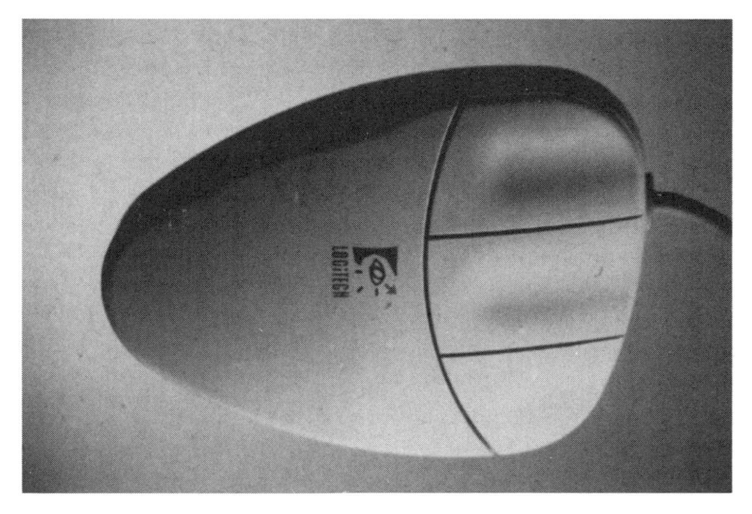

FIGURE 2.11 The bottom of a mouse.

On the top of a mouse are one, two, or three buttons that are used to select items pointed to with the cursor. The movement of the cursor and the use of the mouse buttons enable the user to perform computer functions without using the keyboard. Depending on the software in use, a mouse can access menus, select commands, draw lines, and move items around on the screen.

A mouse is usually connected to an interface port in the system unit by a thin cord. Some mouses, however, do not require a cord. One cordless mouse transmits signals to a receiver plugged into the computer. It operates like a television remote control and requires a clear line of sight to the receiver. Another type of cordless mouse operates like a cordless telephone and is shown in Figure 2.12. Low frequency radio waves are sent to the mouse's receiver, which is connected to the computer. This type of mouse does not require a clear line of sight to its receiver.

5. Track Balls, Integrated Pointing Devices, and Touch Pads

Portable computers often use pointing devices other than a mouse to increase portability. **Track balls** are similar to an upside-down mouse and are either clipped to the side of the portable computer or are part of the computer itself. The ball is mounted in the computer or a plastic box. As the user spins the ball, the pointer moves in the direction and at the speed of the ball's motion. An **integrated pointing device** is mounted in some portable computers. It resembles an eraser on the end of a pencil and moves the pointer in the direction that it is pressed. Buttons similar to mouse buttons are found near the track ball and integrated pointing device for selecting items on the screen. **Touch pads** are touch-sensitive pads that are mounted in the portable computer. Moving a finger across the pad will cause the pointer to move in the same direction on the screen. Some touch pads have adjacent buttons for selecting items. Others allow you to select items by tapping or double tapping the touch pad.

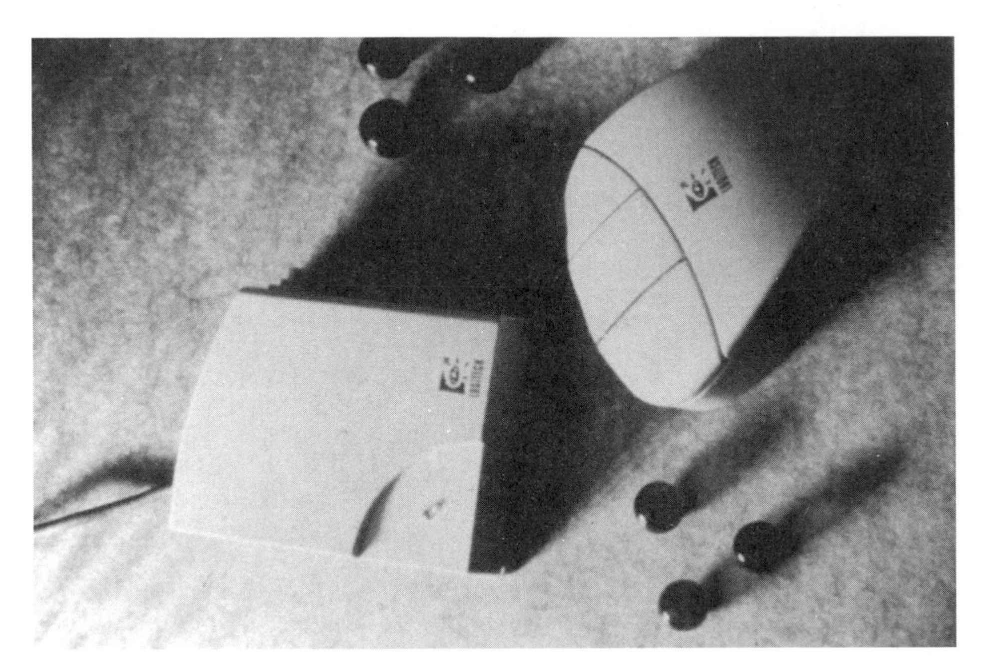

FIGURE 2.12 A cordless mouse, which transmits signals to the computer using radio waves, and its receiver.

6. Bar Code Readers

A **bar code reader** is another type of input device. It scans a bar code and transmits the code to the computer. With a bar coding system, a distinct bar code is developed for every book, file, document, or other item of information. When the bar code is scanned with a light pen or other bar code reader, the computer recognizes the item that corresponds to that bar code. The computer then acts on the information according to the program software.

In general, the bar code reader has been most widely used by supermarkets. More and more, however, law libraries, law offices, and courts are all discovering the capabilities of bar coding. Some law offices bar code their files for easy reference; law libraries bar code their books for easy check-out and return; and some courts bar code their files and case filings for quick retrieval and record tracking.

7. Touch Screens

Touch screens are special monitors that allow a user to input information by touching the screen with a finger or an electronic pen. Sports announcers and meteorologists use electronic pens on touch-sensitive monitors to map out plays and indicate weather flows and temperatures. These monitors contain an invisible grid system that enables the computer to recognize the coordinates of the location where the finger or electronic pen touches the screen.

Some courts use touch screens for public access to the court's indices of cases. The case indices contain the case type, the case number, the parties' names, the date the case was filed, and the nature of the action. You will need to use these indices when checking to see if a person or entity has been involved in other litigation or when you have the parties' names but not the case number. The case number is required if you desire to view the court's file on the case. The monitor displays the types of cases available (civil, criminal, probate, domestic, etc.) and the user touches the appropriate picture. An alphabet then appears for the user to press in a party's name. The computer then displays alphabetically the index entries for the cases including and surrounding the name entered.

8. Speech Recognition

Speech recognition is the ability of a computer to understand and interpret speech. The operator's voice is captured by a microphone and converted into digital signals recognized by the computer. Speech recognition can be used by physically challenged people to turn on lights, televisions, stereos, and the like. Speech recognition enables the legal professional to dictate work directly into the computer. As the technology evolves, this input device is recognizing more words and is becoming more affordable for law office use.

9. Handwriting Recognition

Handwriting recognition is the ability of a computer to understand handwritten characters and symbols. A special pad or screen recognizes contact made on its surface and translates the handwritten letters and characters into computer code. Computers without keyboards have been developed that will recognize printed characters and symbols, such as check marks. These computers are often used for inventory control because they are small and can be carried like a note pad. Numbers, words, and symbols can be entered into the computer and recorded into memory. The hand-held computer can then be connected to a larger computer to download the collected information.

E. OUTPUT DEVICES

An **output device** is a piece of computer hardware used to communicate the results of the computer's processing to the user. Some of the various types of output devices are discussed below.

1. Monitors

Monitors, also called "cathode ray tubes" (CRTs) and "video display terminals" (VDTs), are the most common type of output devices. A monitor resembles a television screen.

The two main types of monitors are:

Monochrome: Two-color displays similar to a black and white television screen. These monitors primarily offer green, black, or amber displays.
Color: Monitors offering three or more colors in their displays.

Graphics adapters can enhance the color and graphics capabilities of a monitor.

2. Printers

Printers are output devices that print a "hard copy" of data results onto paper. The printer's speed can be measured in characters per second (CPS) or in pages per minute (PPM).

There are two classifications of printers, impact and nonimpact.

a. Impact Printers

Impact printers actually strike the paper like a typewriter. Common impact printers are daisy wheel and dot matrix printers.

Daisy wheel printers produce a letter-quality product, although they are limited to the characters present on the character wheel. They are slow, noisy, and do not have extensive graphics capabilities.

In the past dot matrix printers were commonly used in law offices for producing draft copies of documents. These printers operate at a high rate of speed and require minimal maintenance. A configuration of dots is used to produce letters and graphics. Dot matrix printers can be very noisy and are not always capable of producing letter-quality output.

b. Nonimpact Printers

Nonimpact printers do not strike the page with the printing mechanism. Common nonimpact printers are the laser and ink jet printers. Both of these types of printers have models that can print colors.

Laser printers use a laser to place a charge on a magnetic plate, which then causes toner to be formed into the characters and graphics that are then adhered to the paper. These printers produce a letter-quality document and are fast and quiet. A 20-page document can be printed in under three minutes with a laser printer.

Ink jet printers are similar to dot matrix printers in that characters are represented in a dot pattern on the page. Ink jet printers shoot their ink at the paper instead of making contact. Special paper may be required with these printers to prevent the ink from running. There are many ink jet printers that provide a final product that is very comparable to laser printer output.

3. Plotters

Plotters are graphics printers that create images using drawing pens. The pens, which come in assorted colors, are chosen by the plotter's drawing arm. The plotter rolls a piece of paper in and out of the device, allowing the drawing arm to draw with a particular color. When the plotter is finished with a color, it replaces the pen and grasps the next color.

Plotters are used extensively by the architecture and engineering professions. They can be used by legal professionals to create charts, graphs, and demonstrative evidence; however, they are not a standard law office item.

4. Speakers

With the advent of **multimedia** computing, speakers have become a common output device on home computers. Multimedia merges text, sound, pictures, and motion in games, presentations, and other productions generated by your computer. Speakers are not standard law office equipment, but they may be found in offices that use voice recognition software or multimedia applications.

F. COMMUNICATIONS

Computers can communicate with one another through telephone lines or cables. A modem allows computers to use telephone lines to communicate with other computers. Computer networks link two or more computers through cables to communicate with one another. Electronic mail is used to send information or files to another computer user.

1. Modems

Modems are devices that allow one computer to communicate with another through telephone lines. The modem in the sending computer translates the computer's digital signals into analog signals to travel over telephone lines. The modem in the receiving computer translates the analog signals from the telephone line back into digital signals.

The traditional modem is limited to the transfer of files and text between two computers. Modern modems are available with the ability to send and receive faxes. Even more advanced modems, called "DVSD" (Digital Simultaneous Voice and Data) modems, allow voice and data or faxes to travel over a telephone line simultaneously. This enables you to speak with the person on the other end of the modem line while data is being transmitted or received.

An external modem resides outside of the computer's system unit and attaches by cable to a port at the back of the system unit. An internal modem is a circuit board that is inserted into an expansion slot in the system unit. A telephone jack in the circuit board is accessible at the rear of the computer. To use the modem, a user can unplug a telephone and plug the cord into the back of the computer.

A communications software package is necessary to operate a modem. With a modem, the legal professional can transfer data to and from an off-site computer or can access a database such as LEXIS or WESTLAW. Modems that can send and receive faxes require fax communication software.

2. Local Area Networks (LANs)

Local area networks (LANs) are a means of connecting computers and hardware devices within an office. A LAN lets computers share information and peripheral devices such as printers.

A typical LAN will have **workstations** located throughout an office. In a LAN configuration called "peer to peer," the workstations are cabled together in a formation that allows them to access information from each other. In a LAN configuration called "client/server," the workstations are cabled together and access and store information on a main workstation called the **file server.** In most cases, each of the workstations is a microcomputer that contains a network "card" in one of its expansion slots. Cable is run throughout the office connecting the workstations and the file server.

The file server in the client/server LAN can be a powerful microcomputer or a minicomputer. The file server's hard disk is where the data files for the office will be stored. Each workstation can access and store information on the file server and can use any printers or other devices attached to the network.

3. Wide Area Networks (WANs)

Wide area networks (WANs) connect networks of computers in distant locations through dedicated telephone lines. A wide area network can enable a large law firm with offices in San Francisco, Los Angeles, and Washington, D.C. to connect all of its computers to share information and send electronic mail.

4. Electronic Mail

Electronic mail, or **"E-mail,"** is the use of a computer to send and receive messages to and from other users. When their telephones are busy or they are in a meeting, a message can be left in their electronic mail mailbox. The next time they check their computer or check their mailbox, a message will appear that they have received new mail. They can read their mail and then respond to, delete, forward, print, or save the message.

G. SUMMARY

The computer's hardware is the tangible parts of the computer. These parts include the system unit, secondary memory storage devices such as a magnetic disk, input devices such as the keyboard, and output devices such as printers.

The computer's system unit contains the central processing unit, circuit boards, a hard disk, and diskette drives. The central processing unit consists of an arithmetic/logic unit, a control unit, and a main memory unit. The arithmetic/logic unit performs the computations required by the computer. The control unit directs the data through the computer. The main memory unit contains permanent data storage (ROM) and temporary data storage (RAM). A single electronic piece of data is called a bit and 8 bits make up a byte, which represents a single character.

Secondary memory storage devices include magnetic disks, magnetic tape, and optical disks. Secondary memory is where files created by the user can be stored, and from which they may be retrieved.

Input devices allow the user to transmit data to the computer. The most common input devices are the keyboard and mouse. Output devices allow the user to see the results of the computer's processing. The most common output devices are the monitor and printer.

Communication between computers can be accomplished by modem or through computer cables. A modem enables a computer to communicate with another computer through telephone lines. A local area network (LAN) is a configuration of several computers cabled together to share a common bank of information and hardware. A wide area network (WAN) allows communications between distant offices using a dedicated telephone line. Electronic mail is a message or correspondence sent from one person to another through a computer.

KEY TERMS

arithmetic/logic unit, 18
bar code reader, 34
bit, 20
byte, 20
CD-ROM disk, 27
central processing unit (CPU), 18
control unit, 18
cursor, 31
digital video disk (DVD), 28
direct access, 26
disk drive, 23
diskette, 24
electronic mail (E-mail), 38
expansion slots, 17
file server, 38
floppy disk, 24
function keys, 30
gigabyte, 20

handwriting recognition, 35
hard disk, 23
hardware, 17
imaging, 32
input device, 30
integrated pointing device, 33
keyboard, 30
kilobyte, 20
local area network (LAN), 38
magnetic disk, 21
magnetic tape, 26
main memory unit, 19
megabyte, 20
microprocessor, 21
modem, 37
monitor, 36
mouse, 32
multimedia, 37
optical character recognition, 32
optical disk, 27
output device, 35
plotter, 37
printer, 36
punched card, 31
RAM, 20
read/write head, 23
ROM, 19
scanner, 32
secondary memory storage, 21
sequential access, 26
speech recognition, 35
system unit, 17
template, 31
terabyte, 20
touch pad, 33
touch screen, 34
track balls, 33
wide area network (WAN), 38
workstation, 38
WORM, 29
write protect tab, 25

QUESTIONS

1. What are the three components of a CPU?
2. Define ROM and RAM and explain the difference between them.
3. Give an example of a secondary memory storage device.
4. What is the difference between direct access and sequential access in the reading and writing of data to memory?
5. What is write protection?
6. Give an example of two input devices.
7. Give an example of two output devices.
8. What is a local area network?

DISCUSSION QUESTIONS

1. How are the computers you are using with this course configured? Are they individual computers, or are they connected with cables in a local area network? Are the diskette drives 5¼-inch, 3½-inch, high density, or low density?
2. How often should a law office back up its computer system? Why does it make more sense to back up to magnetic tape cartridges rather than diskettes? What are the advantages of removable hard disks?

CHAPTER

3

Computer Software

This chapter will discuss the different categories of computer software and the software used by legal professionals. **Software** is the term for the coded instructions used to run the computer in a given task. Legal professionals use software developed for all types of businesses, in addition to the software developed specifically for the law.

Programming is the act of creating software. You do not need to learn how to program a computer. Software can be purchased to perform almost any task. In the law office, you will use software to create documents, manage cases, and organize evidence. You will also use software to run your computer and organize your computer files. This chapter will cover

- the four categories of computer software
- software commonly found in the law office
- software copyrights and ethical considerations

A. SOFTWARE DEFINED

Computer software consists of the coded instructions that direct the actions of the computer. A computer cannot operate without software. Software can allow you to type documents into the computer and send them to a printer; software can create graphs from numbers typed into the computer; and software can also sort and search through a large bank of data stored in the computer. Software can be created to perform almost any task performed by humans. The coded instructions within the software are the steps necessary to perform the task.

B. SOFTWARE CATEGORIES

There are four categories of computer software:

- **Computer languages** are the codes that create operating systems, utility programs, and application programs.
- **Operating systems** are a collection of programs that manage the operation of the computer.
- **Utility programs** help to operate your computer more efficiently.
- **Application programs** are designed for a specific purpose, such as word processing, time and billing, spreadsheet creation, and database management. They allow the user to perform personal and business-related tasks.

1. Computer Languages

Computer languages are specialized software used to create computer programs. They create the appearance of a program, its method of processing, and the appearance of output. The software takes the written code and compiles it into digital instructions that are understood by the CPU. The operating systems, utility programs, and application programs are like books that tell the computer how to perform a task; computer language software allows you to write the words that make up the books.

Computer languages can be compared to human languages. Different computer languages have different ways of, for instance, adding 2 + 2. They all come up with the same answer; they just go about it in a different manner.

A program in the BASIC programming language could add 2 + 2 with the following commands:

```
10 A=2
20 B=2
30 C=B+A
40 PRINT A;"+";B;"=";C
50 END
```

When the program is run, the following result appears:

```
2 + 2 = 4
```

It is unlikely that you will be doing any programming in the legal profession. Most programs you will use in your work can be purchased at a software store or through a software company.

In addition to BASIC, some other examples of computer languages are COBOL, FORTRAN, Pascal, C++, Machine Language, and Assembly Language. Several microcomputers have the BASIC programming language installed in their ROM. DOS also includes it in its program files. Additional programming language software can be purchased for microcomputers at software stores.

2. Operating Systems

An **operating system** is a collection of individual software programs, each of which performs a unique task, and is used to manage a computer. Operating systems include programs that

- copy files
- delete files
- format magnetic disks
- rename files
- list the files on a disk
- copy magnetic disks
- compare magnetic disks
- create disk directories
- move between directories

Some operating systems also include utility programs, such as programs for undeleting files and unformatting magnetic disks.

An operating system is the link between the computer hardware and software. Without an operating system, the computer can only use those programs that have been installed in the computer's ROM by the manufacturer. Remember that the ROM is fixed and cannot be altered by normal computer operations. If you think of your computer as a table, the operating system is the tablecloth. It must be on the table in order to begin placing the software dishes (WordPerfect, etc.) on it.

Common operating systems used by microcomputers and minicomputers are DOS, Macintosh®, Windows NT, Windows 95, OS/2, and UNIX.

a. DOS

DOS (disk operating system) is the most commonly used operating system for microcomputers. There are two types of DOS, PC-DOS® and MS-DOS®. Both systems were developed by Microsoft Corporation and are very similar. PC-DOS is owned by IBM and is only found on IBM-brand computers. MS-DOS is available for brands of computers that are IBM-compatible. DOS will be discussed in detail in Chapter 4.

Common DOS commands are:

COPY	used to copy files from one location to another
ERASE	used to erase a file from a disk
FORMAT	used to prepare a magnetic disk to store information
CHKDSK	used to analyze a magnetic disk and produce its current status

```
TODAY... Sun 11-01-1992                                        TIME...23:53:00.09
C:\TEXT>chkdsk a:

   1213952 bytes total disk space
    600064 bytes in 15 user files
    613888 bytes available on disk

       512 bytes in each allocation unit
      2371 total allocation units on disk
      1199 available allocation units on disk

    655360 total bytes memory
    525120 bytes free

TODAY... Sun 11-01-1992                                        TIME...23:53:09.21
C:\TEXT>
```

FIGURE 3.1 A DOS command.

The CHKDSK command is shown in Figure 3.1.

Microsoft **Windows**® is an **operating environment** that takes DOS and changes its appearance to the user. Pictures of documents, called "icons," pull-down menus, and windows take the place of the command structure seen on a DOS screen. Figure 3.2 shows an example of a Windows screen.

FIGURE 3.2 The Windows Program Manager.

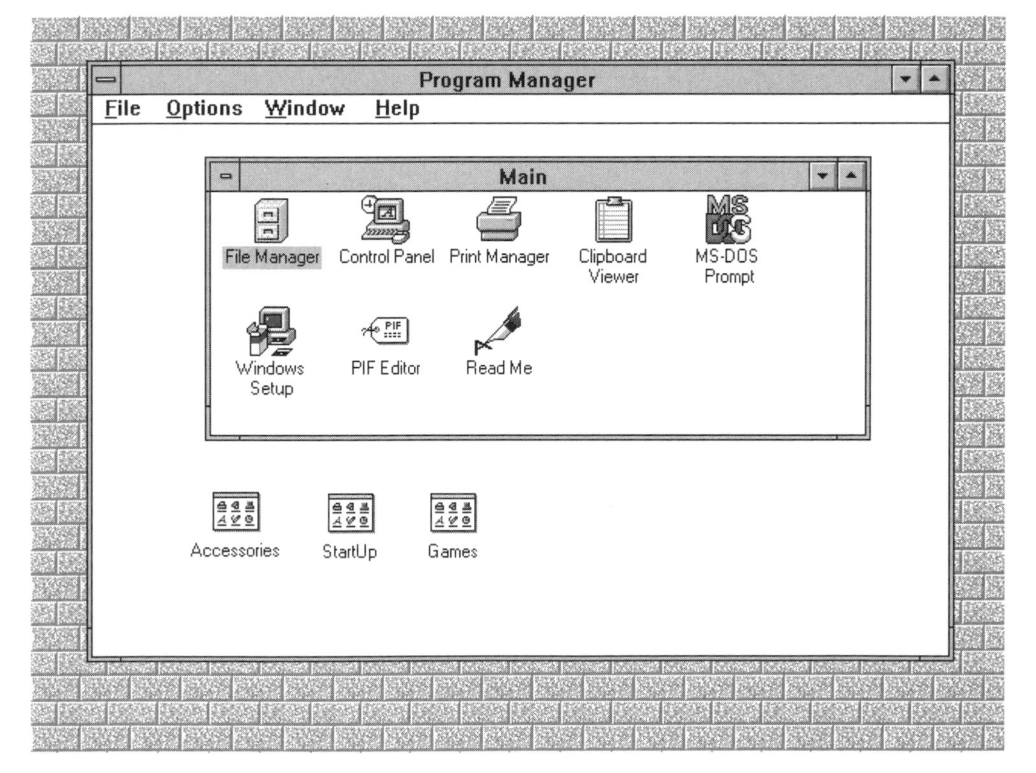

Windows also gives the user the ability to work in more than one program at a time. For example, you may be working on a document in WordPerfect in one window and on a spreadsheet in Lotus 1-2-3 in another window.

b. Windows 95

Microsoft **Windows® 95** is an operating system that improves on the DOS and Windows operating environment combination. This operating system is very similar in appearance and feel to the operating system of a Macintosh. Windows 95 is a 32-bit operating system. This allows it to run 32-bit applications, which are faster and more efficient than those applications written for DOS and Windows. An example of the Windows 95 main screen is shown in Figure 3.3.

FIGURE 3.3 The Windows 95 desktop.

c. Macintosh

Macintosh computers have an operating system with a graphical operating environment. An example of a Macintosh screen is shown in Figure 3.4. One uses a mouse to select icons and menus. The Macintosh line of microcomputers was the first to use windows to display applications, icons to represent utilities and

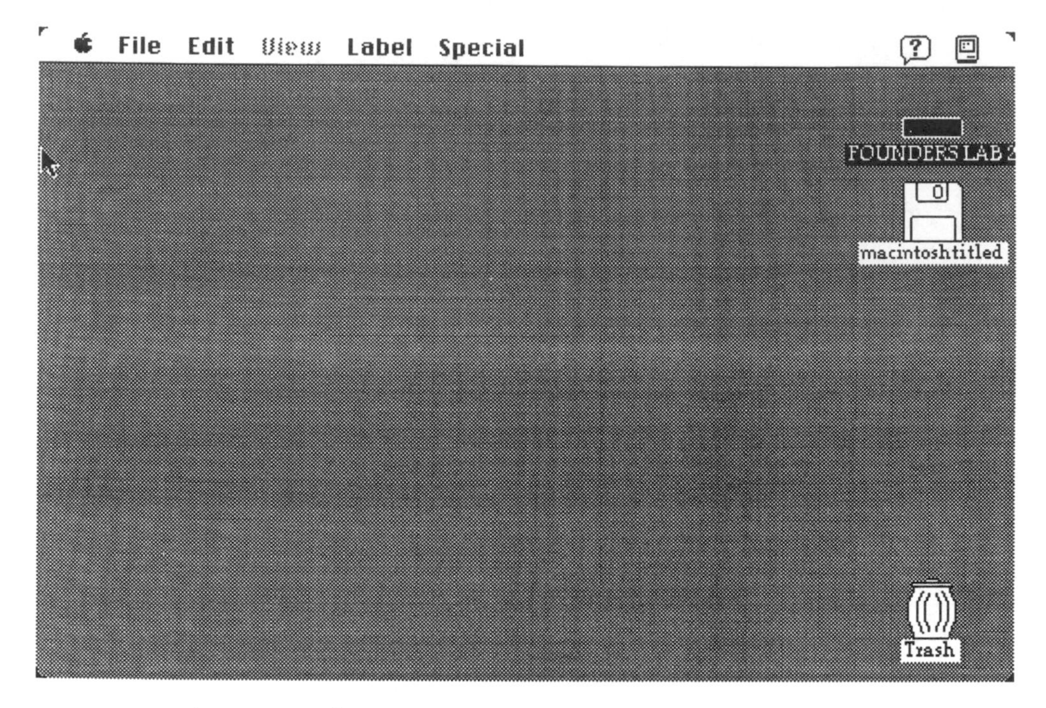

FIGURE 3.4 The Macintosh operating system with its graphical operating environment.

applications, and a mouse for moving the cursor on the screen. This operating system is very similar to the Windows 95 operating system.

d. OS/2

OS/2 is an operating system developed by IBM and appears much like Windows 95. OS/2 is a 32-bit operating system and can run many programs created for DOS and Windows as well as those written for OS/2. OS/2 operates efficiently on systems with limited RAM (4 megabytes minimum) and takes full advantage of systems with more RAM.

e. UNIX

UNIX is an operating system traditionally popular with computer programmers, scientists, and engineers. It can be a complicated operating system to a computer novice due to its command structure. It is used in the law office with some minicomputer and microcomputer systems.

3. Utility Programs

Utility programs help you operate your own computer more efficiently. These programs help to run, enhance, create, or analyze other programs and hardware. Programs that can undelete a file, unformat a disk, debug a program, or perform a task such as tape backup fall into this category.

4. Application Programs

Application programs assist in the performance of business-related and personal tasks. This category of software includes programs that perform word processing, create spreadsheets, create databases, manage cases, produce bills, and provide entertainment (game programs). Some examples of application programs are Word-Perfect, Word, Quattro Pro, and Paradox.

C. LAW OFFICE SOFTWARE

Legal professionals use a wide variety of software. Some of this software is created specifically for the legal business, and some of it is applicable to any type of business. This section will discuss the most commonly used software types and how they are used by the legal professional.

1. Accounting and Time and Billing Software

Law firms usually purchase their first computer in order to automate the office's accounting and word processing functions. Law office accounting and **time and billing software** packages keep track of the time of the billers within the office and their respective rates.

Law is a service business. In order to receive income, the law office must generate an itemized billing statement for the client. To do this, a legal professional keeps track of the time spent working on specific matters for each client. An individual matter is the reason for which the client is seeking the services of the firm. It can be anything from a lawsuit or a corporate merger to a tax problem. The legal professional uses a **time sheet** or a **time slip** to record the time spent on each matter. A time sheet is a document, usually prepared daily, that is used to enter the client and matter name, the services performed, and the time spent performing the services. An example of a time sheet is shown in Figure 3.5 below. A time slip is prepared for each task or group of tasks performed on a particular matter during a day. An example of a time slip is shown in Figure 3.6. Time sheets and time slips will either be prepared in writing and submitted to the accounting department, or they will be entered directly into the computer by the legal professional.

As a paralegal, you will be required to keep track of the time that you spend

FIGURE 3.5 A sample time sheet.

TIME SHEET

DATE: 9/3/96 NAME: Sue Smith

CLIENT/MATTER	DESCRIPTION	HOURS
Wright/PI 29001	Review discovery requests; Draft responses to requests for admissions; Draft portion	3.60
	of responses to interrogatories; Telephone conference with client re responses to Interrogatories (555-4321 12 min.)	
Holman/Corp. 35021	Draft amendment to corporate bylaws; Prepare minutes from board meeting of	2.10
	8/31/96 from secretary's notes.	
Dunham/PI 42001	Legal research re possible negligent infliction of emotional distress cause of	1.25
	action; Draft memo to DSL.	
	Total	6.95

TIME SLIP

DATE: 9/3/96 NAME: Sue Smith

CLIENT/MATTER: Wright/PI 29001 HOURS: 3.60

DESCRIPTION:
Review discovery requests; Draft responses to requests for admissions;
Draft portion of responses to interrogatories; telephone conference
with client re responses to interrogatories (555-4321 12 min.)

FIGURE 3.6 A sample time slip.

working on each matter for a client. Time is measured in tenths or hundredths, depending on the firm's policy. When you begin working on a matter for a client, you note the time that you begin. As you work, you may note on your time sheet or time slip the different tasks that you are performing. When you are finished with the task or move on to another matter, you note the time that you stopped working on the initial matter. You then compute the time spent on that matter and convert it into a decimal number. A sample conversion chart is shown below:

Minutes	Decimal	Minutes	Decimal
5	.10	35	.60
10	.20	40	.70
15	.25	45	.75
20	.35	50	.80
25	.40	55	.90
30	.50	60	1.00

Your office may have a policy providing for a set minimum on certain services such as telephone calls. Many firms charge a minimum of .20 of an hour for each telephone call because, in order to take or place a call, you must end what you are working on, reorganize your thoughts to focus on the subject of the call, and then prepare youself to continue your work once the call is completed. The .20 minimum accounts for that time. Of course, calls lasting more than 10 minutes will be billed according to their true time consumption.

Once the time sheet or time slip entries have been placed into the time and billing software, the computer organizes them by client and matter to prepare the billing statements. Different legal professionals within the office will bill their time at different rates. The software recognizes each individual's initials and computes the amount due for the services accordingly. The accounting department will add any additional expenses, such as copying, postage, telephone calls, and computerized legal research, to the bill and prepare a preview of the billing statement. The billing preview is reviewed by a person in charge of the client's matters to check that the figures are accurate and that the client is not being overcharged for a specific service. The reviewed bill is then returned to accounting for finalization and transmittal to the client. A sample final billing statement is shown in Figure 3.7. When the client pays the bill, the payment is entered into the time and billing software to adjust the client's account.

Many time and billing software packages also can produce accounting and management reports such as accounts receivable reports, individual client account reports, work in progress reports, individual and firm productivity reports, and

FIGURE 3.7 A sample billing invoice.

Marshall, Hanson, and Dewey
12345 Main Street
Carson City, Nevada 80009

September 30, 1996

Jason P. Wright
1122 Pine Lane
Carson City, NV 80009

Re: Wright v. Potter

Date	Description of Services Rendered	Init.	Time	Amount
9/3/96	Review of discovery requests; Draft responses to requests for admissions; Draft portion of responses to interrogatories; Telephone conference with client regarding responses to interrogatories.	SBS	3.60	$288.00
9/10/96	Draft remainder of responses to interrogatories.	SBS	2.75	$220.00
9/15/96	Finalize responses to requests for admissions and interrogatories.	LDR	1.10	$247.50
9/28/96	Conference with client re status of case and trial strategy; Prepare memo to file re case.	LDR	2.50	$562.50

Miscellaneous charges: $ 6.50
Copy costs: $3.50
Telephone charges: $3.00

Total Amount Due: $1,324.50

Thank you,

MARSHALL, HANSON, AND DEWEY

unbilled time reports. These reports assist the firm in determining the productivity of individuals, the firm, and the accounting procedures as a whole.

2. Word Processing Software

Word processing software packages allow a firm's secretarial staff, as well as legal professionals, to draft documents using a computer. The advantages of word processing over the traditional typewriter are the ease of document revision and the wide range of word processor features available, such as spell checking and graphics creation. For example, a paragraph can be inserted in a 40-page contract and the contract reprinted in a matter of minutes using a word processor. The same task would take hours with a typewriter. An example of a word processing software package is WordPerfect. Word processing is discussed at length in Chapter 7.

3. Document Generation

Document generation is the creation of a template document or form for frequently used documents. Figure 3.8 shows an example of a template document.

FIGURE 3.8 A template document.

[Date]

[Client Name]
[Client Street]
[Client City], [Client State] [Client Zip]

Dear [Client Title Name]:

Enclosed is a retainer agreement employing the law firm of Hanson and Hanson to represent you in an action for injuries suffered by you resulting from [Incident] which occurred on [Incident Date]. Please sign the retainer agreement and return it to this office as soon as possible.

Thank you for retaining the firm of Hanson and Hanson.

Sincerely,

[Attorney]
HANSON AND HANSON

Client and case information is entered into a database for use with the template. Documents are then generated by integrating the case information with the template. Figure 3.9 shows a generated document.

Many of the documents created in a law office are forms. Oftentimes letters, retainer agreements, contracts, articles of incorporation, bylaws, minutes, complaints, answers, affidavits, court orders, proofs of service, and other documents contain "boilerplate" language. The only parts of these documents that change are the facts specific to a given client or case. With a document generator you can take one of these documents and create a template by identifying the places where the variable information belongs. Once the template is developed, an input form is created for entry of the variable information. The information from the input form is then combined with the template to generate the document.

FIGURE 3.9 A generated document. (Underscoring added to figure for emphasis.)

July 22, 1996

Mary Smith
54 Main Street
Los Angeles, California 90007

Dear Mrs. Smith:

Enclosed is a retainer agreement employing the law firm of Hanson and Hanson to represent you in an action for injuries suffered by you resulting from slipping and falling on leaves and debris while walking on a sidewalk which occurred on April 11, 1996. Please sign the retainer agreement and return it to this office as soon as possible.

Thank you for retaining the firm of Hanson and Hanson.

Sincerely,

James T. Keel
HANSON AND HANSON

4. Electronic Spreadsheet Software

Electronic spreadsheet software packages are used by legal professionals to create spreadsheets for a variety of applications. An electronic spreadsheet is similar to an accountant's pad with its preprinted columns and rows. With an electronic spreadsheet, however, you can insert or remove columns or rows and make them larger or smaller. You can also enter formulas in the places where you would normally put the total that you have manually computed on a calculator. When information within the spreadsheet is changed, the software will automatically recalculate each formula and display a new total.

Legal professionals use electronic spreadsheets for in-house accounting and management and for calculating "what if" scenarios. "What if" scenarios involve creating a spreadsheet and then altering the information within the spreadsheet to analyze the results. For example: "What if we increase John's billing rate to $140 an hour. Will that give us the necessary income to purchase the computer system?" A spreadsheet with the income and expenses of the firm could be altered to show the change in John's income after the new rate. The effect of the change in John's billing rate to $140 per hour would immediately be reflected in a new income total. All of the computations within the spreadsheet that were dependent on John's billing rate would change automatically.

The "what if" scenario can also be a valuable tool in the areas of estate and tax planning and family law.

a. Estate Planning

Estate planners can create a spreadsheet with the income and expenses of a family. The spreadsheet can then be altered to observe what effect the death of the family's primary wage earner would have on the income and expenses of the family. Perhaps a larger life insurance policy would be warranted to compensate for the lost income.

b. Tax Planning

Tax planners can create a spreadsheet showing a corporation's income and deductions and the computed taxes based on this information. The tax planner can then add a deduction or increase the corporation's income and observe the effect on the tax liability.

c. Family Law

Family law practitioners can use electronic spreadsheets to assist with, among other things, the division of assets in a marital dissolution action. Columns are created for the asset names and the value of assets assigned to the husband and to the wife. The distribution of assets can then be altered to observe the effect on the total value attributed to each person. (See Figure 3.10.)

5. Damage Calculation Software

Programs are available to the legal professional to assist in calculating present and future damages and in structuring settlements. For example, Advocate Software's

DISSOLUTION OF SIMPSON

ITEM	PETER	SUSAN	NOTES
Residence		$125,000	$325,000 value less mortgage
Cabin	$142,000		$300,000 value less morgage
Investments:			
Savings	$18,500	$18,500	Total value $37,000
Stock	$6,000	$6,000	Total value $12,000
Personal Property:			
Peter's Car	$12,200		Blue Book value
Susan's Car		$10,300	Blue Book value
Recreation Equipment	$1,250	$1,250	Total value $2,500
Computer Equipment	$2,700		
Household Furnishings:			
Television		$300	
VCR		$250	
Stereo	$750		
Living Room		$2,400	
Dining Room		$3,500	
Bedrooms		$2,600	
Family Room		$900	
Cabin Furniture	$4,200		
Refrigerator		$500	
Microwave		$100	
TOTALS	$187,600	$171,600	

FIGURE 3.10 A spreadsheet dividing the assets in a marital dissolution.

PI Economist will calculate damages in personal injury, medical malpractice, and product liability cases. The user completes information in a Case Information Screen, and the program then calculates the individual's work life and life expectancy. Lost earnings and future loss of earnings, medical costs, and miscellaneous other costs are factored by the computer to produce a report on the damages. Rates of inflation and other factors may be adjusted to perform "what if" scenarios using the program. A sample of a report generated with this program is shown in Figure 3.11.

JOE ATTORNEY, ESQ.
Attorney at Law
335 Main Street San Diego, CA 92110
(619) 555-1212

Personal Injury Economic Damages Report
Plaintiff: Ima Shirley Hurting
Report Produced On 07/10/1996 Prepared by: Betty D. Typer

Case Information

Trial or Settlement Date: 08/04/1996
Plaintiff's Sex: Female
Birthdate: 05/05/1955
Race: White
Injury Date: 02/01/1991

Worklife Expectancy (as of injury date): 20.38 years.*
Life Expectancy (as of injury date): 45.15 years.**
Retirement Age: 56.13
Age at Death: 80.9

Discount rate (adjusted for inflation) for high present value: 2%
Discount rate (adjusted for inflation) for low present value: 4%
Compound interest rate for past damages: 6%

Damages Summary

Type of Damage	Present Values			Future Values	
	Past	Future From (Low)	Future To (High)	Past	Future
Lost Earnings	$ 150,072	$ 575,544	$ 683,967	$ 127,844	$ 820,226
Fringe Benefits	56,243	201,226	238,683	47,799	285,716
Household Chores	130,857	554,552	713,299	114,162	956,531
Medical Costs	12,346	256,439	366,600	9,226	553,956
Other Costs	19,758	57,518	60,922	14,764	64,651
Total Damages	$ 369,276	$ 1,645,279	$ 2,063,471	$ 313,795	$ 2,681,080
Grand Total Damages		$ 2,014,555	$ 2,432,747	$ 2,994,875	

* Worklife Expectancy calculated from tables in "A Markov Process Model of Work Life Expectancies Based on Labor Market Activity in 1992-93", Journal of Legal Economics, American Academy of Economic & Financial Experts, pub, Vol 5, Number 3, Winter, 1995.

** Life Expectancy calculated from tables from "National Center for Health Statistics, Vital Statistics of the United States, 1991; vol. II sec. 6 Life Tables" Washington: Public Health Service, 1995.

FIGURE 3.11 A damage calculation report.

6. Document Management Software

As computers have made their way into the law office in large numbers, saving and retrieving documents on a local area network has become a problem. In order to save or retrieve a document, you must specify the correct drive, directory, and file name. This requires an understanding of DOS that many people in the law office just do not have. This lack of knowledge, coupled with poor computer network management, can lead to files with unintelligible file names being stored in the wrong directories. It also makes it difficult to locate a file that you want to retrieve.

To alleviate this problem, software companies have developed **document management software.** Document managers, as they are sometimes called, are written to make it easier to save and retrieve files. The law office installs the document manager on the network and sets up categories of information that the user will fill in each time a document is saved. When the document is saved, the user will be prompted to enter information, such as his or her initials, client name, client number, case name, document title, and document type. In many instances, the document manager will assign a file name to the document and place it in the proper directory. The drive letter, directory path, and file name are often placed in a footer on the document so that anyone with a printed copy can locate it. To retrieve the document into the word processor by using the document manager, the file name can be entered or a search of one or more categories can be conducted. For example, if you know that you drafted a contract for a specific client but you cannot remember where it was saved or what its file name is, you can enter the client's name, your initials, and the document type (e.g., contract). The document manager will search through the categories of each of the documents on the network and provide you with a list of the files you have created for that client that are contracts. Selecting the correct one will open the file into the word processor.

Document management software is not necessary in a small office with adequate computer training for its employees and good network management. In larger firms, however, it almost becomes a necessity to purchase this software to manage the documents on the network.

7. Case Management Software

Case management software assists in keeping track of information regarding each of the firm's clients and cases. This information includes

- names, addresses, and telephone numbers of case counsel
- names, addresses, and telephone numbers of clients
- a list of a case's pleadings
- a list of due dates, conferences, and court hearings for all cases

This software lets the legal professional have all case information available on the computer and reduces the need to constantly search through files to find telephone numbers and addresses. The programs can also perform conflict of interest checks, keep case and office calendars, and maintain databases of case information. Many programs will also link with your word processor to provide client addresses and other information.

An example of case information in a case management program is shown in Figure 3.12.

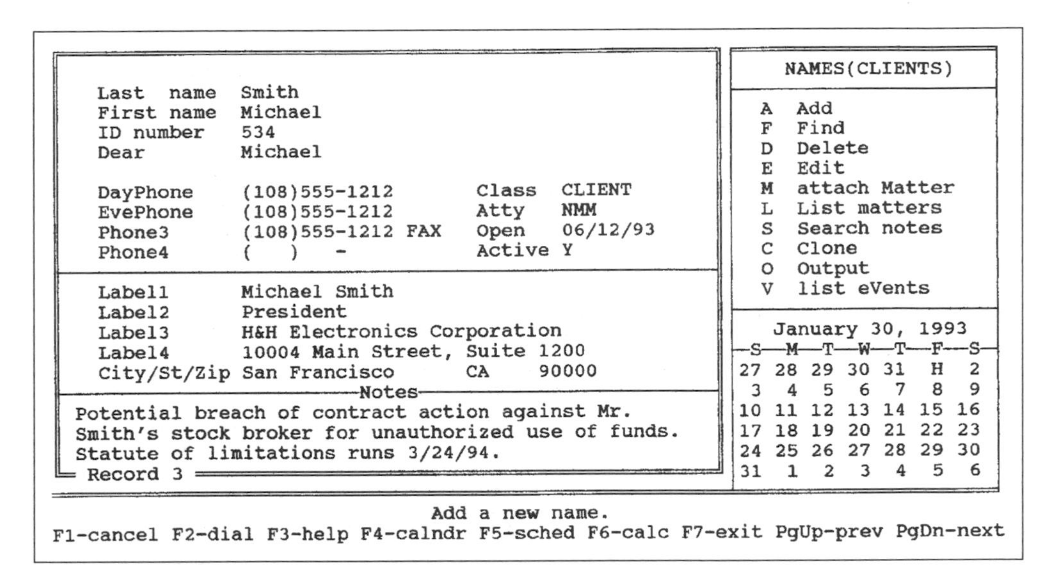

```
Last  name   Smith
First name   Michael
ID number    534
Dear         Michael

DayPhone     (108)555-1212       Class   CLIENT
EvePhone     (108)555-1212       Atty    NMM
Phone3       (108)555-1212 FAX   Open    06/12/93
Phone4       (   )   -           Active  Y

Label1       Michael Smith
Label2       President
Label3       H&H Electronics Corporation
Label4       10004 Main Street, Suite 1200
City/St/Zip  San Francisco       CA      90000
                       Notes
Potential breach of contract action against Mr.
Smith's stock broker for unauthorized use of funds.
Statute of limitations runs 3/24/94.
Record 3

NAMES(CLIENTS)
A  Add
F  Find
D  Delete
E  Edit
M  attach Matter
L  List matters
S  Search notes
C  Clone
O  Output
V  list eVents

 January 30, 1993
 S  M  T  W  T  F  S
27 28 29 30 31  H  2
 3  4  5  6  7  8  9
10 11 12 13 14 15 16
17 18 19 20 21 22 23
24 25 26 27 28 29 30
31  1  2  3  4  5  6

Add a new name.
F1-cancel F2-dial F3-help F4-calndr F5-sched F6-calc F7-exit PgUp-prev PgDn-next
```

FIGURE 3.12 Client information entered in a case management program.

8. Calendaring Software

Calendaring software can vary from programs that maintain an individual's calendar to programs that maintain case calendars and firm calendars. Calendaring software can be purchased alone or as part of a case management program.

Calendaring software programs notify the user of upcoming due dates, either on the screen or by a printed calendar or report. These dates are entered into the program by a legal professional, a secretary, or the person in charge of the firm's calendar.

Specialized calendar programs will compute due dates automatically. For instance, "Fast Track" calendaring programs are designed to compute due dates for pleadings and conferences in jurisdictions that require an attorney to bring a case to trial in a short amount of time. With these programs, the user inputs the filing date of a complaint or answer, and the computer then calculates the due dates of further pleadings, discovery cutoffs, court conferences, and other information. A calendar input screen and calendar are shown in Figures 3.13 and 3.14.

9. Forms Software

Forms software enables a legal professional to use a computer to complete the preprinted legal forms used by the various courts. The forms are preprogrammed into the software. A selected form is displayed on the computer monitor in order to input and revise information. (The form itself cannot be altered.) The completed form is sent to a laser printer, which prints it just as though the actual form had been completed with a typewriter. The advantage of this software is that an error

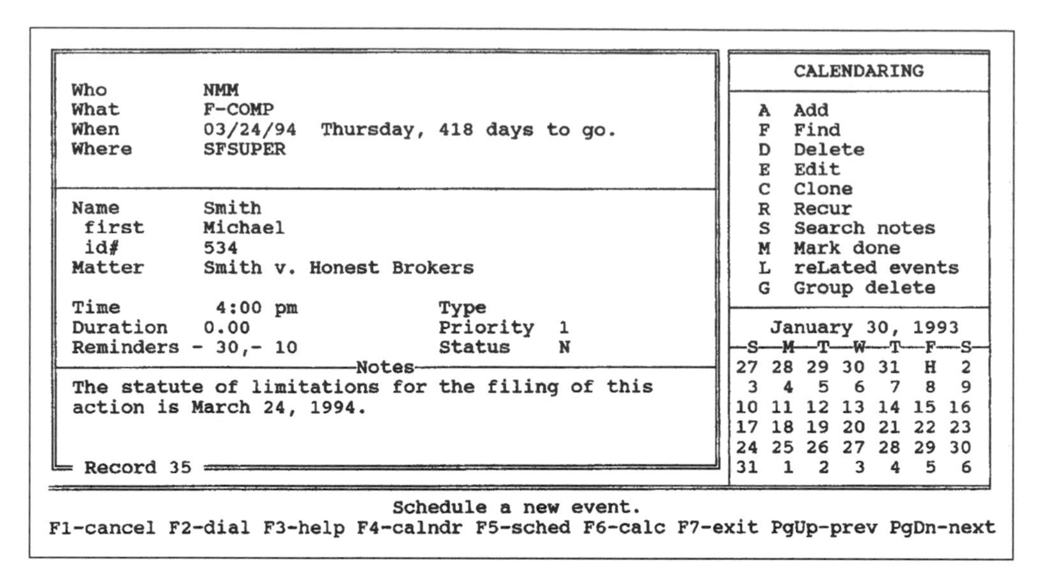

```
Who        NMM                                      CALENDARING
What       F-COMP                                   A  Add
When       03/24/94  Thursday, 418 days to go.      F  Find
Where      SFSUPER                                  D  Delete
                                                    E  Edit
Name       Smith                                    C  Clone
 first     Michael                                  R  Recur
 id#       534                                      S  Search notes
Matter     Smith v. Honest Brokers                  M  Mark done
                                                    L  reLated events
Time        4:00 pm          Type                   G  Group delete
Duration   0.00              Priority  1
Reminders - 30,- 10          Status    N            January 30, 1993
-------------------Notes-------------------         S  M  T  W  T  F  S
The statute of limitations for the filing of this   27 28 29 30 31  H  2
action is March 24, 1994.                            3  4  5  6  7  8  9
                                                    10 11 12 13 14 15 16
                                                    17 18 19 20 21 22 23
                                                    24 25 26 27 28 29 30
 Record 35                                          31  1  2  3  4  5  6

                        Schedule a new event.
F1-cancel F2-dial F3-help F4-calndr F5-sched F6-calc F7-exit PgUp-prev PgDn-next
```

FIGURE 3.13 A calendar input screen.

```
  Sun       Mon                M A R C H   1 9 9 4            Fri       Sat
  27        28         1         2         3         4         5
                             March 24, 1994
   Day When      Time      Hrs What      Who        Where     Client
  6 Th  03/24/94  4:00 pm 0.00 F-COMP    NMM        SFSUPER   Smith
    Alt-Z)oom
  13        14        15        16        17        18        19
  20        21        22        23        24        25        26
  27        28        29        30        31         1         2
   3         4     January 30, 1993   AT-A-GLANCE
D-new date  W-change Who (All)      A-add E-edit C-clone P-print  V-view
F3-help     R-recur  L-reLated      Del-delete   Alt-F-filter Alt-M-Mark done
```

FIGURE 3.14 A calendar with the items displayed for the highlighted date.

can be corrected on the computer and the form sent again to the printer. This eliminates the need to retype entire forms.

Different forms of software packages are available for each jurisdiction and area of law (e.g., civil forms, family law forms, and probate forms). This type of software requires a laser printer with sufficient memory to store several typefaces.

Therefore, it is important to check the firm's printer capabilities before purchasing the software.

10. Deposition Summarization Software

Summarizing depositions is a task that most legal assistants will perform at least once in their careers. When a deposition is taken, a shorthand reporter takes down everything that is said and produces a transcript of the proceedings. The transcript is typed on ruled and numbered pleading paper for easy page and line number reference during court proceedings. A legal assistant is usually asked to summarize the transcript by reading through it and summarizing the responses to lines of questioning, noting the page and line numbers where the answer is given. The process of summarizing a deposition manually is very time-consuming. **Deposition summarization software** makes this process easier. Most shorthand reporters will provide an ASCII (DOS text) disk of the transcript along with the bound volume. ASCII disks can be read by almost every word processor and deposition summarization software program. The deposition summarization software displays the transcript on the computer screen. The user reads through the transcript and highlights pertinent passages. With a keystroke or mouse click, the highlighted text is copied into the summary document and the page and line numbers are automatically inserted. The final summary document is created with the correct page and line references and with minimal typing.

11. Document Imaging

Document imaging is the scanning of documents and pictures onto an optical disk (WORM disk). Large litigation cases may have hundreds of thousands of pages of evidentiary documents. Storing these documents within the office takes up valuable office space. Getting them all into the courtroom presents another obstacle. Document imaging solves this problem. Document imaging uses a scanner to take a picture of each document and place it on an optical disk. A single optical disk the size of a compact disk can hold thousands of pages. As the document is scanned, an abstract of the document or the full text of the document is entered into a database linked to the imaging software. Documents are retrieved onto the computer screen by a document number reference or by a search within the abstract or full-text database. Many programs of this type also provide the ability to bar code the images. The documents can then be retrieved to the screen by scanning a bar code with a light pen. The original paper documents, once scanned, can be sent off to outside storage. They will need to be retrieved for introduction into evidence at trial, but any copies necessary before that time may be printed from the optical disk. Special hardware is required to scan the documents onto the optical disk. Many firms, therefore, have outside companies come in and scan the documents onto the optical disks. These companies charge a fee per image scanned. Once an image is scanned onto the optical disk, the disk becomes a ROM disk and cannot be altered.

12. Database Management Systems

Database management systems (DBMSs) are software programs that help manage databases containing an abstract, image, or full text of a document or piece of information. A **database** is an organized collection of related information. There are two main types of databases: those that contain a summary or abstract of information and those that contain the full text or image of the information.

Database management systems are effective litigation tools for

- client lists
- case lists
- conflict of interest checks
- docket and calendar control
- evidence management
- forms file management

a. *Summary Databases*

Summary databases, also called "flat file," "relational," "bibliographic," "abstract," and "index" databases, store a summary of a document or item of information. Examples of everyday summary databases are a telephone book and a library card catalog. The telephone book contains three pieces of information (name, address, and telephone number) about people and businesses within a given area. A library card catalog contains the title, author, subject, catalog number, and other information for each book and periodical in that library.

Summary databases are made up of files, fields, and records. The database *file* is the complete database for a client list, case list, or other collection of information. The *field* is each item category summarized from the information. The *record* is the group of fields for each document or item in the database. Using the telephone book example, the telephone book is the database file, the fields are name, address, and telephone number, and the record is the group of fields for each person or entity listed in the telephone book.

A litigation support summary database, used to keep track of all evidentiary documents for a case, stores a summary record for each piece of evidence. Fields for the database could be

document number
document type
date
author
author company
recipient
recipient company
summary
file location

These fields would make up each record in the database. In generic summary database software programs such as Paradox, Access, and dBase, the fields are determined by the user when the database is created. In many of the programs that have been written specifically as litigation support tools, the fields are already set up for litigation documents.

Creating a summary database is similar to filling out an index card for each item of the database. To enter a document into this database, you would look at the document and enter data for each field. For example, Figures 3.15 and 3.16 show a piece of evidence and how it would be entered into this database.

A search of a summary database involves selecting one or more of the fields and identifying the information you are searching for within the fields. Some examples of search requests are shown below.

All evidence dated before March 18, 1993.	DATE < 03/18/93
All evidence written by John Smith.	AUTHOR = Smith, John
All evidence dated before March 18, 1993, and written by John Smith.	DATE < 03/18/93 AND AUTHOR = Smith, John

b. Full-Text Databases

Full-text databases contain the full text or images of documents. A document scanner is the common way to enter the document text or image into the computer.

When searching a full-text database, the user forms a search looking for key words that will be found in the body of the desired documents. The computer processes the request and lists or displays documents that contain the key words. Full-text databases can be databases that are maintained by an outside source (e.g., LEXIS and WESTLAW), or purchased on compact disks, or scanned to a magnetic disk, tape, or optical disk.

Image databases store a picture of a document or photograph on an optical disk. The documents or photographs are scanned onto the disk with a scanner. An image database cannot be searched like a regular full-text database using key words, because the computer does not recognize the individual words in the image. Many companies that supply imaging technology also provide a way to store the full text of the imaged document so that full-text searching is possible. Imaging databases that do not have accompanying full-text capabilities may be searched like a summary database. When setting up the image database, the user may define fields that will be used with the database documents. As a document or photograph is scanned onto the optical disk, the field information pertaining to that image may be entered by the user.

Full-text databases on CD-ROM (Compact Disk-Read Only Memory) are used to store volumes of legal texts and information. Anywhere from 250,000 to 500,000 pages of text can be stored on a single compact disk.

WOOLFOORD CHEMICAL CORPORATION
5555 Toxic Way
Anywhere, Minnesota 00900

April 25, 1990

Barry Nerdly, Commissioner
Minnesota Air Quality Management
123 Main Street
Anywhere, Minnesota 00900

Re: Commissioner's Report A-457

Dear Barry:

I enjoyed speaking with you last week at the fund raising dinner for your re-election. Your work with Air Quality Management has been outstanding, and I am sure that the voters will support you for another term as Commissioner.

I am writing to you because I am concerned about the findings in the above-referenced Commissioner's Report. The report states that my company "willfully" burned hazardous waste materials at night over the past two years. It further states that the materials were burned at night so that "the black smoke emitted from the smoke stacks would not be visible." I am concerned because there is no basis for these allegations. My company does not burn hazardous waste materials. The waste materials generated by the plant are trucked to the coast for disposal at sea. My office will be happy to supply you with the invoices for the disposal.

I know that you will take some time to review the Report before it is released to the public. The statements contained therein about my company are wholly unsubstantiated and should be eliminated.

Thank you for your reconsideration, and good luck in the upcoming election.

Very truly yours,

SMILEY WOOLFOORD, PRESIDENT
WOOLFOORD CHEMICAL CORPORATION

248

FIGURE 3.15 An evidentiary document to be entered into a database.

```
DOC_NO       248
DOC_TYPE     Letter
DATE         04/25/90
AUTHOR       Woolfoord, Smiley
AUTHOR_CO    Woolfoord Chemical Corporation
RECIPIENT    Nerdly, Barry
RECIP_CO     Minnesota Air Quality Management
SUMMARY      Letter requesting that the Commissioner reconsider
             the findings of Commissioner's Report A-457,
             denying any burning of hazardous materials, and
             hinting at political support for the
             Commissioner's re-election if references to
             Woolfoord Chemical were deleted from the Report.

FILE_LOC     5609.2.10
```

FIGURE 3.16 The database entry for the document in Figure 3.15.

West Publishing Company offers many of its case reporters on compact disks. West's California Reporter, which is comprised of over 200 volumes, is contained on three compact disks. A compact disk drive and special software are required to access the disks and search them using full-text methods. These disks can be searched using full-text methods because the individual characters, as opposed to a page image, are stored on the disk. With office space at a premium, many office law libraries contain shelves of bound volumes and a shelf of numerous other volumes on compact disks. The legal professional is able to travel with an entire set of state codes or digests on a few compact disks in his or her briefcase.

A detailed explanation of summary and full-text databases is given in Chapter 9.

13. Communications Software

Communications software is a type of application program that allows a computer to communicate with another computer or another machine (such as a fax machine).

a. Modem and Fax Communications

Simple communications software for use with modems has the ability to send and receive files between computers using the telephone lines. The modem is a piece of computer hardware that enables the actual communication. Communications software is necessary in order to use the modem.

Some communications packages allow the user to actually operate another computer from a remote location. A person can be working on a computer at home or on a business trip and dial up the office computer. When the remote computer connects to the office computer, the remote computer can perform many of the tasks that you would be able to perform if you were seated at your office desk. Modems and communications packages are very useful to the legal professional. The office computer and its files are only a telephone call away from the legal professional's home computer or laptop computer. Likewise, documents or pleadings created by the legal professional can be transmitted and retrieved to the office's computer whether the legal professional is at home, in a hotel room, or spending a day at the park.

Fax circuit boards ("fax boards") can be purchased alone or as part of a modem ("fax modems"). They enable a user to send files through the telephone lines to fax machines. They also allow the computer to receive faxes. The downside to these fax boards is that, while they are able to send computer files to a fax machine, preprinted forms and signed documents require an external fax machine or a scanner to scan them into the computer.

b. Network Communications

Networking software allows several microcomputers to communicate through a local or wide area network. The local area network, as explained in Chapter 2, enables connected computers to interact, share information, and share printers and other hardware. A wide area network connects computers in distant offices through a dedicated telephone line. A network circuit board (network card) is inserted into an expansion slot in each of the workstations of the network. The network software then governs the operation of the network, allowing for the sharing of files and peripherals and the transmittal of electronic mail.

D. COMPUTER SOFTWARE COPYRIGHTS AND ETHICAL CONSIDERATIONS

Computer software and its accompanying manuals are copyrighted by the owner or creator of the software. A license to use the software and manuals is granted to a purchaser of the software package. This license normally covers only one computer or workstation. Further licenses must be purchased to install the program on more computers or workstations. Even network versions of programs (versions that allow more than one person to use the software at once) require the purchase of licenses for each workstation using the program.

A software license agreement is breached when copies of the software or its manuals are sold or distributed without the permission of the copyright holder. Title 17, §117, of the United States Code states that it is not copyright infringement to make a copy of a computer program *provided that* it is necessary to make the copy in order to run the program, or *provided that* the copy is for archival (back-up) purposes. The purchaser of a software program, therefore, may only make a copy of the program disks if such a copy is necessary to run the program *or* as a backup for the original disks. Any other unauthorized copies are illegal and subject to federal copyright infringement laws.

You will find that people may request copies of a program you have purchased. Making these copies is illegal. If it is the firm's software, you should not copy it even with the firm's approval. Whether you will make the copy of your own software for others is a matter of personal ethics. Remember that the person who wrote the software spent numerous hours developing, testing, and marketing the program. Unauthorized copies deprive the author of much earned royalties.

"Public domain software," "shareware," and "freeware" are software that are not always copyrighted. Copies of these programs are usually free or have a nominal fee associated with using them. The program will usually inform the user whether it is copyrighted and what copying, if any, is permitted.

E. SUMMARY

Computer software is the term used to describe the instructions that run the computer. The four categories of computer software are computer languages, operating systems, utility programs, and application programs. Computer languages are used to create the three other types of software. Operating systems manage the activities of the computer and allow other software to communicate with the computer's hardware. Utility programs help to operate a computer more efficiently. Application programs perform specific business or personal tasks.

Software used by legal professionals can be software developed for specific legal applications or software also used by other types of businesses. Common types of software used in the law office include time and billing software, word processing software, electronic spreadsheet software, document management software, imaging software, database software, and specific legal software such as case management, deposition summarization, form generation, and calendaring programs.

When using any of this software, it is important to consider the copyright rules and regulations. Legally, you may make one copy of a software program for back-up purposes in case your original program disks are damaged. Making any other copies, however, is a violation of copyright laws.

KEY TERMS

application program, 47
calendaring software, 57
case management software, 56
communications software, 63
computer language, 42
database, 60
database management systems (DBMSs), 60
deposition summarization software, 59

document generation, 51
document imaging, 59
document management software, 56
DOS, 43
electronic spreadsheet software, 52
forms software, 57
full-text database, 61
Macintosh, 45
operating environment, 44
operating system, 43
OS/2, 46
software, 41
summary database, 60
time and billing software, 47
time sheet, 47
time slip, 47
UNIX, 46
utility program, 47
Windows, 44
Windows 95, 45
word processing software, 51

QUESTIONS

1. What is software?
2. Name the four categories of software and give an explanation of each.
3. Pick one type of software used by legal professionals (e.g., case management software) and explain how it could be used to help you in your job.
4. When is it legal to make a copy of a software program?
5. What type of software would you use to itemize the income and expenses in a conservatorship action? The court wants to see the date, payee or payor, item category, and amount of every item of income and expense incurred last year on behalf of the conservatee.

DISCUSSION QUESTIONS

1. Discuss the type of operating system, application programs, and utility programs that are used on the computers you will use in this course.
2. Many software packages are expensive, between $150 and $1,500. Software companies claim that they must charge these high prices because so many illegal copies of their software are distributed among friends and acquaintances. This means that a person who legitimately purchases a software package is, in effect, paying for the illegal copies made by others. Would lowering the price of a software package to around $100 cause more people to purchase legal versions of the software and reduce piracy? Would the software company be able to maintain its profit margin?

PART

II

Operating Systems and Environments

CHAPTER

4

DOS

As discussed in Chapter 3, an operating system is a collection of programs used to manage and run a computer. The operating system is the link between the computer's hardware and software; without it, the computer can only use those programs the computer manufacturer has installed in the computer's ROM. You need to learn about operating systems in order to understand the workings of the computer and to perform everyday functions, such as saving, copying, and retrieving files you have created. In this chapter we will discuss the common operating system for microcomputers: DOS (disk operating system).

In Chapter 5 we will discuss Windows, an operating environment for DOS. An operating environment is software that presents an operating system in a different manner. Windows has become very common in law offices, although some offices continue to use only DOS. In Chapter 6 we will discuss the Windows 95 operating system. This operating system is similar to the Windows operating environment and also offers access to DOS. Its advantages: Its 32-bit operating system is capable of running faster software, and it streamlines many of the computing functions, such as the installation of software and new hardware.

All three of these chapters are useful for your general computer education. However, your instructor and your computer system will dictate which of the three chapters you will study. Because Windows is just another way of viewing DOS and Windows 95 follows many DOS rules, Windows and Windows 95 users should study Chapter 4 in addition to Chapter 5 or 6.

A. INTRODUCTION

DOS (disk operating system) is the operating system found on many microcomputers. Its commands are helpful to learn even if the computer you are using has a Windows-type operating environment or operating system. DOS commands are accessible from DOS-based operating environments, operating systems, and application programs. A knowledge of how DOS structures disks is also necessary to save and open documents that you create.

1. Disk Organization

Magnetic and optical disks are the primary media used to store computer files. These disks are housed in **disk drives,** which are given labels by DOS. DOS can also divide the disk into storage places, called "directories," where the user can store related files. Drive labels, moving between drives, and directories are all discussed below.

a. Drive Labels

DOS labels a computer's disk drives with letters. The diskette drives are normally labeled A: and B: and the hard disk drive is labeled with any other letter from C: to Z:. Some hard disk drives are partitioned into more than one letter drive. Therefore, even though you have only one hard disk, it may be identified, for example, as C:, D:, E:, and Z:. Your other types of drives, such as a CD-ROM drive, will also be assigned a letter.

When you are in DOS, a prompt will be displayed on the screen with a flashing cursor where you may enter commands. The DOS prompt identifies the disk drive letter, the current directory (in this example it is the root directory, indicated by the backslash), and is followed by a greater than symbol, >.

C:\> _

The underline symbol in this example indicates the flashing cursor.

b. Moving Between Drives

Sometimes it will be necessary to move from one drive to another to issue a command. To move to a new drive, at the prompt type the desired drive letter followed by a colon and press the [Enter] key.

Example: A:[Enter]
Moves to the A: drive.
C:[Enter]
Moves to the C: drive.

c. Directories

Hard disks and diskettes may be organized and divided into **directories.** Directories are storage places for software files. The main directory on every disk is called the **root. Subdirectories** of the root are created to help organize your files.

The root directory is identified by the backslash character, \ . Imagine the root directory as a filing cabinet. The directories off of the root (its initial "branches") are the separate drawers of the filing cabinet. Yet further directories can be created, much as one places separations within a file drawer. A directory is a "subdirectory" of its parent; therefore, the initial directories branching off of the root are called subdirectories of the root directory.

The directory structure of a disk is referred to as the **tree.** A typical tree for a hard disk could look like the one below.

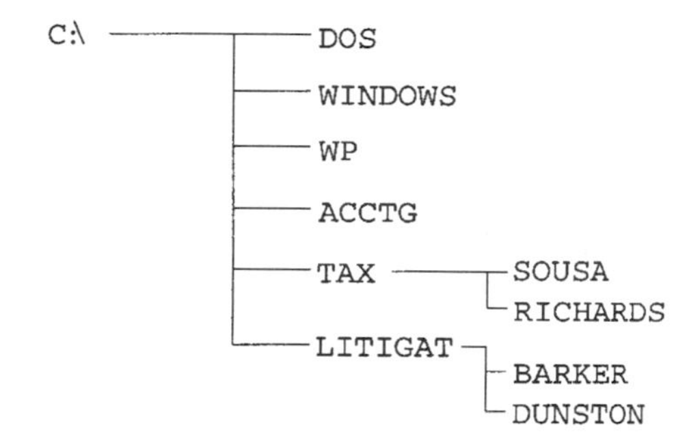

In the example above, the root is indicated by the backslash after the drive letter. The directories DOS, WINDOWS, WP, ACCTG, TAX, and LITIGAT are subdirectories of the root. The TAX and LITIGAT directories are further divided. The directories SOUSA and RICHARDS are subdirectories of the TAX directory. The directories BARKER and DUNSTON are subdirectories of the LITIGAT directory. Sousa and Richards would be clients of our hypothetical firm's tax department. Barker and Dunston would be clients of the litigation department.

When referencing a disk drive using DOS, the letter of the drive is followed by a colon: for example, C:. The directories of the disk are separated by the backslash character (\). The root directory of a C: drive is C:\, and the DOS directory is C:\DOS. Similarly, the WINDOWS directory would be referred to as C:\WINDOWS. The TAX subdirectory called "SOUSA" would be referred to as C:\TAX\SOUSA.

The actual program files that make up DOS, Windows, and WordPerfect would be stored in the \DOS, \WINDOWS, and \WP directories. They are kept separated from other files so that they can be easily deleted from the system when a new version of the program is purchased. The new version would be placed in the same directory after the old version has been erased. The SOUSA and RICHARDS directories will hold the documents that you create for their tax cases. The BARKER and DUNSTON directories will hold the documents that you create for their litigation matters. Making directories and moving between them will be discussed later in this chapter in the DOS Commands section, under MD and CD respectively.

PRACTICE TIP

If the DOS prompt is only displaying the directory letter with a prompt, i.e., C>, the display may be changed to show the current directory, i.e., C:\> or C:\DOS>. The DOS command to change the display is:

PROMPT PG

This command should be included in the computer's AUTOEXEC.BAT file to execute automatically whenever the computer is turned on.

2. Files

Files are software codes that make up purchased programs or that you create when you save a document, database, spreadsheet, or other item. When documents, databases, spreadsheets, and other types of files are created using application software, the user will be asked to give the file a name. DOS will accept file names that contain from *one to eight characters followed by an optional period and a one- to three-character extension.* For example:

FILENAME.EXT

Some software programs automatically supply an extension to file names. For example, Lotus 1-2-3 applies .WK1 as an extension to all file names so that the program will recognize worksheet files by looking for this extension. The following are examples of file names accepted by DOS:

DEMAND.LTR

12/3/96.BRF

TRIALBRF.1

RESUME

File names may be input in uppercase or lowercase letters. In addition to letters and numbers, the following characters may be used in a file name or extension:

! @ # $ % & ( ) - _ ‘ ’ { }

The most important rule to follow when creating a file name is to create a name that will identify the work not only to the user but also to anyone else who may need to locate it.

When you name a file, you may also need to identify the drive letter and directory where it will be placed. If you do not, the file will be placed in the directory that is currently open or the default directory selected by the application.

To save the Barker complaint that you have just created in WordPerfect, you would identify the drive containing the directory for the Barker files, the directory in which to place the file, and the file name. An example is shown below.

C:\LITIGAT\BARKER\COMPLNT

B. DOS COMMANDS

DOS commands may be entered in uppercase or lowercase letters. The [Enter] key is pressed after typing the complete command form in order to execute the command. DOS commands can perform many functions, including listing, copying, moving, renaming, and deleting files. They can also create directories on your disks into which related files are placed.

DOS commands may be divided into three categories:

- commands that act on directories
- commands that act on files
- commands that act on disks

The main commands that you will need to learn are divided into their categories below.

DIRECTORIES	FILES	DISKS
dir dir/p dir/w md cd rd	copy rename erase del	format diskcopy

The format command will be discussed first. The remaining commands will be discussed in order, by category.

1. Formatting Disks—FORMAT

Magnetic disks can be purchased blank or preformatted. **Formatting** a disk prepares it to be used by the computer's operating system and checks for any defects on the disk surface. The format command creates sectors and tracks on the disk to enable the operating system to store and locate information.

Low density and high density diskettes are formatted with different forms of the format command. This is necessary because the disks can hold different quantities of data. When formatting a low density (double density) disk in a high density disk drive, a special command is needed to tell DOS to format at low density. DOS recognizes the disk drive as high density and will automatically format the disk at high density unless otherwise instructed. A high density disk may also be formatted at low density with the same command. The format command is normally performed by typing FORMAT A: or FORMAT B:.

NOTE

It is very important to note that formatting erases *all previous information stored on a disk. Check with your instructor or supervisor regarding their procedures for formatting disks. Never type the word* format *and press the [Enter] key.*

It is a common business practice to erase the format command from the office computer system. This prevents the accidental erasure of important information by a mistake in using the command. Disks may need to be taken to a designated person in the firm to be formatted, or there may be a menu option on the computer screen that automatically performs this task.

---

2. Displaying a List of Directories and Files

a. DIR

The directory command, DIR, displays a list of all subdirectories and files located in the directory where you execute the command. The drive and directory where you are executing the command is called the "default."

In addition to subdirectories and file names, the command will display <DIR> for a directory and the file size in bytes for each file. The date and time of the last revision of the directory or file are also displayed.

Command Structure: DIR
Example: DIR
Displays a list of all directories and files at the current default drive.

```
C:\>dir

Volume in drive C is DOS500
Directory of C:\

LOTUS              <DIR>     03-05-91    4:51p
DBASE4             <DIR>     03-05-91    4:52p
WP51               <DIR>     03-05-91    4:57p
AUTOEXEC  BAT        196     03-05-91    7:54p
MENU      BAT         31     12-06-90    4:25p
CONFIG    SYS        129     03-05-91    5:29p
          6 File(s)          5187583 bytes free
```

b. Displaying a List of Files in a Directory

To display the contents of a specific directory, the directory name is typed after the DIR command. A backslash is placed in front of the directory name to indicate that it is a branch off of the root.

Command Structure: DIR \[directory name]
Example: DIR \LOTUS
Displays the files and directories located in the LOTUS subdirectory of the root.

```
C:\>DIR \LOTUS

Volume in drive C is DOS500
Directory of C:\LOTUS

.              <DIR>     03-05-91   5:04p
..             <DIR>     03-05-91   5:04p
ACCTG          <DIR>     03-05-91   5:15p
MGMT           <DIR>     03-05-91   5:16p
[LOTUS program files would be listed below]
```

NOTE

The two directories indicated by the single and double periods are found in all subdirectories. The single period directory denotes the directory currently listed. The double period entry denotes this directory's parent directory. The parent directory is the directory under which this subdirectory is created. For example, the parent directory of C:\LOTUS is the root directory C:\.
The directories and files of the parent directory may be displayed from this subdirectory by simply typing:

DIR ..

To display the contents of a subdirectory of a subdirectory of the root, the following command is used:

Command Structure: DIR \[subdirectory\subdirectory]
Example: DIR \LOTUS\ACCTG
Displays the files and subdirectories located in the \LOTUS\ACCTG directory.

c. Displaying a List of Files on Another Drive

To display a list of the directories and files on a drive other than the default drive, the desired drive letter must be specified.

Command Structure: DIR [drive letter]:
Example: DIR B:\
Displays a list of all subdirectories and files at the root of a diskette located in the B: drive.

```
C:\>DIR B:\

Volume in drive B has no label
Directory of B:\

DEMAND     LTR    12568      05-12-92   10:51a
SMITH      CPL    57433      07-25-92    4:52p
SMITH1     ROG    42875      08-05-92    1:57p
SMITH1     RFA    25196      08-05-92    3:44p
SMITHDEP   NOT     2108      08-06-92   10:25a
           5 File(s)          222316 bytes free
```

PRACTICE TIP

Occasionally when you try to view or move to a diskette drive, you will get the message:

Not ready reading drive B
Abort, Retry, Fail?

This can happen if your diskette is damaged or not formatted, or if you have not inserted a diskette into the drive.
Responding by typing the letter A will instruct the computer to try to abort the command. Frequently, however, you will get the "Not ready" message again. If you have not put a diskette into the drive, you should do so and then press "R" for retry. If nothing seems to be working, you should type "F" to return to the hard drive. When you type "F," you receive the message:

Current drive is no longer valid>

Type the letter of your hard drive followed by a colon (e.g., C:) to return to the hard drive.

To display the contents of a directory located on a drive other than the default drive, the desired drive letter must first be specified.

Command Structure: DIR [drive letter]:\[directory]
Example: DIR A:\WORK
Displays the files and subdirectories located on the A: drive in the WORK directory.

NOTE

Remember that DOS commands are not case-specific. The command above could also be typed: dir a:\work *or* DIR a:\WORK *or* dir A:\work

d. Displaying a List of Specific Files

The DIR command may also be used to display file names with common characteristics. For example, I always recommend that letters be named with the extension .LTR. This immediately identifies the file as a letter. To display a list of all files with the .LTR extension, the following command would be used:

Command Structure: DIR [portion of file name]
Example: DIR .LTR
or
Example: DIR *.LTR
Displays all files with the extension .LTR. The wild card character (*) may be used but is not required.

The listing of a single file may also be displayed with this command.

Command Structure: DIR [filename]
Example: At the B:\ prompt, type: DIR DEMAND.LTR

```
B:\>dir demand.ltr

Volume in drive B has no label
Directory of B:\

DEMAND     LTR    12568     05-12-92  10:51a
           1 File(s)         222316 bytes free
```

e. DIR/P

When there are a large number of files and subdirectories at a particular location on a drive, the DIR command can be modified to pause at the end of each screenful of information.

Command Structure: DIR/P
Example: DIR/P
Displays the subdirectories and files located at the default directory, pausing at the end of each screenful of information.

```
C:\>dir/p

Volume in drive C is DOS500
Directory of C:\

LOTUS              <DIR>     03-05-91    4:51p
DBASE4             <DIR>     03-05-91    4:52p
WP51               <DIR>     03-05-91    4:57p
AUTOEXEC  BAT        196     03-05-91    7:54p
MENU      BAT         31     12-06-90    4:25p
CONFIG    SYS        129     03-05-91    5:29p
Press any key to continue . . .
```

Pressing any key will take you to the next screenful of files. This command may be used just like the DIR command.

Examples: DIR/P A:\
DIR/P C:\LOTUS

PRACTICE TIP

The forward slash [/] is used in the structure of commands (e.g., DIR/P). The backslash [\] is used to designate and separate directory names (e.g., C:\LOTUS\ACCTG). An easy way to remember which key is the forward slash and which is the backslash is to think of the forward slash as leaning forward and the backslash as leaning backward.

f. DIR/W

This command provides a wide display of the directories and files. It does not display the <DIR> indication, file size, or date and time of the last revision. This allows the command to display more directory and file names on the screen. In newer versions of DOS, the subdirectory names will appear in brackets.

Command Structure: DIR/W
Example: DIR/W
Displays the subdirectories and files of the current directory in a wide display.

```
C:\>dir/w

Volume in drive C is DOS500
Directory of C:\

LOTUS   DBASE4   WP51   AUTOEXEC BAT   MENU BAT
CONFIG  SYS
          6 File(s)      5187583 bytes free
```

Like the DIR/P command, the DIR/W command can be used in the same way as the DIR command.

Examples: DIR/W A:\
DIR/W C:\LOTUS

PRACTICE TIP

Many students ask what the statement "Volume in drive C is DOS500" *indicates when they use the DIR command. The volume is the name given to the disk. With many format commands, you are prompted to label the disk. In the DIR examples above, the hard disk has been named "DOS500." If your disk has not been labeled, you will see a statement like:* "Volume in drive C has no label."

---

3. Making Directories—MD or MKDIR

Making directories is an essential task in order to keep the computer's disk space organized. The command to make a directory, **MD** or **MKDIR,** is used to perform this task. Either command will work, but it is easier to use MD. A directory name can contain anywhere from one to eight alphanumeric characters.

A law office computer will have a hard disk that needs to be organized to provide directories for software program files, client files, and form files. Creating a directory tree on paper makes it easier to see how the structure will work. For example, a firm may need a directory tree that looks like the following:

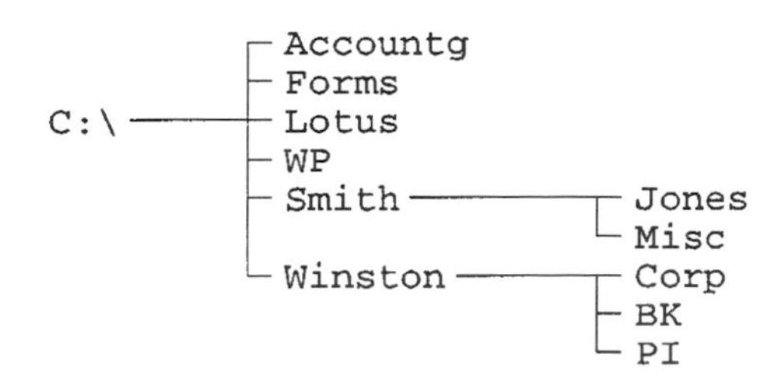

In this example, the software program files for Lotus 1-2-3 and WordPerfect each have their own directories (Lotus and WP). There is also a directory for the firm's forms and for the accounting department's software programs and files (Forms and Accountg). Smith and Winston are clients of the firm. The Smith directory has subdirectories for his lawsuit versus Jones and for miscellaneous other work. The Winston directory contains subdirectories for the Winston Corporation's corporate minutes and documents, the corporation's bankruptcy, and the personal injury lawsuit filed by one of its employees.

The Smith and Winston directories will store the client's retainer agreements and other miscellaneous files. Case files will be stored in the case subdirectories. This enables everyone in the office to quickly locate files pertaining to a particular matter, such as the Winston Corporation's bankruptcy.

Before we create these directories, the tree for our hard disk looks like this:

C:\

At this point, there is only a root directory.

To create the first level of directories from the root, C:\, the MD command is used in the form shown below:

Command Structure: MD \[directory name]
Example: MD \ACCOUNTG
Makes a subdirectory of the root called ACCOUNTG.

The remaining first-level directories are created in the same manner.

MD \FORMS
MD \LOTUS
MD \WP
MD \SMITH
MD \WINSTON

The initial backslash after the MD command instructs DOS to begin at the root directory. Eliminating the backslash from the command instructs DOS to begin at the current (default) directory (where the command is being executed). These first-level directories could, therefore, have been created without using the backslash in the command.

After we have created these first-level directories, our tree looks as follows:

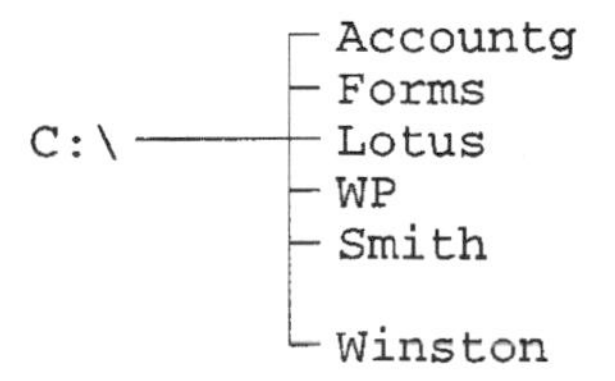

To create the subdirectories under Smith and Winston from the root directory, the path from the root must be specified.

Command Structure: MD \[directory]\[subdirectory]
Example: MD \SMITH\JONES
Creates the subdirectory JONES under the directory SMITH.

Our tree now looks as follows:

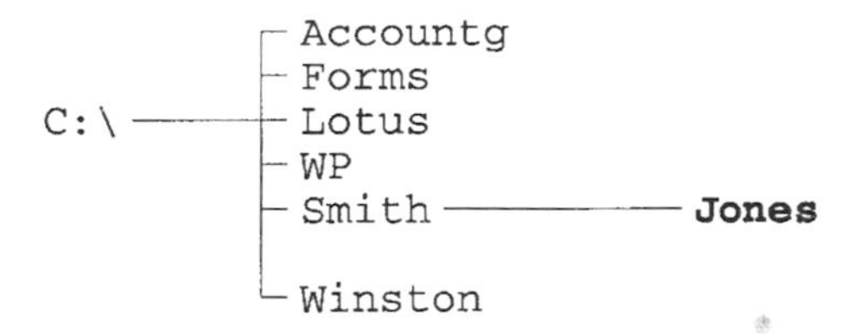

The remaining subdirectories are created by the following commands:

MD \SMITH\MISC

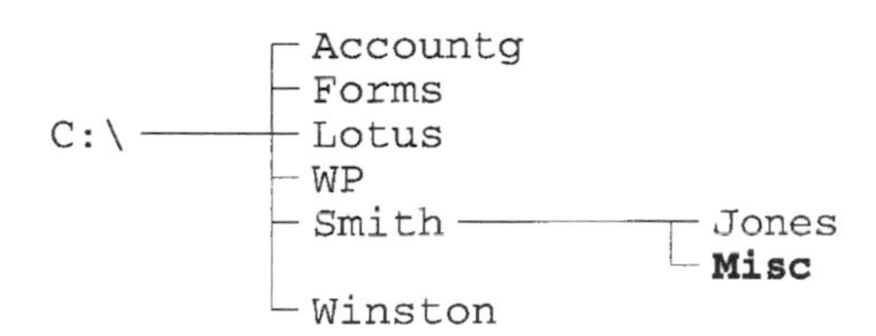

MD \WINSTON\CORP

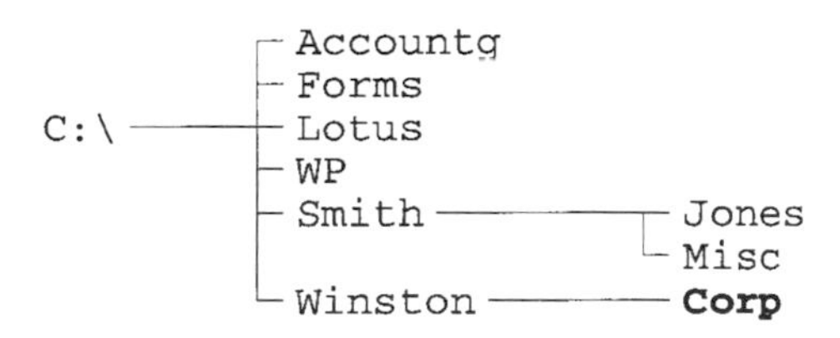

MD \WINSTON\BK

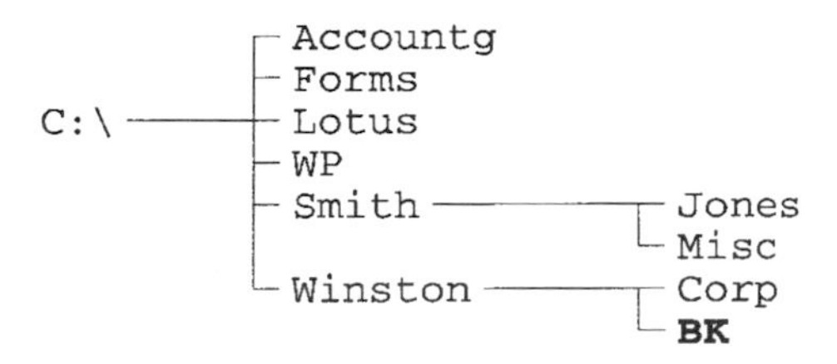

MD \WINSTON\PI

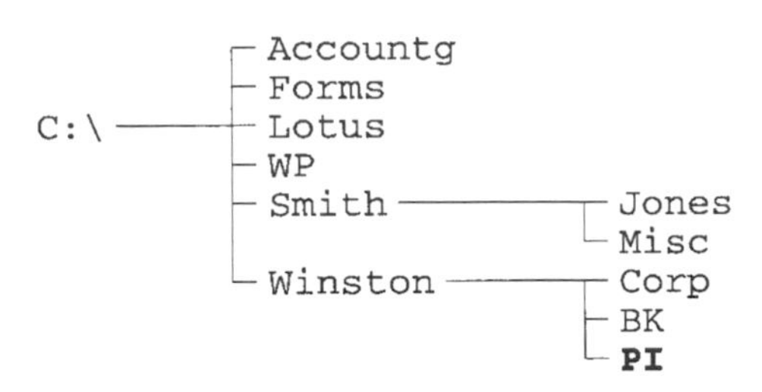

If the subdirectories of Smith and Winston were being created from the Smith and Winston directories (i.e., from C:\Smith> or C:\Winston>), the respective subdirectories could be created as follows:

From C:\Smith> MD JONES
MD MISC

From C:\Winston> MD CORP
MD BK
MD PI

NOTE

The command MD \JONES *from the* C:\Smith *directory would make a new directory under the root directory, instead of under the Smith directory. Remember, the backslash after the MD command tells DOS to begin at the root. The command* MD \Smith\Jones *or* MD Jones *executed from the* C:\Smith *directory will create the subdirectory Jones under Smith.*

A directory can be made on another disk drive by supplying the drive letter before the backslash. For example, from the root of the hard disk, C:\, a directory named Smith may be created on a diskette in the A: drive using the following command:

Command Structure: MD [drive letter]\[directory]
Example: MD A:\SMITH
Creates a subdirectory of the root called SMITH on the A: drive.

4. Changing Directories — CD or CHDIR

The command to change directory, **CD** or **CHDIR,** moves the user around in the directory tree.

Command Structure: CD \[directory name]
Example: CD \WP
Moves the user to the WP directory and makes this directory the default directory.

Once again, the backslash is used to tell DOS to begin at the root directory and to move the user to C:\WP.

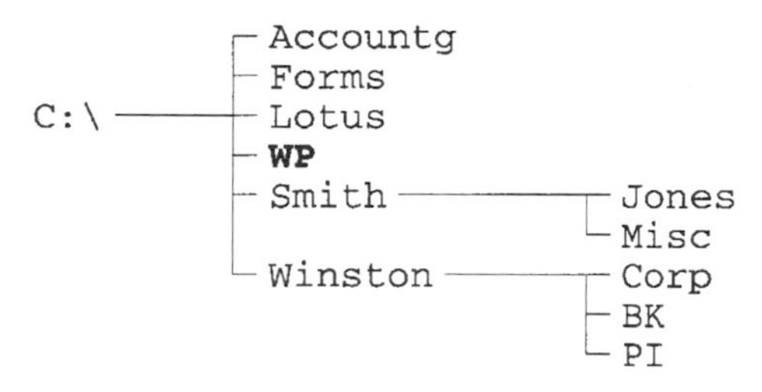

To move from C:\WP to C:\Winston, the following command would be used:

CD \WINSTON

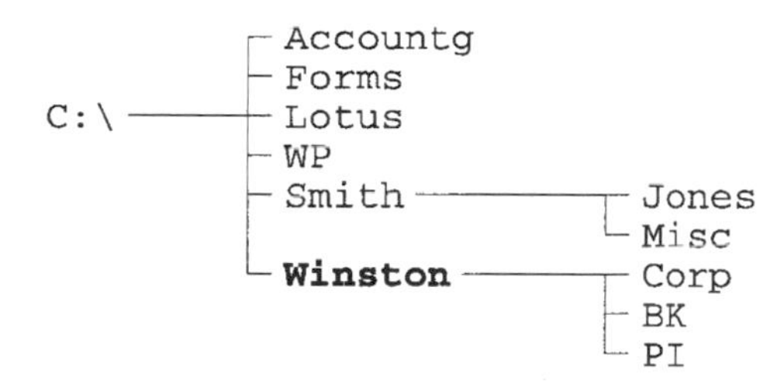

To move to C:\Winston\PI from C:\Winston, either of the following commands could be used:

CD \WINSTON\PI or CD PI

Eliminating the backslash from the CD PI command instructs DOS to begin at the current directory.

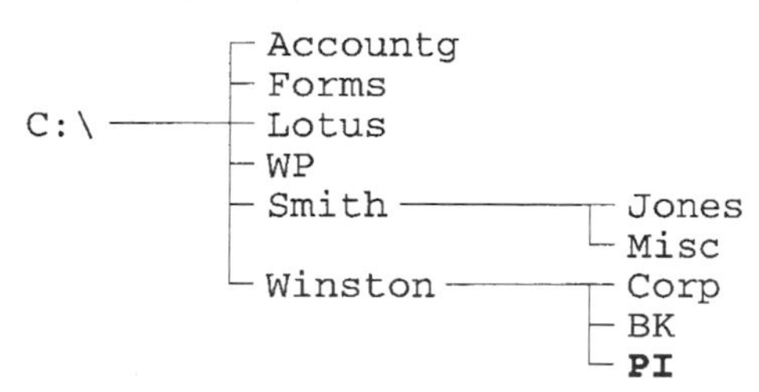

To move from C:\Winston\PI to C:\Smith\Misc, the following command would be used:

CD \SMITH\MISC

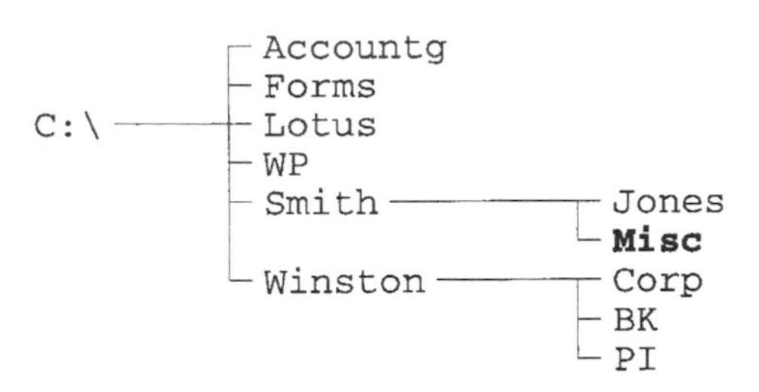

5. Removing Directories — RD

When directories are no longer needed, they should be removed from the disk. For example, assume the Winston Corporation's personal injury suit has been settled. All final paperwork has been completed and the case has been closed. It is time to copy the files in the PI directory onto a diskette and erase them from the PI directory.

NOTE

DOS will not allow a directory to be removed until all subdirectories and files have been removed or deleted.

After the files have been erased, the PI directory is removed with the following command:

Command Structure: RD \[directory]
Example: RD \WINSTON\PI
Removes the subdirectory PI from the WINSTON directory.

From the C:\Winston directory prompt, the PI subdirectory could be removed using:

RD PI

The new tree would look as follows:

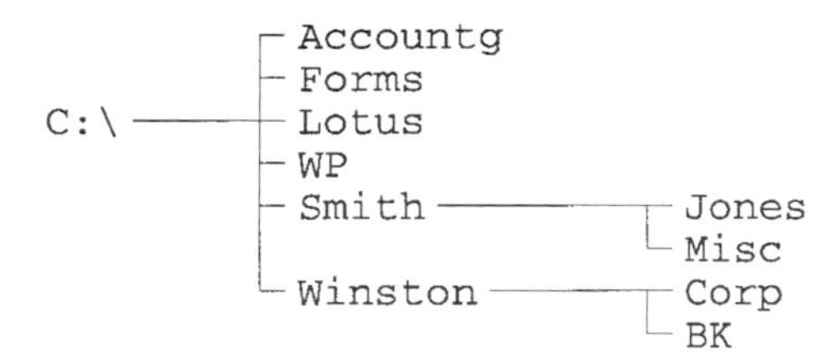

6. Copying Files — COPY

The **COPY** command allows the user to copy a file from one location to another. Copying a file involves identifying

- the file's location and its name
- its desired new location
- a new name for the file (optional)

Command Structure: COPY [file location]\[file name] [new location]\[new file name (optional)]
Example: COPY C:\WINSTON\PI\RESPONSE.DEM A:\ Copies the file response.dem from the PI subdirectory of the Winston directory to the root of a diskette in the A: drive.

There must be a space after COPY and after the file name.

To copy a form for an articles of incorporation document, called "ARTICLES.FRM," from the C:\Forms directory to the C:\Winston\Corp directory, renaming the document "WINSTON.ART," the following command would be used:

COPY C:\FORMS\ARTICLES.FRM C:\WINSTON\CORP\WINSTON.ART

7. Renaming Files — REN or RENAME

To change the name of a file, in instances other than with the COPY command, the **REN (or RENAME)** command is used.

Command Structure: REN [file location][old name] [new name]
Example: REN A:\SMITH.LET SMITH.LTR
Renames the file SMITH.LET at the root of the A: drive to SMITH.LTR.

If we had copied the file ARTICLES.FRM in the previous COPY example without designating a new name, we could use the REN command to rename it as follows:

REN C:\WINSTON\CORP\ARTICLES.FRM WINSTON.ART

We could also have changed directories to \Winston\Corp with:

CD \WINSTON\CORP

and then, from the C:\WINSTON\CORP> prompt, entered the command:

REN ARTICLES.FRM WINSTON.ART

NOTE

Remember that when you do not specify a location, DOS assumes that you want to act on the default directory (where you are in the tree). If you had executed the above command (REN ARTICLES.FRM WINSTON.ART) from the root of the C: drive, DOS would have looked for the ARTICLES.FRM file at the root and given you the message: "File not found."

8. Erasing and Deleting Files—ERASE and DEL

There are two commands for eliminating unwanted files: **ERASE** and **DEL.** They perform the same function and are used with the same structure.

Command Structure: ERASE [file location][file name]
Example: ERASE A:\SMITH.LTR
Erases the file SMITH.LTR from the root of a disk in the A: drive.

Command Structure: DEL [file location][file name]
Example: DEL A:\SMITH.LTR
Deletes the file SMITH.LTR from the root of a disk in the A: drive.

To erase the file WINSTON.ART from the C:\Winston\Corp directory, either of the following two commands could be used:

ERASE C:\WINSTON\CORP\WINSTON.ART

DEL C:\WINSTON\CORP\WINSTON.ART

9. Copying Disks — DISKCOPY

DISKCOPY makes an exact copy of one diskette onto another diskette. The contents (files and directories) of the source disk will be copied onto the target disk.

Command Structure:	DISKCOPY [source drive] [target drive]
Example:	DISKCOPY A: B:
	Copies the contents of a diskette in the A: drive to a diskette in the B: drive.

NOTE

Any existing files or directories on the target disk will be erased.

If you have only one diskette drive, or have a 5¼-inch A: drive and a 3½-inch B: drive and are copying a 5¼-inch diskette, the same drive letter is used at both places in the command. For example:

DISKCOPY A: A:

You will be prompted when to enter the source diskette and when to enter the target diskette. You cannot use the DISKCOPY command to copy to a diskette with a different density.

C. GLOBAL (WILD CARD) CHARACTERS

Global or **wild card characters** are used to execute commands on several files at one time. The global characters recognized by DOS are:

* and ?

* replaces multiple characters
? replaces a single character

If you have named your files with uniform three-character extensions, it becomes very easy to perform DOS commands on them using wild cards. For example, all letters with a .LTR extension could be acted on with *.LTR. Examples using the wild card characters are shown below.

COPY C:\LEGAL*.LTR A:

This command copies all files in the C:\Legal directory that contain the extension .LTR to the A: drive. Files with names such as JAN6.LTR, RETAINER.LTR, and SETTLE.LTR would be copied.

DEL C:\LEGAL*.LTR

This command would delete all files with an .LTR extension from the C:\Legal directory.

COPY A:*.* C:\FORMS

This command copies all files from the root of the diskette in the A: drive to the C:\Forms directory.

The wild card combination *.*, often referred to as "star dot star," acts on all files in a directory. It identifies files with file names containing any characters before the period and any extension.

The ? wild card is not often used because the * character can do everything the ? can do. However, a series of files like the ones listed below could be acted on using the ?.

1SMITH.LTR 2SMITH.LTR 3SMITH.LTR 4SMITH.LTR

COPY A:\?SMITH.LTR C:\FORMS

This command copies the files at the root of the A: drive that have names beginning with any character, followed by "SMITH.LTR" to the C:\Forms directory.

D. RUNNING AN APPLICATION

To run an application in DOS, you must type the command found in the application's executable file name. For example, the executable file name for Windows is WIN.EXE. To start Windows, you would type WIN. The executable file name for Quattro Pro is QPRO.EXE. To start Quattro Pro, you would type QPRO. The manual for the application will give you the command name. If you do not have the manual, you can look in the directory that contains the program for files with the extension .EXE. The command DIR .EXE will display a list of the executable files in the directory. An example of the executable files in a directory containing WordPerfect would be

INSTALL.EXE

WPINST.EXE

WP.EXE

You may have to try more than one command to find the one that starts the program, but you can usually make an educated guess by looking at the file name. In this case, typing INSTALL will begin the process of installing the application. To begin WordPerfect, you would type WP.

E. SUMMARY

DOS is the operating system used by many IBM-compatible microcomputers. Commands are issued in DOS by typing the command at a prompt and pressing the [Enter] key.

DOS lets you make directories in which to store your files. Directory names may be from one to eight characters in length. Files are parts of software programs or documents created in applications. File names may be from one to eight characters in length followed by an optional period and a one- to three-character extension. In order to recognize your files by name within these directories, you need to have specific rules for creating file names. Using uniform file name extensions, such as .LTR for letter and .CPL for complaint, is one of the best ways to structure your file names.

There are DOS commands that prepare a magnetic disk (FORMAT), provide a list of files on a magnetic disk (DIR), make directories (MD), erase files (ERASE), and copy files (COPY). A list of common commands and their structure is provided after the Key Terms list.

KEY TERMS

directory, 70
disk drive, 70
DOS (disk operating system), 69
file, 72
format, 73
global (wild card) characters, 87
root, 71
subdirectory, 71
tree, 71

DOS COMMANDS LIST

Directory Commands

DIR — Displays a list of all directories and files at the default drive and directory.

DIR/P — Displays the directories and files located at the default directory, pausing at the end of each screenful of information.

DIR/W — Displays the directories and files located at the default directory in a wide display.

MD	Makes a directory. Command Structure: MD \[directory name]
CD	Changes the default directory. Command Structure: CD \[directory name]
RD	Removes a directory. Command Structure: RD \[directory name]

File Commands

COPY	Copies a file from one location to another. Command Structure: COPY [file location]\[file name] [new location]\[new file name (optional)]
REN	Renames a file. Command Structure: REN [location][old name] [new name]
ERASE	Erases a file. This command is the same as the DEL command. Command Structure: ERASE [location][file name]
DEL	Deletes a file. This command is the same as the ERASE command. Command Structure: DEL [location][file name]

Disk Commands

FORMAT	Sets up tracks and sectors on a disk so that DOS can store and retrieve information. Command Structure: FORMAT [drive letter]:
DISKCOPY	Makes an exact copy of one disk onto another disk. Command Structure: DISKCOPY [source drive] [target drive]
DISKCOMP	Compares the contents of two disks to see if they are identical. Command Structure: DISKCOMP [drive] [drive]

Other Commands and Wild Card Characters

PATH	Displays the path setup of the computer. When a command is entered at a DOS prompt, DOS will look for the command in the current directory and then will search the directories within the path.
TREE	Displays a list or display of the directories and subdirectories of a disk in the current disk drive.

*	Wild card character that can replace any number of characters in a file name when using a DOS command.
?	Wild card character that can replace one character in a file name when using a DOS command.

QUESTIONS

1. What is a directory?
2. What is a file?
3. From the root of the C: drive, C:\, what command would make a directory called "FORMS"?
4. From the root of the C: drive, C:\, what command would you use to see a list of the files in the FORMS directory?
5. From the root of the C: drive, C:\, what command could you type to copy a file named ANSWER.FRM from the \FORMS directory to the root of a diskette in the A: drive?
6. From the root of the C: drive, C:\, what command could you type to copy all of the files from the FORMS directory to the root of a diskette in the A: drive?
7. From the root of the C: drive, C:\, what command could you type to erase a file named DEMURRER.FRM in the FORMS directory?
8. From the root of the C: drive, C:\, what command could you type to move to the C:\FORMS directory?
9. From the C:\FORMS directory, what are two different ways that you can construct the ERASE command to erase the file in this directory named ANSWER.FRM?
10. From the C:\FORMS directory, what command could you type to move back to the root of the C: drive?
11. From the root of the C: drive, C:\, what command could you type to remove the FORMS directory from the C: drive?

DISCUSSION QUESTIONS

1. Two forms of structuring a law firm's hard disk using directories were shown in this chapter on pages 71 and 79. What other forms of structuring could also be used?
2. Discuss how application programs like WordPerfect can be used to perform DOS commands such as copy, move, rename, and erase or delete.

CHAPTER

5

Windows

Microsoft® Windows® is an operating environment that takes the DOS operating system and presents it in a graphical display. Reviewing the discussion of DOS in Chapter 4 will help you better understand the underlying premises of Windows. The commands used in Windows are DOS commands; they are just presented in a different manner.

One of the main features of Windows is that it allows you to have more than one program open at a time. This is called **multitasking.** For example, you may have one window open with a WordPerfect document and another window open with a Lotus spreadsheet. Windows uses the mouse, icons, windows, and pull-down menus to access software, create documents, and manage files.

This chapter covers

- using the mouse
- the Windows desktop, windows, dialog boxes, and icons
- the management of files with the File Manager
- running and switching between applications
- using the DOS prompt from within Windows

A. USING THE MOUSE

The basic terms connected with using a mouse in Windows are *pointing, clicking, holding, double clicking,* and *dragging.* As you move the mouse, an arrow graphic moves around on the screen. Windows uses the left and right mouse buttons. Some mouses have two buttons and some have three. Mouses with three buttons will not use the middle button in Windows. The basic mouse terms are explained below.

Pointing is using the mouse to move the arrow on the screen to point to an item you want to select.
Clicking is pressing the left mouse button to select an item currently pointed to with the arrow.
Holding is clicking on an item and holding down the mouse button until an item is highlighted, or a screen effect is achieved, and then releasing the button.
Double clicking is pointing to a desired item and pressing the left mouse button twice in quick succession.
Dragging is pointing to an item, clicking and holding down the mouse button, and moving the mouse to drag the item to a new location.

B. THE DESKTOP, WINDOWS, DIALOG BOXES, AND ICONS

1. The Desktop

When you enter Windows, the computer takes you to the desktop. The **desktop** is where the program's windows are placed. The main window open on the desktop is called the Program Manager. Figure 5.1 shows a computer screen with both the Program Manager and the Main program group windows open.

In Figure 5.1 you can also see

- the Program Manager pull-down menus (File, Options, Window, and Help)
- icons for the applications available in the Main program group window
- closed program group windows (Accessories, StartUp, and Games)
- a Control Menu button in the upper left-hand corner (the small square that looks like a file drawer above the word "File" in Figure 5.1)

A closed group window may be opened by double clicking on its icon or by clicking once and selecting Restore from the displayed menu. A window can be closed by either clicking on the Control Menu button in the upper left-hand corner of the window and selecting Close, or by double clicking on the same button.

2. Windows

A **window** contains

- a Title Bar that displays the title of the window
- a Menu Bar in some windows that gives menu options for the window

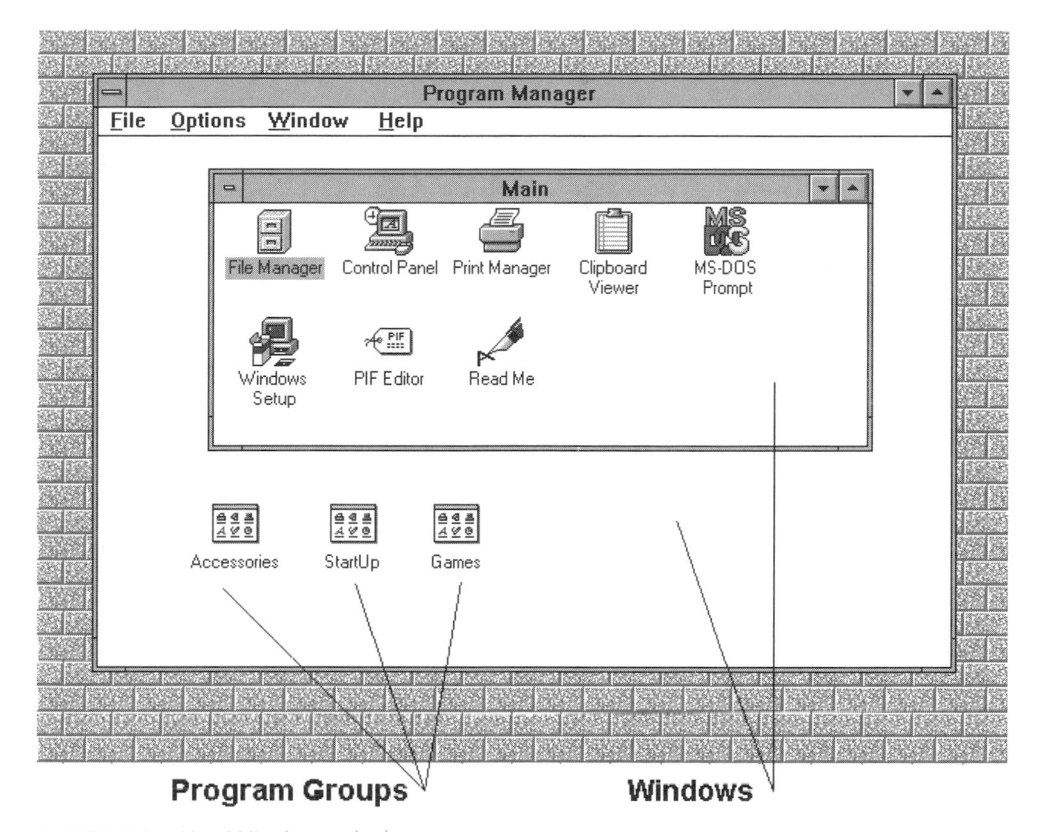

FIGURE 5.1 The Windows desktop.

- a Control Menu button in the upper left-hand corner
- sizing buttons in the upper right-hand corner that will reduce the window to an icon (down arrow), maximize the window to the full screen (up arrow), or restore the window to its previous size (up/down arrow)
- scroll bars on the right and on the bottom of some windows to scroll the display within the window up and down and right and left

3. Dialog Boxes

Dialog boxes are displayed to request information from you or to supply you with information that you might need. You will see dialog boxes when you open or save a file, and when you select many options from the menus in applications. A menu option that displays an ellipsis (. . .) after the command name will generate a dialog box when selected. The Create Directory dialog box is displayed in Figure 5.5 at page 106.

4. Icons

An **icon** is a small picture that represents an application, minimized window, or file. To run an application or to open a minimized window or file, double click on the icon or click once and press the [Enter] key. You can move the icons around on your desktop or in a window by dragging them with the mouse. You can also move an application to a different group window by opening both windows and dragging the icon to the new window. To arrange your icons uniformly in the Program Manager window and in group windows, select Arrange Icons from the Window menu.

C. PROGRAM GROUPS

Program groups are windows in the Program Manager that contain icons for programs and documents. Windows ships with the program groups displayed in Figure 5.1. The Main group contains applications for managing your files and directories (File Manager), setting up your desktop, drivers, and ports (Control Panel), managing your print jobs (Print Manager), and other applications that are important for running Windows. The Accessories group contains applications such as Write (a simple word processor), Paintbrush (a drawing and painting program), and Calculator. The StartUp group contains any application that you want to automatically start up when your Windows session begins. This group window may be empty. You can add new applications to the StartUp group at any time by dragging the application's icon from its current window to the open StartUp group window. The Games group usually contains Minesweeper and Solitaire.

1. Creating New Program Groups

You may create new program groups to hold additional applications that you purchase. Usually when you purchase a Windows application, such as WordPerfect for Windows, it will create its own program group during the installation process. This can become cumbersome, however, when your most frequently used applications are all in separate program groups. I create a program group called "Applications" and drag the icons of my most important applications from their program group windows into my Applications group window. To create the program group "Applications":

- Open the File menu and select New.
- Click on Program Group and click on the OK button.
- At the prompt for the Description, enter the name of the program group ("Applications" for this example).
- Do not enter anything at the Group File prompt.
- Click on the OK button to complete the process.

2. Adding New Application Icons

Occasionally you will need to add an application icon to one of your program groups. This becomes necessary when the software that you have installed does not create its own program group or icon, or when you have accidentally deleted an application's icon. To add an application's icon to a program group, you will need to open the program group's window. When the window is open, click inside the window to make sure that it is the active window. The active window's title bar will be highlighted. Next, follow the steps below:

- Open the File menu and select New.
- Click on Program Item and click on the OK button.
- In the Program Item Properties dialog box, enter a name for the icon at the Description prompt. At the Command Line prompt, type the location (drive and directory) and the executable file name for this application.
- The Working Directory and Shortcut Key options can be left blank.
- Click on the Change Icon button to select an icon for the application.

If you do not know the location of the application's executable file, you can click on the Browse button and go look for it. You can change the properties (description, icon, etc.) of your application at any time by clicking on its icon and then opening the File menu and selecting Properties.

3. Deleting Application Icons and Program Groups

To delete an application icon, click on the icon and press the [Delete] key on the keyboard. To delete a program group, open it up to a window, remove all application icons, and press the [Delete] key.

D. THE PULL-DOWN MENUS

The **pull-down menus** listed across the top of some windows are accessed by pointing at the menu name with the mouse and clicking the left mouse button. A menu will pull down from the menu title. An option is selected within the menu by pointing and clicking on the item. Menu items that appear "grayed out" are not available at this point in your work. Once you have opened one of the menus, you may use the [Right Arrow] and [Left Arrow] keys to open menus to the right and left.

1. Keyboard Access to Menus

To use the keyboard to access a menu, hold down the [Alt] key and press the underlined letter of the menu name. For example, [Alt] + [F] will open the File menu. When the menu has been opened, an option may be selected by pressing the option's underlined letter.

2. Keystroke Access to Dialog Boxes

Some dialog boxes can be accessed directly with a keyboard combination as opposed to being accessed from the menus. For example, clicking on an application icon and pressing [Alt] + [Enter] will open the Program Item Properties dialog box. Using the menus, you would select File, Properties. The quick access keyboard combinations will be displayed next to the options within the pull-down menus.

3. Running an Application from the File Menu

To run an application that does not have an icon, or from a diskette, open the File menu and select Run. The Run dialog box will appear and prompt you for the location and executable file name for the application. If you are not sure of the location or file name, you can use the Browse button to look for them on the disk. Once you have entered the location and file name into the command line, clicking on the OK button will start the application.

4. Saving the Screen Settings

The screen settings in Windows are the settings that record the position of the windows and icons on your desktop. Selecting Save Settings on Exit from the Options menu will save the current screen settings each time you exit Windows. This option can be annoying in that if you leave it on, your screen does not always appear the same when you enter Windows. If the option is on, it will be checked in the Options menu. To turn it off, select it from the Options menu. Once you have your desktop set up to your liking, you can record the settings by selecting Save Settings on Exit from the Options menu, exiting Windows, and then reentering Windows and turning off the Save Settings on Exit option. A quicker way to record your screen settings, avoiding the Save Settings on Exit option entirely, is to set up the desktop the way you like it and then, while holding down the [Shift] key, select File, Exit. Your screen settings will be recorded. You will not exit from Windows.

E. WINDOWS HELP

Help menus are available in many windows. You can access help by opening the Help menu (with the mouse or [Alt] + [H]), or you can highlight a particular command or option and press the [F1] key to get help for that item. Many Help windows contain buttons like Contents, Search, Back, History, Index, and Glossary. You press these buttons by pointing and clicking on them. The underlined topics displayed in Help windows are accessed by pointing and clicking on them.

The Windows Tutorial can be accessed from the Help menu in the Program Manager window. There are two parts to the tutorial. The first part covers the use of the mouse and is good for both beginning users and those who just want to brush up on their mouse skills. The second part covers the basics of using Windows and is helpful to all users. You will also find tutorials in the Help menus of many applications. You may see them referred to as tutorials, wizards, or coaches.

F. THE FILE MANAGER

Managing your files and directories is accomplished in the File Manager application. This application is represented by an icon in the Main group window, as shown in Figure 5.1 on page 95. To access the File Manager, point to its icon and double click the left mouse button. The File Manager window displays the available disk drives and the directories and files of the selected drive. The File Manager window is shown in Figure 5.2.

1. Drive Labels

Since Windows is based on DOS, many DOS rules apply. DOS labels the computer's magnetic disk drives with letters. The diskette drives are normally labeled A: and B:, and the hard drive is labeled with any letter from C: to Z:. Many large hard disks are partitioned into multiple drives. In the examples shown in this chapter, the computer has more than one letter for the hard disk drive. The drives are represented by icons that resemble disk drives. The icons for drives A: through E: are shown in Figure 5.2. The E: drive in Figure 5.2 is a CD-ROM drive.

2. Selecting a Drive

To view the contents of a disk drive, click on the icon for that drive. The directories and files for the drive will be displayed. The D: drive has been selected in Figure 5.2.

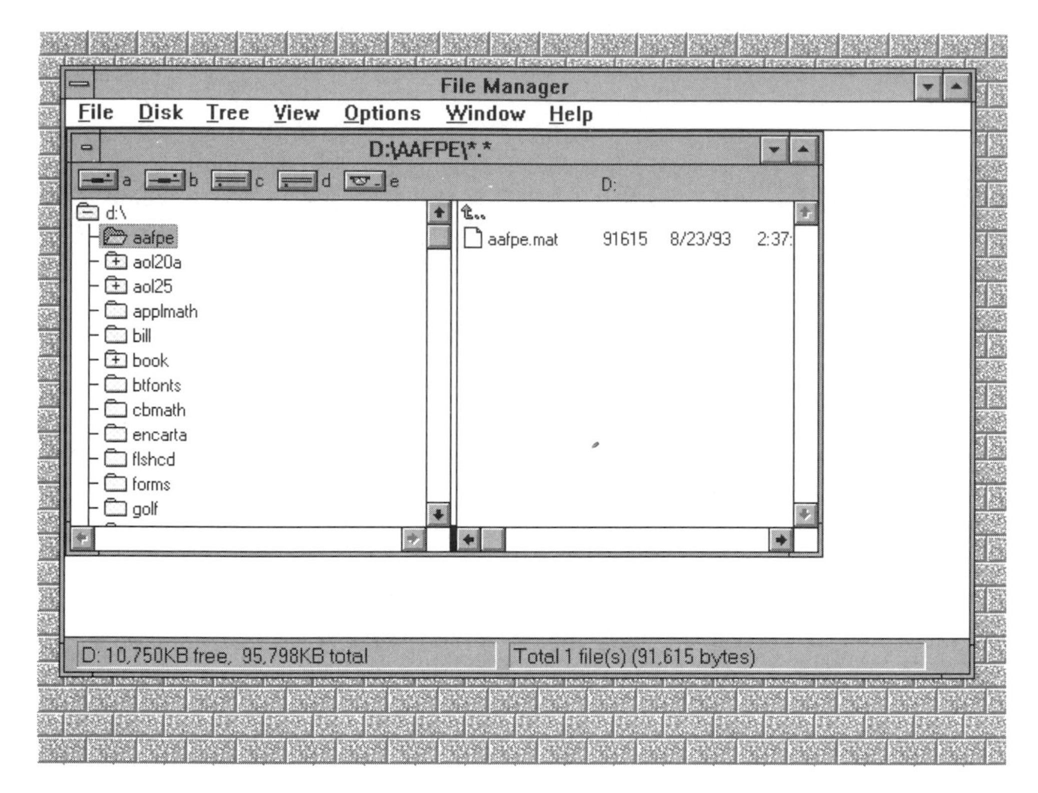

FIGURE 5.2 The File Manager window.

3. Directories

Hard disks and diskettes may be organized and divided into directories. A **directory** is a place where files are stored. The directories in Windows are represented by folder icons. The main directory on every disk is called the root. Subdirectories of the root are created to organize program and document files. The directory structure of a disk is referred to as the tree. The tree for the D: drive on this disk can be seen by selecting the Expand All option in the Tree menu. An expanded tree is shown in Figure 5.3.

When referencing a directory in DOS and Windows, the drive letter is specified, followed by a colon, with backslash characters (\) separating the directory names. A directory name may be anywhere from one to eight characters in length. The root directory of a D: drive is D:\. The subdirectory folder aafpe is referred to as D:\aafpe. The aol20a directory folder shown in Figure 5.3 has several subdirectories. The aol20a directory folder would be referred to as:

D:\aol20a

The download subdirectory of aol20a would be referred to as:

D:\aol20a\download

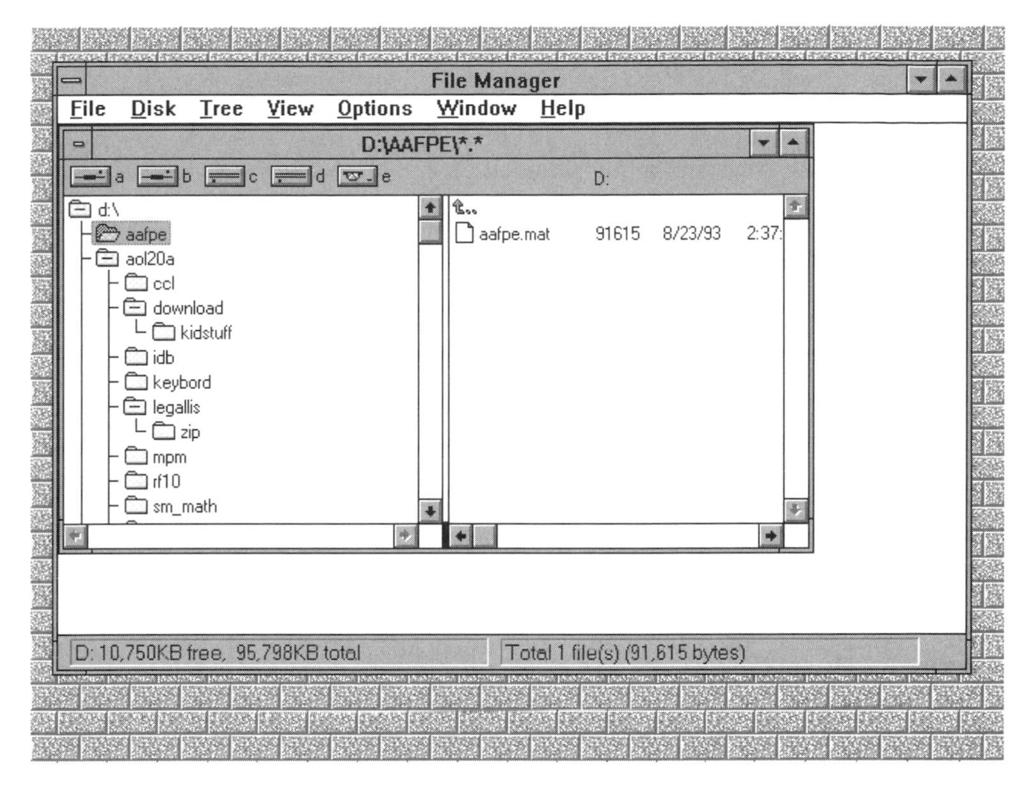

FIGURE 5.3 An expanded directory tree.

4. Files

Files are part of software programs or are created using application software. When you create a new file, you will be asked to give the file a name. DOS will accept file names that contain from one to eight characters followed by an optional period and a one- to three-character extension. An example of a file name is:

FILENAME.EXT

Some software programs automatically supply an extension to file names. For example, Lotus 1-2-3 applies a .WK1 extension to all file names so that the program will recognize worksheet files by looking for this extension. The following are examples of file names accepted by DOS:

DEMAND.LTR

12/3/96.BRF

TRIALBRF.1

RESUME

File names may be entered in uppercase or lowercase letters. In addition to letters and numbers, the following characters may be used to create a file name or extension:

! @ # $ % & ( ) - _ ' ' { }

The most important rule to follow when creating a file name is to create a name that will identify the work not only to the user but also to anyone else who may need to locate it.

In Windows, the files contained in a folder may be seen by clicking on the folder. The aafpe directory folder has been selected in the example shown in Figure 5.3. The one file contained therein is shown on the right half of the screen. A file is identified by its location, the drive letter followed by a colon, the directory name, and the file name. The drive designation, directory name, and file name are separated by the backslash character. The aafpe.mat file in Figure 5.3 would be identified as:

D:\aafpe\aafpe.mat

5. Managing Files and Directories

Options for acting on files and directories are available in the File menu of the File Manager window shown in Figure 5.4.

a. Acting on Files

To perform an action on a file, click on the file name on the right side of the File Manager window and select one of the options from the File menu. You may also perform actions on files by using the mouse. Some of these actions are set out below:

- Open a file by double clicking on the file name.
- Move a file by dragging the file icon to a different folder.
- Copy a file by holding down the [Ctrl] key while dragging the file icon to a different folder.
- Copy a file to another drive by dragging the file icon to the drive icon. (You cannot *move* a file to a different drive by dragging. Windows interprets the drag as a copy regardless of whether you are holding down the [Ctrl] key.)
- Delete a file by clicking on the file name and pressing the [Delete] key on the keyboard.

When you drag a file, if the file icon is displayed containing a plus symbol you are performing a copy. If the icon does not display a symbol, you are performing a move. To move or copy several files using the mouse, hold down the [Ctrl]

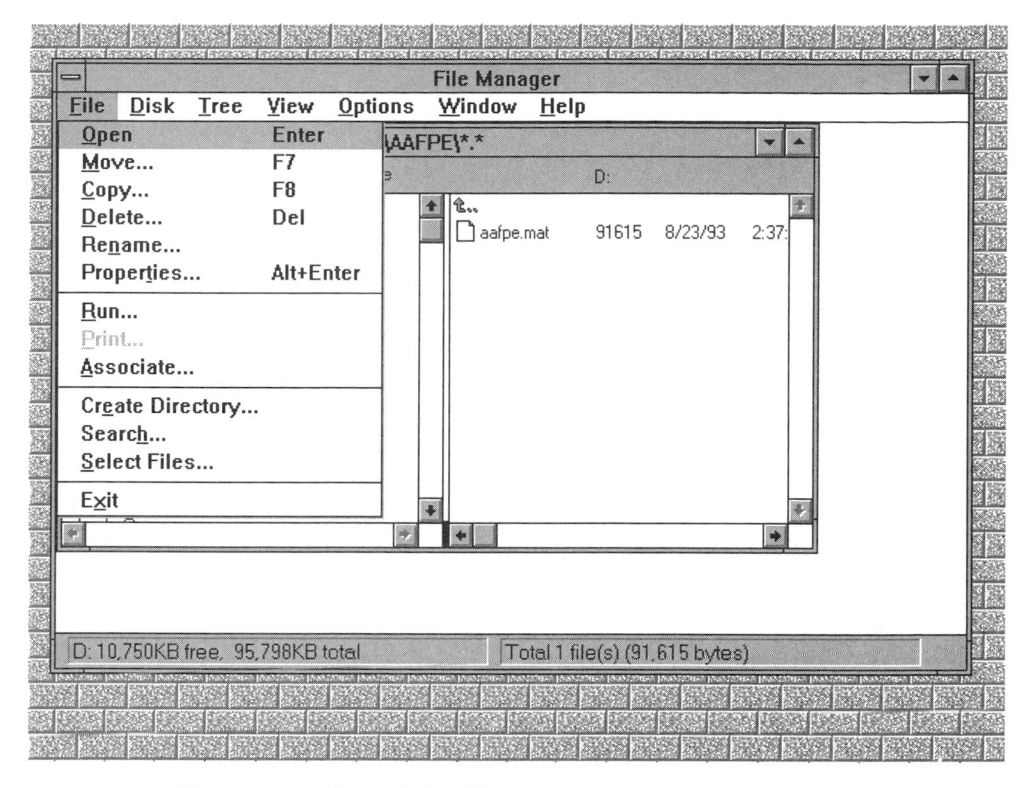

FIGURE 5.4 File menu options of the File Manager.

key and click on the files you want to act on. You can then drag them as a group to the desired new location. You can select all files in a directory by clicking on the first file listed, depressing the [Shift] key, and clicking on the last file listed.

b. Acting on Directories

Clicking on a directory folder on the left side of the File Manager window and selecting an option from the File menu will allow you to perform many actions on the directory folders. New directory folders may be created by selecting Create Directory.

Some actions, such as those listed below, can also be performed using the mouse.

- Move a directory folder and its contents by dragging its icon to a new location.
- Copy a directory folder and its contents by holding down the [Ctrl] key and dragging its icon to a new location.
- Delete a directory folder and its contents by clicking on its icon and pressing

the [Delete] key. (Note that Windows, unlike DOS, *will* allow you to delete a directory that is not empty.)

6. Disk Options

The Disk menu in the File Manager allows you to format, copy, and label your disks.

a. *Formatting a Disk*

Magnetic disks can be purchased either blank or preformatted. Formatting a disk prepares it for use by the computer's operating system and checks for any defects on the disk surface. The **Format** command creates sectors and tracks on the disk that enable the operating system to store and locate data.

NOTE

It is very important to note that formatting erases *all previous information stored on a disk. Check with your instructor or supervisor regarding their procedures for formatting disks.*

It is a common business practice to erase the Format command from the office computer system. This prevents the accidental erasure of important information by a mistake in using the command. Therefore, disks may need to be taken to a designated person in the firm to be formatted.

When you select the Format Disk option, the Format Disk dialog box will be displayed. You will then need to specify the drive letter where the disk is located and the format capacity. Alternatives may be seen by clicking on the arrow buttons to the right of the selections. A format capacity must be specified because low density and high density diskettes hold different quantities of data. A high density disk can be formatted at low or high density. A low (double) density disk can only be formatted at low density. You can label the disk (give it a name) by clicking in the Label option box and typing a name. Click on the OK button when you are ready to begin the format. The File Manager will not allow you to format the hard disk.

b. *Copying a Disk*

You can make an exact copy of a disk onto another disk of the same density using the Copy Disk option of the Disk menu. You will be prompted for the drive letter of the source disk (the one to be copied) and of the destination disk (the one on which the copy will be placed). If you have only one diskette drive, the same letter may be entered for both the source and the destination disk. The program will prompt you to enter the source or destination disk at the appropriate time. The command is executed by clicking on the OK button.

G. A CASE EXAMPLE

I will use an example here to illustrate many of the Windows features. Assume that our firm has just been retained by John Smith to handle a personal injury action. We will

- create a new directory folder for Mr. Smith's files
- save a complaint
- create a subdirectory
- move a file
- copy a file to a diskette
- delete a file and directory folder

1. Creating a Directory Folder

Our first step in the process is to add a new directory folder for the Smith files. To do this, open the File Manager from the Main group window, if you have not already done so. Select the drive where you want the Smith directory to be created by clicking on that drive's icon. Then open the File menu and select the Create Directory option. You will then be prompted for a directory name. If you simply type a name at this point, the directory will be made as a subdirectory of the current directory listed (D:\AAFPE in Figure 5.5). To make our directory as a subdirectory of the root, type the drive letter followed by a backslash and the name SMITH (i.e., D:\SMITH). Clicking on the OK button will complete the creation. Close the File Manager window by opening the File menu and selecting Exit. Close the Main group window by double clicking on its Control Menu button.

2. Entering a Program

Now we need to draft the Smith complaint. Locate the icon for WordPerfect for Windows or another word processor. Enter the application by double clicking on the icon or by clicking on the icon and pressing the [Enter] key.

a. *Saving a File*

After we have typed in some text for our practice complaint, we will need to save the document. Open the File menu and select Save As. In the dialog box

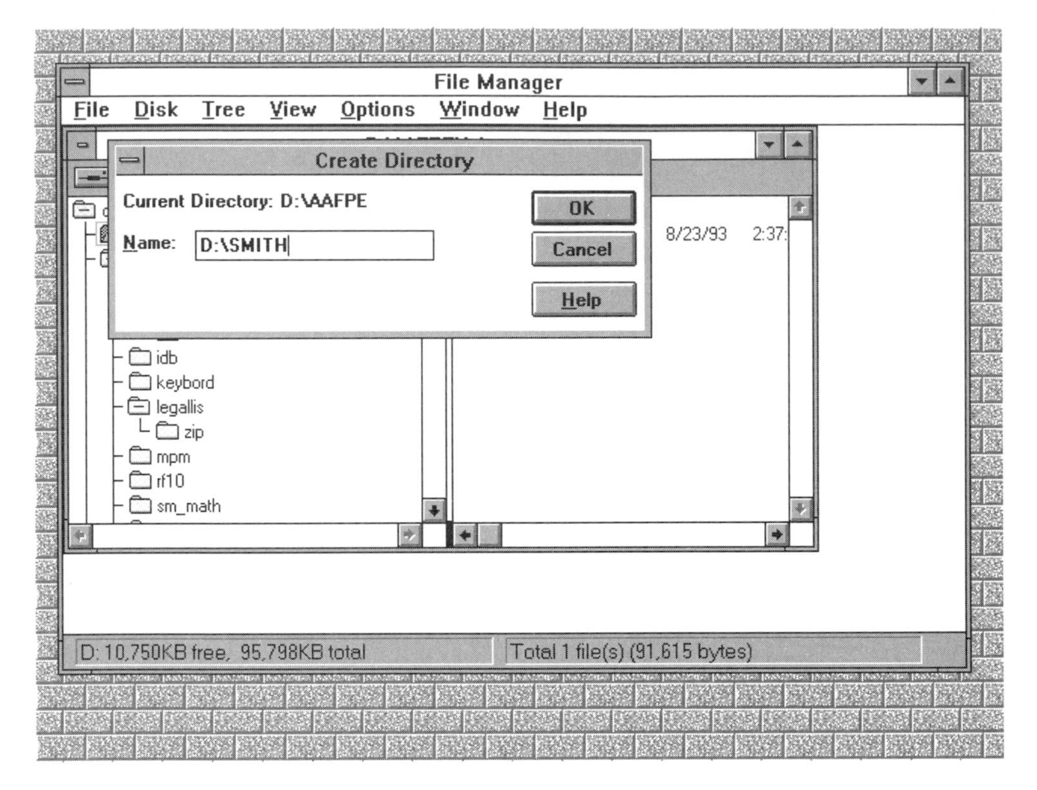

FIGURE 5.5 The Create Directory dialog box.

that appears you will need to type in the drive letter, directory, and file name. See Figure 5.6. Clicking on the OK button will save the file. Another way of identifying the drive letter and directory is to first select the drive letter from the Drives portion of the dialog box. Then you can click on the appropriate directory in the Directories portion of the dialog box. With the SMITH directory opened in this manner, you could simply type in a file name in the File Name area and the file will be placed in the SMITH directory.

b. Exiting the Word Processor

You can close the document by selecting Close from the File menu or by exiting the program. To exit the program, double click on the Control Menu button or select Exit from the File menu.

3. Creating a Subdirectory

We have saved the Smith complaint to the directory D:\SMITH. Our client, Smith, will likely be retaining us on other matters. Therefore, we should create

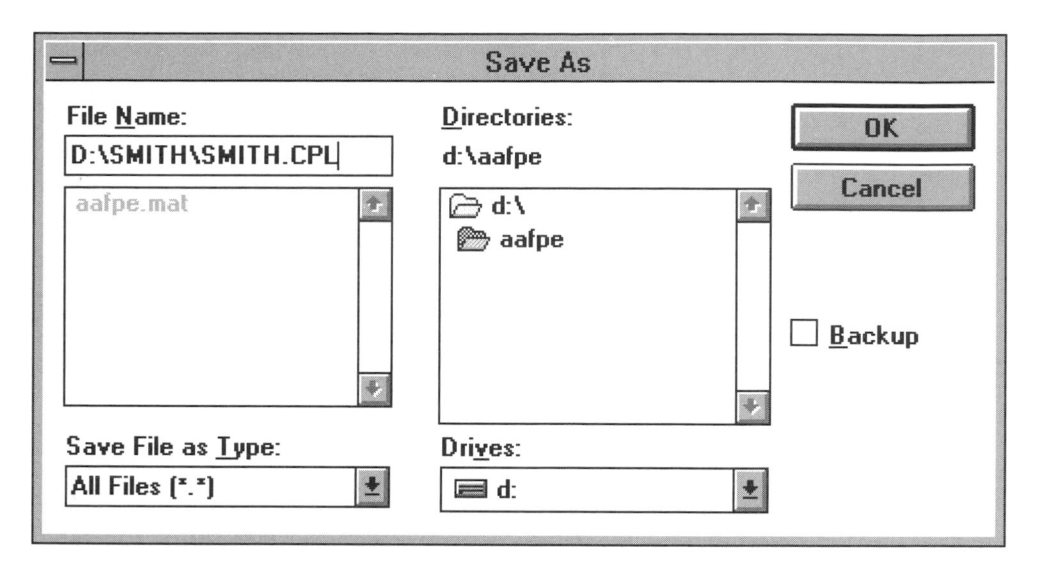

FIGURE 5.6 A Save As dialog box typical to most Windows-based programs.

subdirectories under D:\SMITH for these matters as we are retained. We will now make a new directory under D:\SMITH, where we will store the personal injury case files, and move our complaint to that directory. The new directory under D:\SMITH will be PI and will be identified by DOS as D:\SMITH\PI.

To make this new directory, we need to get back into the File Manager application. In the File Manager window, we click on the SMITH directory folder, open the File Menu, and select the Create Directory option. The Create Directory window is opened, and we type PI. Note that we do not have to type D:\SMITH\PI because we made D:\SMITH the current directory by clicking on it. Windows assumes that we want to create a subdirectory of D:\SMITH. Clicking on the OK button completes the subdirectory creation. Figure 5.7 shows the newly created subdirectory and the File contained in D:\SMITH.

4. Moving a File

We can now move our document, SMITH.CPL, to the D:\SMITH\PI directory folder by clicking on the document's icon, holding down the left mouse button, and dragging the document to the PI folder. Releasing the mouse button brings up the Confirm Mouse Operation dialog box. Clicking on the Yes button will complete the move. We can check to see that our file was moved to the PI subdirectory folder by clicking on the PI folder at the left half of the window, as shown in Figure 5.8. If the PI folder is not displayed, click on the Smith folder, open the Tree menu, and select the Expand Branch option.

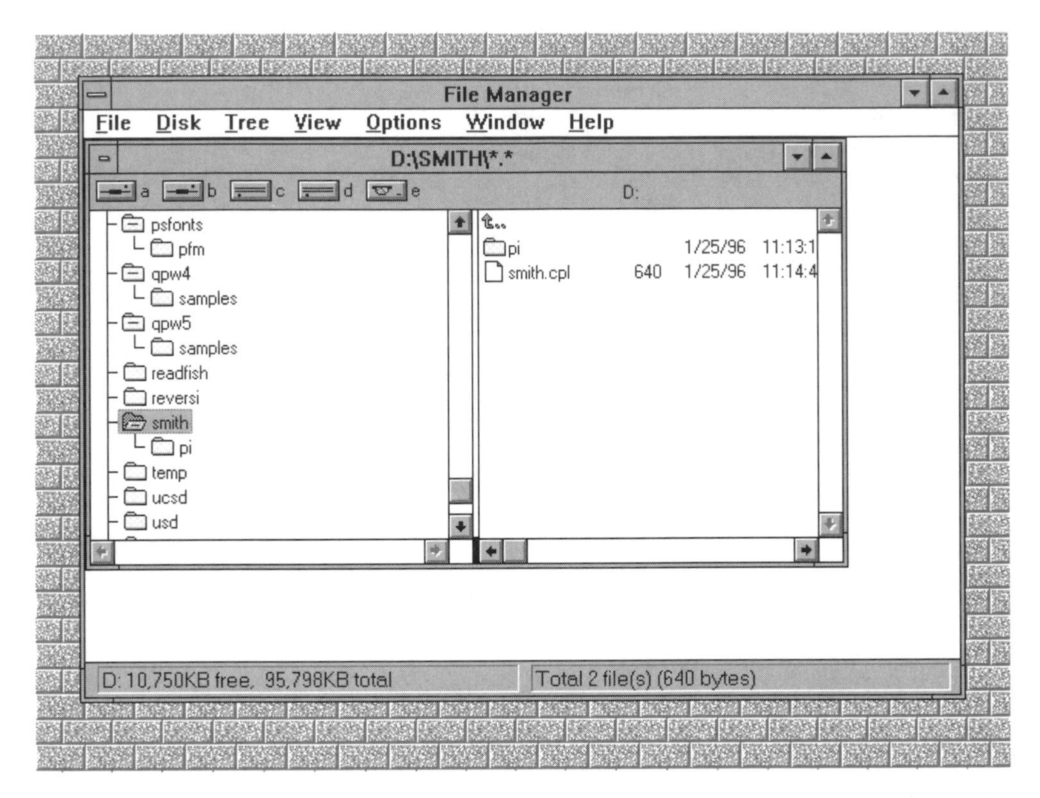

FIGURE 5.7 The contents of the Smith directory are displayed in the right half of the window.

5. Copying a File or Folder to a Diskette

The Smith case settled as soon as the defendants received our complaint. We can now archive the PI directory folder, and all of the files contained therein, to a diskette. To do this, we insert a diskette into drive A: or B:, drag the PI folder icon to the icon for the diskette drive, and select Yes in the Confirm Mouse Operation dialog box. This copies the PI folder to the diskette.

NOTE

Remember that you cannot move a file or folder to a different drive by dragging it to the drive icon; you can only make a copy.

Check to see that the PI folder has been copied to the diskette drive by clicking on the diskette drive icon. Click on the hard drive icon to return to a list of folders and files on the hard disk.

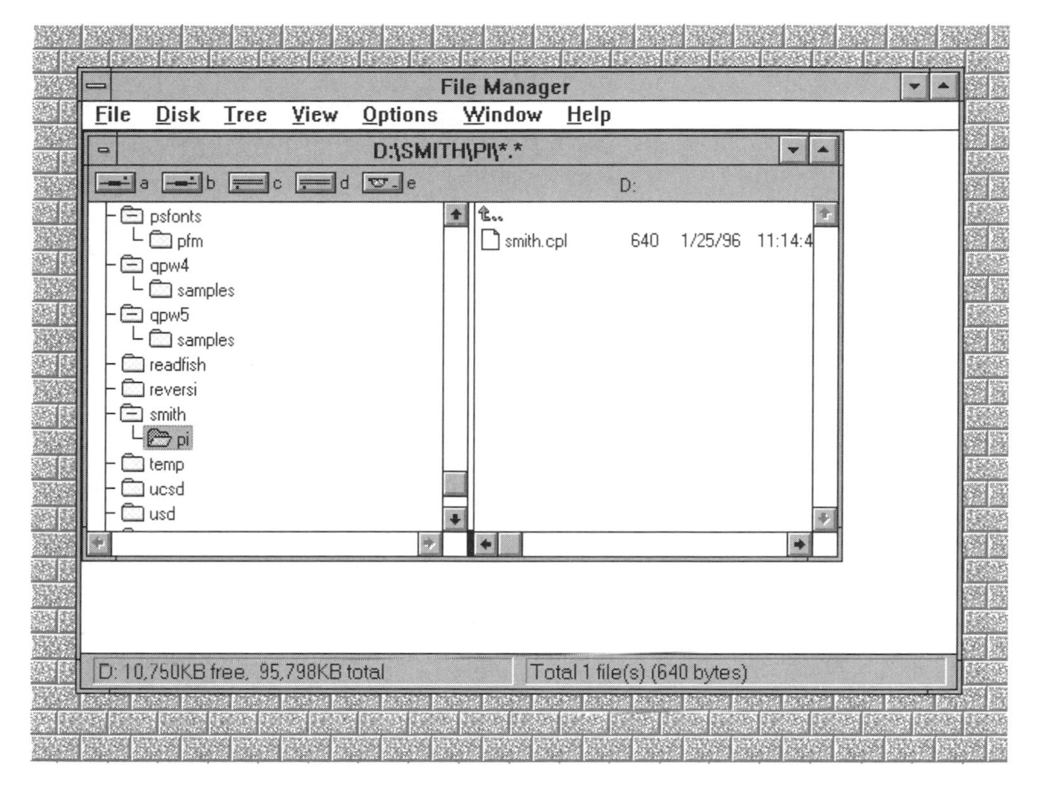

FIGURE 5.8 The PI subdirectory contains the file "smith.cpl."

6. Deleting a File

Now that we know our PI folder and its files are safely stored on a diskette, we may delete the SMITH.CPL file by clicking on it and pressing the [Delete] key.

The Delete dialog box is opened, displaying the file name. Clicking on the OK button will process the deletion. A confirmation window will then appear, asking you to confirm the deletion. Clicking on the Yes button will complete the action.

7. Deleting a Directory Folder

We can now delete the PI directory folder the same way we did our SMITH.CPL file. Click on the PI folder icon and press the [Delete] key. The Delete dialog box will appear. You can process the deletion by clicking on the OK button. You will again be prompted to confirm the deletion. Clicking on the Yes button will complete the process.

PRACTICE TIP

You could have deleted the PI directory folder, and all of its files, by deleting just the folder. Windows does not require that a directory be empty in order to delete it.

To exit back to the Program Manager, select Exit from the File menu.

H. SWITCHING BETWEEN APPLICATIONS

In Windows you may be working in one program and enter another without exiting the first. You can, however, only be active in one window at a time. To switch between programs you can use [Alt] + [Tab], [Alt] + [Esc], or Task List.

When you are in any open window on the desktop, you can press [Alt] + [Tab] to open the Program Manager window on top of your open window. The Program Manager then becomes the active window. You can then select any icon at the Program Manager to open further windows. All the windows you have opened remain open on the desktop even though you may not be able to see them. Pressing [Alt] + [Tab] or [Alt] + [Esc] will cycle you through the windows. [Alt] + [Tab] involves holding down the [Alt] key while pressing the [Tab] key repeatedly. As you press the [Tab] key, the names and icons for different applications are displayed. You may select an application by releasing the [Alt] key. Holding down the [Alt] key and pressing [Esc] will move you through each of the open windows.

The Task List is another way to switch between applications. The Task List is accessed by pressing [Ctrl] + [Esc]. A sample Task List is shown in Figure 5.9. The Task List lists the programs currently open on the desktop. You may select any of them by clicking on the name and clicking on the Switch To button, or simply by double clicking on the name.

If you choose to tile or cascade your windows on the desktop using options found in the Windows menu, the active window is the one with the highlighted title bar. To make another window active, click the left mouse button anywhere within the window. Scroll bars at the bottom or side of a window will allow you to move to see the rest of a window.

I. USING THE DOS PROMPT

Windows provides an icon in the Main group window that will transfer you to the DOS prompt. The DOS Prompt icon is shown in Figure 5.1. From the DOS

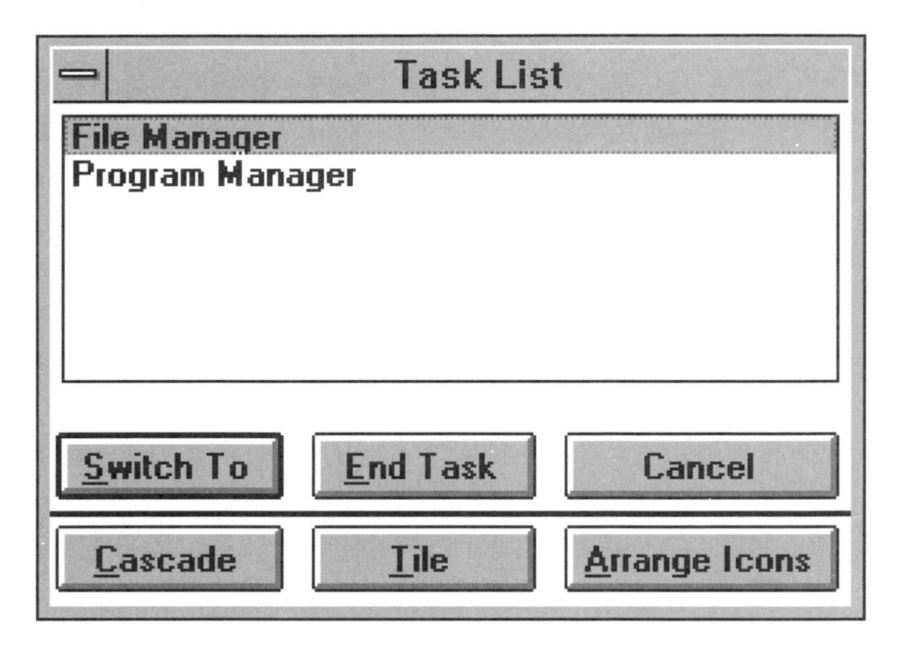

FIGURE 5.9 The Task List dialog box enables the user to switch between open applications and other windows.

prompt you may execute DOS commands. You may also exit to the DOS prompt by exiting Windows from the Program Manager's File menu.

To transfer to DOS, you double click on the DOS icon. You will then be moved to DOS and may execute commands. When you have transferred to DOS from Windows, you may return to Windows by typing "Exit" and pressing the [Enter] key. If you have exited Windows completely by selecting Exit from the Program Manager's File menu, you can start Windows again by typing its executable file name: WIN.

J. EXITING WINDOWS

You should always exit Windows through the File menu to the DOS prompt prior to turning off your computer. This allows the computer to properly close all of the Windows files. To exit Windows, open the File menu at the Program Manager and select the Exit Windows option. The Exit Windows dialog box will appear to confirm the exit. Click on the OK button to exit. This will take you to the DOS Prompt. When you have completely exited Windows in this manner, you must type the Windows command name if you wish to reenter the program. Type "WIN" to start Windows.

K. SUMMARY

Windows is an operating environment that takes the DOS operating system and presents it in a graphical display. DOS conventions, such as file and directory name lengths, apply in Windows.

Windows allows you to use a mouse or the keyboard to access menus and select icons to perform DOS commands. When an application is selected, a window for that item is opened. In Windows, you may have more than one window open on the desktop at once. This allows you to move from one application program to another without having to exit the first application. You can switch between open applications using [Alt] + [Tab], [Alt] + [Esc], or Task List.

An application can be opened by double clicking on its icon. Menus found in open windows can be accessed with the mouse or by holding down the [Alt] key and pressing the underlined letter in the menu name. In the File Manager application you can perform file management tasks such as copying, moving, and deleting files. The File Manager is found in the Main program group. It is important to exit Windows to the DOS prompt prior to turning off your computer so that Windows files are closed properly.

KEY TERMS

clicking, 94
desktop, 94
dialog box, 95
directory, 100
double clicking, 94
dragging, 94
file, 101
format, 104
holding, 94
icon, 96
multitasking, 93
pointing, 94
program groups, 96
pull-down menus, 97
window, 94

QUESTIONS

1. What is a program group?
2. What is an icon?
3. How can you enter an application program, such as WordPerfect for Windows, using the mouse?
4. How do you access the File Manager?
5. From within the File Manager, how do you move a file using the mouse? How do you copy a file using the mouse?
6. How do you close a window?
7. What are the three methods for switching between applications?

DISCUSSION QUESTIONS

1. Discuss the advantages of using Windows rather than the DOS prompt.
2. What effect does the development of Windows have on a law office's purchasing decision when deciding between Macintoshes and IBM-compatible computers?

CHAPTER

6

WINDOWS 95

Microsoft® Windows® 95 is an operating system that takes the DOS and Windows combination and develops it into a user-friendly interface. Windows 95 is very similar to the Macintosh operating system in appearance and feel. It is a 32-bit operating system, which makes it faster than DOS or DOS with Windows. It also supports long file names with software applications written for this operating system, thus eliminating the cryptic file names of DOS and allowing you to describe your document so that it is easy to recognize. Windows 95 also makes the installation of new hardware and software an easy task. Plug and Play hardware can be instantly recognized and configured by the computer upon installation. New software can be added with an Add/Remove Programs application that installs and configures your software, and removes all of the program files (wherever they may be) when you wish to remove the software.

This chapter covers

- using the mouse
- Windows 95 basics
- the Start menu
- running a program
- managing your files in My Computer and in the Windows Explorer
- exiting Windows 95

A. USING THE MOUSE

A mouse is essential when using Windows 95. If you do not have a mouse, or prefer to use the keyboard, see the MouseKeys option in the Help menu. The basic terms connected with using a mouse in Windows 95 are *pointing, clicking, holding, double clicking,* and *dragging.* As you move the mouse, an arrow graphic moves around on the screen. Windows 95 uses the left and right mouse buttons. Some mouses have two buttons, some have three. Mouses with three buttons will not use the middle button in Windows 95. The basic mouse terms are explained below.

Pointing is using the mouse to move the arrow on the screen to point to an item you want to select.
Clicking is pressing the left mouse button to select an item currently pointed to with the mouse arrow.
Holding is clicking on an item and holding down the mouse button until an item is highlighted, or a screen effect is achieved, and then releasing the button.
Double clicking is pointing to a desired item and pressing the left mouse button twice in quick succession.
Dragging is pointing to an item, clicking and holding down the mouse button, and moving the mouse to drag the item to a new location.

B. WINDOWS 95 BASICS

1. The Desktop

The Windows 95 desktop, shown in Figure 6.1, features a Start button and a taskbar at the bottom of the screen and icons for important features. The Start button will activate programs and various Windows 95 features. As you open programs, their icons and titles will appear on the taskbar to allow you to easily switch between them. The icons that appear on the desktop itself will differ according to the setup of your computer. The two icons that you will always find on the desktop are the icons for My Computer and the Recycle Bin. The **My Computer** icon takes you to windows that display the contents of your disk drives and folders that contain your software applications. The **Recycle Bin** is where your deleted files are placed. The files are not actually removed from the disk until you have emptied the Recycle Bin. You can double click on the Recycle Bin to display its contents.

2. Windows

When you activate an application, a "window" opens. A **window** in Windows 95 contains

- a Title Bar that displays the application's icon and its name
- Sizing buttons in the upper right-hand corner that will reduce the window to an icon on the taskbar, maximize the window to the full screen, restore the window to medium size, and close the application (the "X" button)

FIGURE 6.1 The Windows 95 desktop.

- a Control Menu button, the application's icon, in the upper left-hand corner that performs the same features as the Sizing buttons
- a Menu Bar in some windows that gives menu options for that window
- Scroll Bars on the right and on the bottom of some windows to scroll the display within the window up and down and right and left

The Control Panel window is shown in Figure 6.2.

3. Dialog Boxes

Dialog boxes are displayed to request information from you or to supply you with information that you may need. You will see dialog boxes when you open or save a file, and when you select many of the options from the menus in a window. A menu option that displays an ellipsis (. . .) after the command name will generate a dialog box when selected. The Run dialog box is shown in Figure 6.3.

Dialog boxes in Windows 95, and in programs written for Windows 95, will contain buttons in the upper right-hand corner for help and for closing the dialog

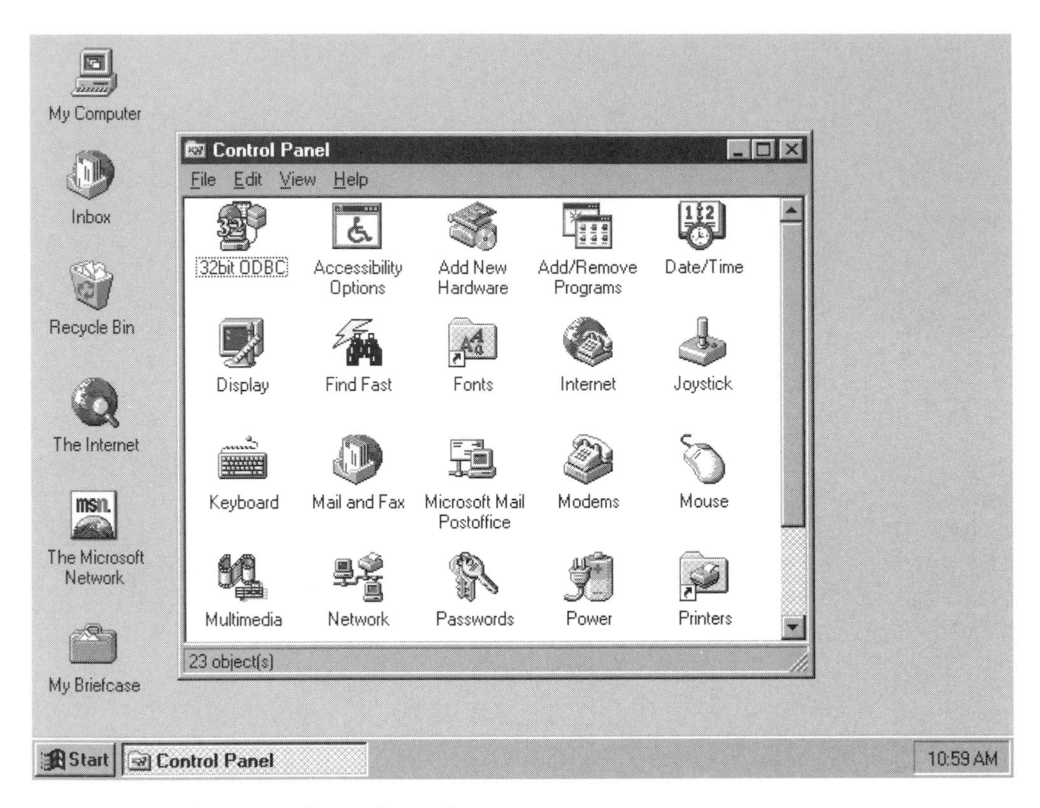

FIGURE 6.2 The Control Panel window.

box. Clicking on the Help button, represented by a question mark, attaches a question mark to your mouse pointer. Clicking on items within the dialog box will bring up a short explanation of the items. The button represented by the "X" will close the dialog box.

4. Icons

An **icon** is a small picture that represents a piece of hardware, a folder, a program, or a file. To run a program from the Start menu or open it from the taskbar, you will click on its icon. To run a program or open a file from a window or the desktop, you will need to double click on its icon. You can move icons around on your desktop or in a window by dragging them with the mouse. You can also move icons to menus, folders, and other places by dragging the icon to the new location.

5. Shortcuts

A **shortcut** is a way to quickly access a program or file. You can add shortcuts to the desktop, the Start menu, and to folders. To create a shortcut, click the right mouse button on the icon for the program or file and select Create Shortcut from

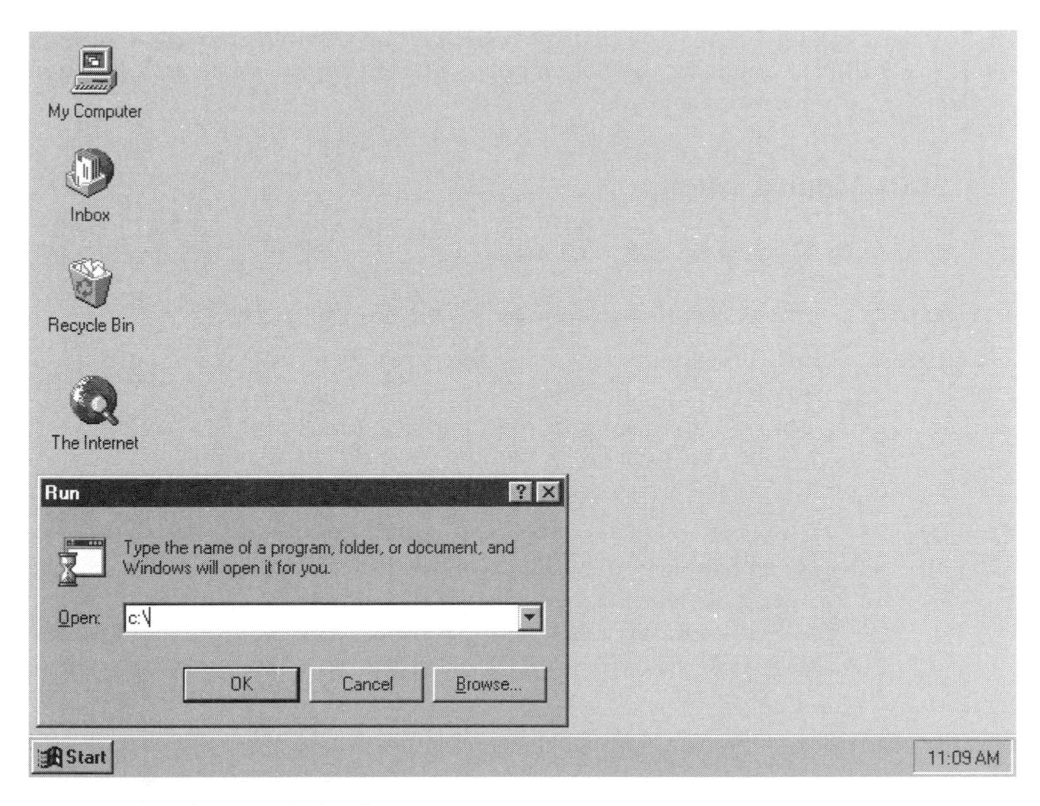

FIGURE 6.3 The Run dialog box.

the menu that appears. Then drag the shortcut icon to the desired location. The actual program or file is not moved. A shortcut icon on the desktop or in a window will display an arrow in its lower left-hand corner.

6. Properties

Just about every item that you see on the Windows 95 desktop, and within My Computer and the Windows Explorer, contains properties that you can change. To change properties of the desktop, such as the background color or font used with your menus, point at the desktop and click the right mouse button. A menu will appear with the Properties option. You can also change the properties of other items on the desktop by clicking on them with the right mouse button. To change the properties of an item when in My Computer or the Windows Explorer, click on the item and select Properties from the File menu.

C. THE START MENU

You can access the basic features of Windows 95 in the Start menu. To open the Start menu, click on the Start button at the bottom of the screen. The Start menu is shown in Figure 6.4. Menu options that have an arrow to the right of their names will display another menu. This submenu will appear when you point at, or click on, the menu option.

1. Start Menu Options

The options that appear on the Start menu are

Programs Lists programs that you can start from the menu.

Documents Lists documents that you have opened recently. This is a quick way to access a file. Note that not all programs can add files to the list. You may have recently worked on a file using a program that was not written for Windows 95 and find that the document is not on this list.

Settings Gives you a submenu with options for the Control Panel, Printers, or taskbar properties. The Control Panel is where you can change your hardware settings, change the settings of Windows 95, and add and remove software applications. The Printers window displays your available printers and allows you to add new printers to

FIGURE 6.4 The Start menu is used to activate most programs.

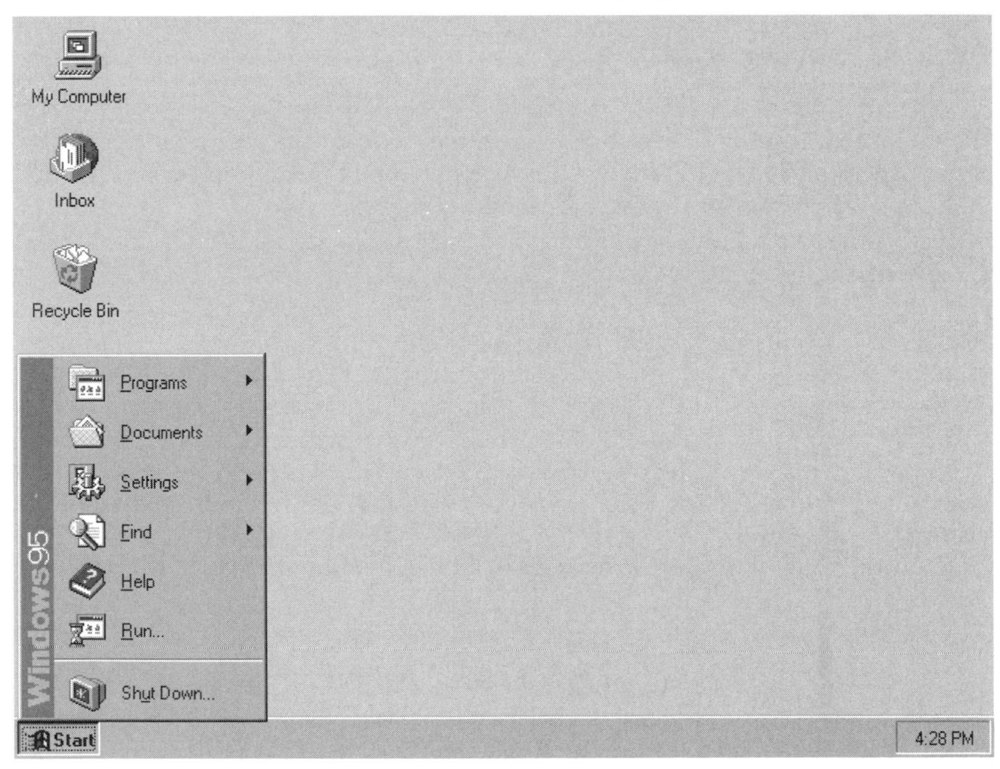

Windows 95. The taskbar properties dialog box allows you to change the appearance of your taskbar and to customize the Start menu.

Find Helps you find a file or folder on the computer's disk drive.

Help Provides help for the features of Windows 95. This option also contains a tour of Windows 95 that teaches some of the basic features of the operating system.

Run Opens a program, folder, or file. This option is often used when you need to run a program from a diskette, or when the program does not have an icon on the desktop and is not listed under Programs in the Start menu. Folders and files can also be opened by typing their location in the command line. This dialog box is shown in Figure 6.3 on page 119.

Shut Down Allows you to shut down the computer or reboot into Windows 95 or DOS.

You can add a program, like your word processor, to the top of the Start menu by double clicking on the My Computer icon and opening the folder containing the files for the program. When you locate the file that starts the program, drag its icon to the Start button. You can also locate the same file in the Windows Explorer and drag it to the Start button.

2. The Programs Option

Under the Programs option of the Start menu you will find program folders containing related software programs. Program folders are created to hold shortcuts to access your programs easily, and are similar to the program groups found in DOS with Windows. The Accessories and StartUp program folders ship with Windows 95. You will also find an icon to access the DOS prompt and the Windows Explorer in the Programs option. Accessing the DOS prompt allows you to execute DOS commands. The **Windows Explorer** is similar to the File Manager in DOS with Windows. For people who are used to working with the File Manager, the Windows Explorer provides a familiar method for managing the files and folders on the computer's disk drives.

The Accessories program folder contains games, system tools for operating your computer more efficiently, a calculator, the Paint program, a primitive word-processor, and many other programs. The StartUp program folder holds programs that you want to start automatically when you enter Windows 95.

3. Adding and Deleting Program Folders

To add or delete a program folder from the Programs option, use your right mouse button to click on the Start button. From the menu that appears, select Open. Double click on the Programs folder that appears in the open window. A window will open that contains your program folders. To add a new folder, open the File menu, point to New, and click on Folder. A new folder will appear in the window and allow you to change its name. Press the [Enter] key to complete the process. To delete the folder, click on the folder and press the [Delete] key. The folder and its shortcuts will be transferred to the Recycle Bin.

4. Adding and Deleting Shortcuts from a Program Folder

To add or delete a shortcut from a program folder, use your right mouse button to click on the Start button. Select Open from the menu that appears. Double click on the Programs folder, then double click on the program folder that you want to use. To add a shortcut to the program folder, open the File menu, point to New, and click on Shortcut. The Create Shortcut wizard will guide you through the rest of the process. To delete a shortcut, click on it and press the [Delete] key.

D. RUNNING A PROGRAM

Windows 95 can run programs written for DOS, Windows, and Windows 95. These programs include your word processor, spreadsheet, database, checkbook manager, and games.

1. Starting a Program

You can start a program from the Start menu, from a shortcut icon that you have placed on the desktop or elsewhere, from My Computer, or from the Windows Explorer.

- To start a program listed in the Start menu, click on the Start button and click on the program's icon. To start a program from the Programs option of the Start menu, click on the Start button, point to Programs, point at the program folder that contains the program, and then click on the program name.
- To start a program from a shortcut on the desktop or in a folder, double click on the program's icon.
- To start a program from the My Computer window, double click on My Computer. When the My Computer window opens, double click on the disk drive that contains the program's files. Open the folder that contains the file and look for the file that executes the program. When you find this file, double click on it to start the program.
- To start a program from the Windows Explorer, click on the Start button, point at Programs, and click on Windows Explorer. In the Windows Explorer window, locate the folder that contains the program and find the program's executable file. When you find the file, double click on it to start the program.

2. Pull-Down Menus

When you enter a program, it will be contained within a window. The **pull-down menus** listed across the top of some windows are accessed by pointing at the menu name with the mouse and clicking the left mouse button. A menu will pull down from the menu title. An option is selected within the menu by pointing and clicking on the option. Menu options that appear "grayed-out" are not available at this point in your work. Once you have opened one of the menus, you may use the [Right Arrow] and [Left Arrow] keys to open menus to the right and left.

To use the keyboard to access a menu, hold down the [Alt] key and press the underlined letter of the menu name. For example, [Alt] + [F] will open the File menu. When a menu has been opened, an option may be selected by pressing the option's underlined letter. Some dialog boxes can also be accessed with the keyboard. These quick access keystroke combinations will be displayed next to the options within the pull-down menus.

3. File Names

A new feature available in Windows 95 is the ability to use file names that exceed eight characters and that contain spaces. This ability to use long file names is only available in programs that have been written for Windows 95. If the program that you are using was not written for Windows 95, the name that you give your file is limited to one to eight characters followed by an optional period and a one- to three-character extension. For example, **walters.rog.** In programs written for Windows 95, a file name can consist of up to 255 characters, including spaces. It cannot contain the following characters:

\ / : * ? “ < > |

The same document mentioned above could be saved in a program written for use with Windows 95 with a long file name such as **interrogatories for the walters case.**

4. Specifying a Path When Opening and Saving Files

When you open or save a file, you need to specify the drive letter, folders, and subfolders that contain the file and the file's name. This direction to the location of the file is called the **path.** To specify a path for a file, you type the drive letter followed by a colon (:) and a backslash (\). You then type the names of the folder and any subfolders that contain the file, separating the folder names with backslashes. The last thing that you type is the file name, preceded by a backslash. An example of a path for a document named **answer.frm** contained in the **\forms** directory on the **C:** drive would be **c:\forms\answer.frm.** If the name of your document contains spaces or is longer than eight characters, the path must be enclosed in quotation marks. For example, if the same file mentioned above had the name **specific answer form,** the path would be **"c:\forms\specific answer form."**

5. Opening a File

When you enter a program such as WordPerfect, it is set up for you to begin a new document. If you would like to open a document that exists on one of your disks, open the File menu and select Open. In the dialog box that appears, type the file's path in the space provided and click on the button that will open the file. If you do not know the name of the folder containing the file or the file's name, you can often click on the folders contained within a portion of the dialog box or on a browse button. When you click on the folders in the dialog box or within the browse feature, the files within them will be displayed. When you find the file, click on it and then click on the button that will open the file.

6. Saving a File

Most programs have two save options in the File menu, Save and Save As. The Save option will prompt you for a file location and name if the file has not yet been saved. If the file has been saved before and has a name, the Save option will quickly save your latest changes to the document. The Save As option prompts you for a file location and name. If you only provide a file name, the file will be placed in the folder that is currently open. To place it in a different folder, either specify the path or click on the desired folder in part of the dialog box to make it the current folder. Once you have made this folder the current folder, you just need to type a file name into the space indicated.

7. Exiting a Program

To exit a program, open the File menu and select Exit. You can also use the "X" in the upper right-hand corner of the window to exit the program. Either option will prompt you to save the file currently open in the program if you have not saved the latest changes.

E. THE MY COMPUTER WINDOW

The computer icon displayed on the desktop called "My Computer" accesses windows that display the contents of your computer. Double clicking on the My

Computer icon takes you to a window that displays the icons for your disk drives, the Control Panel, and Printers. This window is shown in Figure 6.5.

Double clicking on one of the drive icons will display the folders and files found on that drive. Double clicking on the Control Panel icon will allow you to change your computer's settings. Double clicking on the Printers icon will let you set up new and existing printers on your system. The contents of the hard disk are displayed in Figure 6.6.

By double clicking on any of the folder icons, you can open a window displaying the contents of that folder. Double clicking on a file icon will start a program if the file is an executable file, or open a document into a program. If My Computer does not recognize a connection between the document and a program, a list of the programs on your computer will be displayed for you to select from. The document will then be opened into the program and a link between the two will be established so that next time you double click on the document icon it will automatically be opened into the program.

1. Managing Folders and Files

You can manage your folders and files in My Computer or in the Windows Explorer.

FIGURE 6.5 The My Computer window.

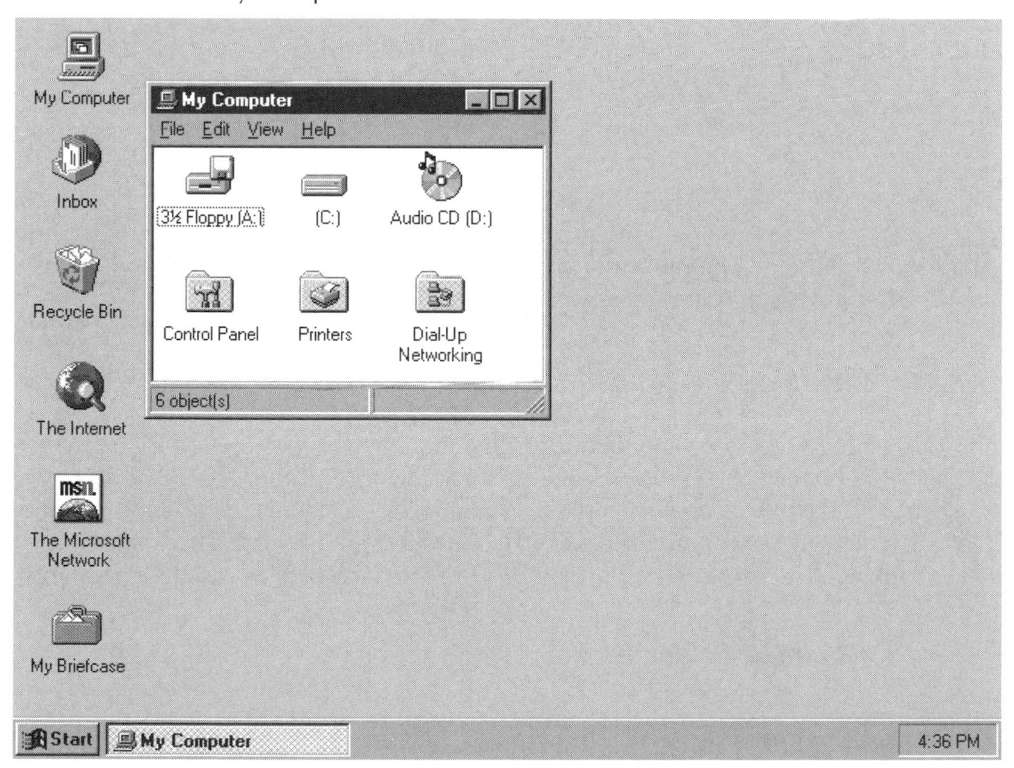

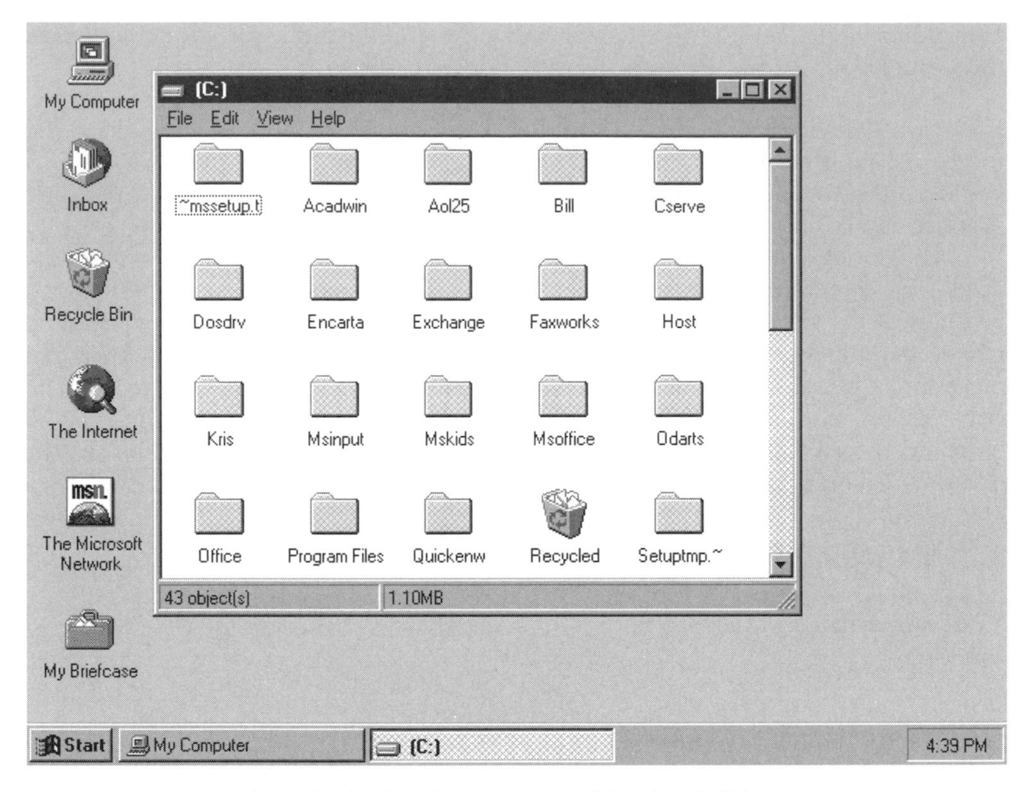

FIGURE 6.6 A window displaying the contents of the hard disk.

a. Adding a New Folder

In My Computer, a new folder can be added by opening the folder in which you want to create the new folder, opening the File menu, pointing to New, and clicking on Folder. The new folder appears with a generic name. Type a name for the new folder and press [Enter].

b. Changing the Name of a Folder or File

To change the name of a folder or file, click on its icon, open the File menu, and select Rename. Type the new name and press the [Enter] key. Another way to change the name is to click on the icon, and then click on the icon's name. Type the new name and press [Enter]. Be careful not to double click on the icon when you do this. Pause after you click on the icon before clicking on its name.

c. Moving a Folder or File

To move a folder or file from one location to another, click on the folder or file, open the Edit menu, and select Cut. Open the folder that you want to move the folder or file to, open the Edit menu, and select Paste. You can also use the mouse to move a folder or file by dragging its icon to the new location.

d. Copying a Folder or File

To copy a folder or file from one location to another, click on the folder or file, open the Edit menu, and select Copy. Open the folder that you want to contain the folder or file, open the Edit menu, and select Paste. You can also use the mouse to copy a folder or file by dragging its icon to the new folder while holding down the [Ctrl] key. A plus symbol displayed in the icon as it is being dragged lets you know that your are performing a copy instead of a move.

e. Acting on Multiple Folders and Files

To move or copy multiple folders or files, hold down the [Ctrl] key while you select the icons. If you want to select all of the icons in a window, or some icons that are listed next to each other, click on the first icon, hold down the [Shift] key, and click on the last icon in the sequence.

f. Copying to a Diskette

To copy folder or files to a diskette, select their icons, open the File menu, point to Send To, and click on the diskette drive.

g. Deleting Folders and Files

To delete a folder or file, click on its icon and press the [Delete] key. You can also delete a folder or file by dragging its icon to the Recycle Bin. If you hold down the [Shift] key while you are dragging the icon, the folder or file will be deleted directly from your computer without being placed in the Recycle Bin.

2. Formatting a Diskette

Formatting a disk removes all information on the disk and maps a new grid onto the disk. You should not try to format your hard disk unless you really know what you are doing. To format a diskette, place it in the diskette drive and open the My Computer window. Click on the icon for the diskette (being careful not to double click on it), open the File menu, and select Format. Select the correct capacity for your diskette, select any other options, and then click on the Start button.

3. Creating Shortcuts

You can create a shortcut to a file in My Computer by opening the folder in which to place it, opening the File menu, pointing to New, and selecting Shortcut. Instructions will appear on the screen to help you create the shortcut. You can also click on the file's icon, open the File menu, and select Create Shortcut. A shortcut for the file will appear in the open window. You can then drag it to the desired folder or to the desktop.

F. THE WINDOWS EXPLORER

The Windows Explorer displays the drives, folders, and files located on your computer. You can use it as an alternative to the My Computer icon and perform many of the same actions within it. To access the Windows Explorer, click on the Start button, point to Programs, and click on Windows Explorer. An example of the Windows Explorer window is shown in Figure 6.7.

FIGURE 6.7 The Windows Explorer.

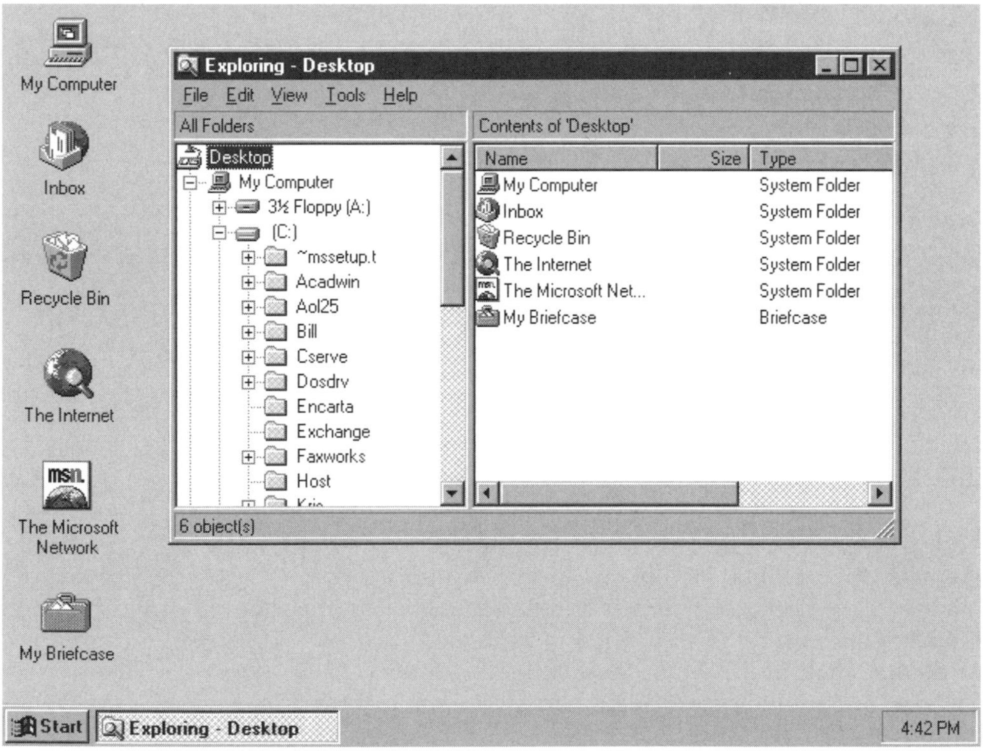

1. Viewing the Tree

The **tree** in the Windows Explorer is the display of drives, folders, shortcuts, and files that appears at the left side of the window. You can expand or minimize the tree by clicking on the plus or minus symbols displayed to the left of the branches. The contents of an item that you click on in the tree are displayed on the right side of the window.

2. Managing Folders and Files

The methods used to manage folders and files are the same as those used in the My Computer window and can be found in Section E on pages 125 to 127.

3. Creating Shortcuts

You can create a shortcut to a file in the Windows Explorer by opening the folder that you want to place it in, opening the File menu, pointing to New, and selecting Shortcut. Instructions will appear on the screen to help you create the shortcut. You can also click on the file's icon, open the File menu, and select Create Shortcut. A shortcut for the file will appear in the open folder. You can then drag it to a new folder or to the desktop.

G. EXITING WINDOWS 95

It is very important that you shut down Windows 95 properly before turning off your computer to avoid losing or damaging files. To shut down Windows 95, close all of your open windows, click on the Start button, and select Shut Down. You will be given three options in the dialog box that appears. You can shut down Windows 95, restart the computer in Windows 95, or restart the computer in the DOS mode. When you shut down Windows 95, a message will appear telling you to wait while your computer is being shut down. When you receive the message that it is safe to turn off your computer, you can do so. Restarting the computer in Windows 95 will reboot the computer for you and take you back into Windows 95. Restarting the computer in the DOS mode will reboot the computer to the DOS prompt. Typing WIN will take you back into Windows 95.

H. SUMMARY

Windows 95 is a 32-bit operating system that improves on the DOS and Windows combination. On the Windows 95 desktop you will find icons for the My Computer window and the Recycle Bin. You may also find icons for the other features and shortcuts to documents and programs. At the bottom of the desktop is the Start button and the taskbar. The Start button opens the Start menu, giving you quick access to many features. The taskbar displays the names of your open windows to allow you to easily switch between them.

To start a program, you double click on its icon on the desktop, select it from the Start menu, or select it from a program folder in the Programs option of the Start menu. To exit a program, you open the File menu and select Exit, or click on the "X" in the upper right-hand corner of the window.

Both the My Computer window and the Windows Explorer help you to manage your files. The My Computer window is accessed by double clicking on the My Computer icon on the desktop. The Windows Explorer is accessed by opening the Start menu, pointing to Programs, and clicking on Windows Explorer.

To avoid losing and damaging files, you must exit Windows 95 prior to turning off your computer. To exit, open the Start menu and click on Shut Down. Select "Shut down the computer?" and click on the Yes button. Wait until you get a message that it is safe to turn off the computer before turning off the power.

KEY TERMS

clicking, 116
dialog box, 117
double clicking, 116
dragging, 116
holding, 116
icon, 118
My Computer, 116
path, 123
pointing, 116
pull-down menus, 123
Recycle Bin, 116
shortcut, 118
tree, 129
window, 116
Windows Explorer, 116

QUESTIONS

1. What is a shortcut?
2. How do you put the shortcut for a program onto the desktop?
3. There is a file in the \PETERS directory on the C: drive called PETERS.LTR. What is this file's path?
4. There is another file in the \PETERS directory on the C: drive that was created with a program written for Windows 95. It has a long file name and is called PETERS PROPERTY SETTLEMENT. What is this file's path?
5. How do you create a new folder to add to the Programs option of the Start menu?
6. How do you copy a file from one folder to another using the mouse?
7. How do you copy a file to a diskette?

DISCUSSION QUESTIONS

1. Discuss the advantages of using the Windows 95 operating system rather than DOS with Windows.
2. How could you set up file-naming parameters for an office that is using long file names? Some uniformity needs to be maintained so that the contents of the file are recognizable to all in the firm by looking at the file name.

PART

III

Applications

CHAPTER

7

Word Processing

Word processing is the act of creating documents with a computer. Although often viewed as a secretarial function, word processing is used by legal professionals for drafting pleadings and other legal documents, memoranda, and simple letters. Many legal professionals are drafting the text of documents on word processors as an alternative to pen and paper or dictation. The advantage of word processing is that you can see the document as you are typing and can readily move sentences and paragraphs to improve the document's appearance and readability. Word processing also allows legal professionals to avoid spending time waiting for a secretary to type a document.

This chapter will explain the basic terms and functions of word processing. These terms and functions are generic to most, if not all, word processing programs. The most basic terms, *inserting* and *deleting,* are all that you need to know to begin using a word processor. More terms and functions are learned with every new document you create.

This chapter covers:

- how you will use a word processor
- basic terms and functions of a word processor
- using columns
- using tables
- merging documents
- creating macros
- printing documents

A. WORD PROCESSING

Word processing is the use of a computer to generate a document. A **document** is computer-generated text. Law offices use word processors to create and revise letters, contracts, pleadings, forms, and anything else that requires placing words or characters in printed or electronic form. A word processor is similar to a typewriter but with many more capabilities and features. A word processor can delete and insert words; move, copy, insert, and delete blocks of text; check spelling within a document; and store the document for later use and revision.

Word processing can be performed using a dedicated word processor or a word processing software program. **Dedicated word processors** are computers that do word processing exclusively or that have other limited capabilities. Dedicated word processors are typically minicomputers with terminals (monitor and keyboard) cabled throughout the office. The keyboards have keys that are labeled for word processing functions, such as bold, underline, and print. Word processing software programs are packaged programs that you can purchase to add to your computer system. These programs are available for all three categories of computers, although the most popular programs, WordPerfect and Microsoft Word, are most commonly used with microcomputers and minicomputers.

B. HOW THE LEGAL PROFESSIONAL USES A WORD PROCESSOR

A word processor is not strictly a secretarial tool. Many law offices are placing computers with word processing capabilities on or near the desk of every secretary, paralegal, and attorney in the office. You should use a word processor for drafting documents and completing forms on the computer. When you have hand-written or dictated a draft of a document, it should be entered into the word processor by a secretary. You should not spend your billable time entering this text.

Portable computers allow you to take your word processor with you to the law library, to the courthouse, to meetings, and on business trips. Documents can be drafted and then transferred to the office computer system by copying them to a diskette or by using a modem to connect to the office computer through the telephone lines.

C. COMMON WORD PROCESSOR TERMS AND FUNCTIONS

1. Word Wrapping

The first feature that distinguishes the word processor from its predecessor, the typewriter, is its ability to **word wrap.** Word wrapping occurs when the word processor continues the text to the next line without the user having to press a return key. This enables you to type without having to watch the screen to see when you are approaching the right margin. At the end of a paragraph, you will press the [Enter] key to return to the left margin to begin the next paragraph.

2. Cursor

The **cursor** is the flashing line character or box that indicates where data will be placed on the screen when entered from the keyboard. The cursor can be moved around the screen with the mouse or the [Arrow] keys. It can also be moved with the [Space Bar], [Backspace], and [Enter] keys.

3. Insert and Typeover

Most word processing programs allow the user to type in one of two modes: insert or typeover. Changing between the two modes is usually accomplished by pressing the [Insert] key.

Insert. In the **insert** mode, text that already exists will be pushed to the right as new text is entered. In the sentence shown below, we will be entering the word "Defendant" before "John Smith."

Plaintiff alleges that John Smith . . .

In the insert mode, we will move the cursor to the space before the "J" in "John" and begin typing. As we type in this mode, "John Smith" and the remainder of the text will move to the right.

Plaintiff alleges that **Defenda**_ John Smith . . .

Typeover. In the **typeover** mode, new text entered at the cursor will overwrite existing text and spaces. Therefore, as we type "Defendant," "John Smith" disappears.

Plaintiff alleges that **Defenda**ith . . .

4. Highlighting Text

Highlighting text is the marking or selecting of text so that you may perform some action or function on the highlighted text as a whole. Highlighting the text by dragging the mouse pointer over it, or inserting codes at the beginning and end of the text, identifies the portion of the text you want the word processor to act on. When you select a command—such as move, copy, or underline—the word processor acts on the entire highlighted block of text. A block of text is a group of words or characters that have been highlighted.

5. Deleting Characters, Words, and Blocks of Text

When editing a document, you will need to delete characters, words, and highlighted blocks of text. Deletions are most often accomplished with the [Delete] and [Backspace] keys.

The [Delete] key will delete the character directly above or to the right of the cursor. The [Backspace] key will delete the character to the left of the cursor. These keys can be held down to delete several characters in quick succession. When deleting large amounts of text, highlight the text and select a Delete command or press the [Delete] key.

6. Moving and Copying Text

Moving or copying text involves highlighting the text and then selecting a Move or Copy command. Moving a block of text removes it from its present location and places it in a new location as indicated by the user. Moving is also referred to as "cutting and pasting." In most Windows-based word processors, moving is accomplished by highlighting the text, selecting a cut option, moving the cursor to the new location, and selecting a paste option. You can also move text with the mouse by highlighting the text, positioning the mouse arrow inside the highlighted text, and dragging the text to the new location.

Copying text leaves the current text intact but allows the user to place a copy of that text at another location within the document. Copying is also referred to as "copying and pasting." In most Windows-based word processors, copying is accomplished by highlighting the text, selecting a copy option, moving the cursor to the new location, and selecting a paste option. You can also copy text with the mouse by highlighting the text, positioning the mouse arrow inside the highlighted text, and dragging the text to the new location while holding down the [Ctrl] key.

7. Boldfacing, Underlining, and Italicizing Text

Each word processing program will have a menu option, a button, a key, or a key combination that will change the text from its normal appearance to boldfaced, underlined, or italicized text. Boldfacing, underlining, and italicizing are accomplished by selecting the option to activate the feature, typing the text, and then turning off the feature. If the text has already been typed into the document, you can highlight the text and then select the feature.

a. *Boldfacing*

To draw attention to a word or group of words, you may type text in a **darker** than normal type. This darker type is called **boldface type.** Boldface type is not often used in pleadings or legal memoranda, but you will use it within contracts, corporate documents, letters, and internal office documents.

b. *Underlining*

Underlining a word or passage of text is another way of adding emphasis in your document. Underlining is often used in legal documents with case names, such as Miller v. Superior Court, and with Latin words and phrases, such as supra and ex parte.

c. *Italicizing*

Italicizing a *word* or *passage of text* can also add emphasis within your documents. Italicizing and underlining are often interchangeable in legal documents. You just need to be consistent throughout the document.

8. Justification

Justification is the positioning of the text in relation to the left and right margins of the page. Left justification positions the text flush against the left margin and leaves a jagged right margin. Right justification positions the text flush against the right margin and leaves a jagged left margin. Full justification positions the text flush against both the left and right margins. Center justification centers the text between the margins. Justification is accomplished by selecting a justification feature and then typing the text. You can also highlight blocks of text and select a justification feature for the block.

9. Centering

Centering places text at the center of the printed page.

Centering

This may or may not be the center of your monitor, so do not be alarmed if the centered text does not look quite right on the screen. The text will appear centered when the document is printed. A line centering feature will center only the current line of text. After selecting this feature and typing the text, pressing the [Enter] key will return you to the left margin of the page. If you need to center multiple lines of text, you can use center justification. This feature will center all lines of text until you change back to left or full justification.

10. Tabbing and Indenting

Word processors have tab stops that are pre-set at approximately every half inch. Pressing the [Tab] key or selecting an indent option will bring the text in to the first tab stop. If you press the [Tab] key or select the indent option multiple times, the text will be brought in that number of tab stops. The tab stops can be adjusted within a document.

The [Tab] key is used to indent the first line of a paragraph or to indent a heading or other item. At the beginning of a paragraph, you will press the [Tab] key to indent the first line to the first tab stop. As you type, the remaining text of the paragraph will word wrap back to the left margin.

There are several other ways to indent a paragraph. A basic indent feature will indent the entire text of the paragraph to a tab stop. A double indent feature will indent the text of the paragraph in from both margins to a tab stop. A hanging indent will indent all of the paragraph except the first line. Examples of each of these three indent styles are shown below.

> An indent feature will indent the entire text of a paragraph to the first tab stop if selected once, or multiple tab stops if selected more than once.

> A double indent feature will indent the paragraph in one tab stop from both margins, and multiple tab stops if selected more than once.

A hanging indent sets the first line of the paragraph against the left margin and indents the remainder of the paragraph.

11. Page Breaks

Word processing programs will end a page of text based on a page length that has been pre-set in the program. This pre-set page length may be changed for an individual document by changing top and/or bottom margins.

There will be times, however, when you want to end a page at a point other than the pre-set length. This breaking of the page, called a "hard" or "manual" **page break,** stops the page where the user indicates and leaves the pre-set page length intact in the remainder of the document. The document shown in Figure 7.1 breaks the page at an awkward point. A hard page break should be placed so that the "II" and "ARGUMENT" appear on the following page. In WordPerfect, this would be accomplished by moving the cursor to the beginning of the line containing "II," and pressing [Ctrl]+[Enter].

JOHN DOE, ESQ.
DOE AND DOE
1234 Herring Street
San Diego, California 99999
(619) 555-1212
State Bar No. 99999

Attorney for Plaintiff, JOSEPH MADISON

SUPERIOR COURT OF THE STATE OF CALIFORNIA

IN AND FOR THE COUNTY OF SAN DIEGO

JOSEPH MADISON, Plaintiff, vs. HOWARD HOOPER, HOOPER LIGHTING, INC., a California Corporation, and DOES 1 through 50, Inclusive, Defendants.	CASE NO.: 34567 PLAINTIFF'S RESPONSE TO DEFENDANT'S MOTION FOR ORDER TRANSFERRING ACTION DATE: June 22, 1996 TIME: 9:00 a.m. DEPT: 24

I.

STATEMENT OF THE CASE

Plaintiff, JOSEPH MADISON, filed the Complaint in this action on May 1, 1996. Plaintiff alleges in the Complaint that the Defendants, and each of them, failed to perform their obligations under a contract for the installation of lighting in Plaintiff's warehouse. Specifically, the Complaint alleges that Defendant, HOOPER LIGHTING, INC., installed lighting that was in violation of city and county building codes. It further alleges that Defendant, HOWARD HOOPER, made false representations to Plaintiff. Plaintiff filed this action in San Diego County, the location of the warehouse. Defendants have filed this motion to have the action moved to Riverside County, where they reside.

II.

ARGUMENT

FIGURE 7.1 When the pre-set page length of a document breaks the page at an awkward place, a hard page break can be used to break the page at a different position.

12. Spell Checking

Most word processing packages come with a feature for checking the spelling in a document. This feature should not replace the proofreading of the document, however, because **spell checking** will not pick up a mistake when the mistake is a recognizable word.

The spell check feature looks at each word in the document and compares it to the words found in its dictionary. When the spell checker finds a word that does not match any word in the dictionary, it pauses and allows you to correct the word, replace it with one from a displayed list of similar words, or skip the word. You will use the skip option often when the spell checker stops on names and on legal terminology that is not contained within the dictionary. There is often an option to add these words to a dictionary so that the spell checker will not stop on the word when you use it in your documents.

13. Thesauruses

Some word processing packages are equipped with a **thesaurus** feature. The thesaurus provides the user with synonyms for a word the user would like to change. An example of WordPerfect's thesaurus for the word "document" is shown in Figure 7.2.

14. Fonts

Fonts are different type styles. *Italics*, smaller type, different styles, and appearances are all possible with your word processor's font capabilities. The fonts that you can

FIGURE 7.2 WordPerfect's thesaurus screen for the word "document."

```
document=(n)
 1 A •certificate          document-(v)
   B •charter               5   •certify
   C •credential                •prove
   D •license                   •substantiate
                                •support
 2 E •chronicle
   F •record               document-(ant)
   G •register              6   •plagiarize

 3 H •deed
   I  diploma
   J •voucher

 4 K •draft
   L  folio
   M  manuscript
   N •text

1 Replace Word; 2 View Doc; 3 Look Up Word; 4 Clear Column: 0
```

use with your word processing program are limited by the fonts that your printer can print. Your word processor may come with all sorts of fonts, but you will need a printer with the capability to print them.

D. SAVING AND OPENING DOCUMENTS

1. Saving a Document

Saving a document places the characters temporarily stored in the computer's RAM onto some type of secondary storage device. To save the document, you will need to specify the disk drive and directory where it will be stored, and you will need to give the document a name.

In DOS and Windows word processors, document names must comply with the DOS specifications of one to eight characters followed by an optional period and a one- to three-character extension. For example, a demurrer in the Halstyn case could be saved to the root of a diskette in the A: drive as follows:

A:\HALSTYN.DEM

This is a descriptive document name, which makes it easy to recognize what the document contains. In Windows 95 word processors, long file names can be used. An example of the same document saved to the root of the A: drive with a long file name would be:

A:\Halstyn Demurrer

Many word processors have two save options, Save and Save As. The Save option will prompt you for a file location and name if the file has not yet been saved. If the file has been saved before and has a name, the Save option will quickly save your latest changes to the document. The Save As option prompts you for a file location and name. If you only provide a file name, the file will be placed in the folder that is currently open. To place it in a different folder, either specify the path or click on the correct folder icon in part of the dialog box to make it the current folder. Once you have made the folder into the current folder, you just need to type a file name into the space indicated. It is a good practice to save a document every few pages as you are typing. Then, in the event that the computer fails, all that will be lost is the material you have not yet saved.

2. Back-up Options

Some word processors, such as WordPerfect versions 5.1 and later, have a **back-up** feature, which allows you to set the program to automatically save a document at timed intervals. In the event that power is lost to your computer, or someone turns your computer off without exiting the word processor, the back-up copy is stored for your retrieval the next time you enter the program.

3. Opening a Document

When you want to open a document into a word processing program, you will need to specify the drive and the directory or folder where the file is located and the file's name.

For example, I may want to retrieve the Smith complaint. The Smith case is a personal injury action. All of the documents for this case are stored in the PI subdirectory of the SMITH directory on the C: drive. All of our complaints have the extension .CPL so I know that the document's name is most likely SMITH.CPL. The directory tree below illustrates the location of the document.

```
                     ┌─ \PI
          ┌─ \SMITH ─┘    SMITH.CPL
C:\ ──────┘
```

To open SMITH.CPL, you would access the proper command in the word processing program and identify the document as:

C:\SMITH\PI\SMITH.CPL

The document would then be opened into the program for editing.

In Windows word processors, a dialog box will appear when you select the Open command. In the space for the file name you can specify the entire path and file name, or you can open directory folders and look for the file. The directory folders appear in a portion of the dialog box. Clicking on the folders lists the files contained therein in another part of the dialog box. To see folders and files that are on different drives, there is often a portion of the dialog box that allows you to change the drive letter.

E. COLUMNS

Columns features allow you to create columns in your documents. There are two basic types of columns: newspaper and parallel.

Newspaper columns are read from top to bottom. When the bottom of the page is reached, the column continues at the top of the same page. This is an example of newspaper columns.

Parallel columns, in contrast, are read from left to right and are commonly used by legal professionals for creating pleading captions and deposition summaries. An example of parallel columns is shown in Figure 7.3.

F. TABLES

Another way to create columns of data is to create a **table.** A table is made up of columns and rows, the intersection of which forms cells. A cell can contain text or numbers. A table looks very similar to an electronic spreadsheet but contains many word processing attributes. For instance, text will word wrap within a cell, and the row will increase in size to accommodate the text. You can use tables to summarize depositions and to create office forms, billing statements, and calendars. For documents that need calculations performed on the numbers within the table, formulas can be created.

When you create a table, you will specify the number of columns and rows that you need. Columns or rows can be added or deleted, and the column size can be adjusted through menu options. A table will appear on your screen with lines separating the columns and rows. In some word processors, the lines will appear in the printed document, in others they will not. Lines can be added or removed or their appearance altered to create different effects in the table. A deposition summary created using tables is displayed in Figure 7.4. The lines of the table were left in the document to make the deposition summary easy to read. If the lines were removed, the deposition summary would look like the one in Figure 7.3.

FIGURE 7.3 A deposition summary created using parallel columns.

SUMMARY OF THE DEPOSITION
OF
LEONARD WILKINS, M.D.

Taken January 26, 1992.

Page:Line	Summary
1:5 to 2:23	Opening remarks and instructions to the witness.
2:27 to 4:12	Dr. Wilkins resides at 3322 Mockingbird Lane, in Wilkinsville, Iowa. His business address is 45 Main Street in Wilkinsville. Dr. Wilkins' family has lived in Wilkinsville for over 150 years.

SUMMARY OF THE DEPOSITION

OF

LEONARD WILKINS, M.D.

Taken January 26, 1992

Page:Line	Summary
1:5 to 2:23	Opening remarks and instructions to the witness.
2:27 to 4:12	Dr. Wilkins resides at 3322 Mockingbird Lane, in Wilkinsville, Iowa. His business address is 45 Main Street in Wilkinsville. Dr. Wilkins' family has lived in Wilkinsville for over 150 years.

FIGURE 7.4 A deposition summary created using a table feature. The lines can be removed if desired.

G. MERGING

Merging is the process of taking one document and integrating it with another document. Form letters and mailing labels are commonly created using merge functions. With most merges a **shell document** is created and then merged with a **secondary file** that contains information necessary to create individual documents. An example of a shell document is shown in Figure 7.5. The shell is created with fields to indicate where information will be inserted from the secondary file. The secondary file for this document would be a list of names and addresses and a salutation. An example of a secondary file for this shell is shown in Figure 7.6.

When the shell document and the secondary file are merged, a separate letter will be created for each of the records in the secondary file. The merged letters will appear as those shown in Figure 7.7.

Some firms use merging to assemble documents. Contracts, pleadings, and other documents with standard language can be created using a merge function. This process is more complicated than the form letter example. Many documents, such as contracts, have standard provisions that are either constant or change according to the parties and circumstances involved. The standard provisions are identified and stored in a secondary file. The primary file is much like the form letter example but will contain more merging features. When the merge is executed, the word processor will prompt the user to select paragraphs from the secondary file. When the merge is complete, an individualized document has been created.

Some word processors have merge documents that prompt you for information instead of pulling the information from a secondary file. A sample of such a merge for a California corporation's articles of incorporation is shown in Figure 7.8.

SMITH AND SMITH
Attorneys at Law
1234 Hampton Avenue
La Jolla, California 99999
(619) 555-1212

February 20, 1997

^Field 1^
^Field 2^

Re: Jones v. Jones, San Diego Superior Court Case No. 444536

Dear ^Field 3^:

Enclosed herewith please find our client's responses to the interrogatories propounded on January 23, 1997. If you have any questions, please do not hesitate to contact me.

Sincerely,

JOHN Q. SMITH, ESQ.
SMITH AND SMITH

JQS/kb
Enclosure

FIGURE 7.5 A shell document with fields where information will be placed.

H. MACROS

A **macro** is a group of keystrokes that are recorded, identified with a key combination or name, and then executed with the key combination or name. For example, say that you end every letter with:

Sincerely,

Wilson Baker, Esq.
TRIBBLE & DOWNEY

```
John Simpson, Esq.^End of Field^
34 Rome Avenue
La Jolla, California  99999^End of Field^
Mr. Simpson^End of Field^
^End of Record^
============================================================
Marvin Pearce, Esq.^End of Field^
Fenner & Pearce
64 Honor Avenue
San Diego, California  99999^End of Field^
Mr. Pearce^End of Field^
^End of Record^
============================================================
James Franklin, Esq.^End of Field^
Marshall and Franklin
22 Windship Lane
San Diego, California  99999^End of Field^
Jim^End of Field^
^End of Record^
============================================================
```

FIGURE 7.6 A secondary file containing the names, addresses, and salutations to be inserted into the shell document.

FIGURE 7.7 The merging of the three records from the secondary file with the shell document creates three separate letters.

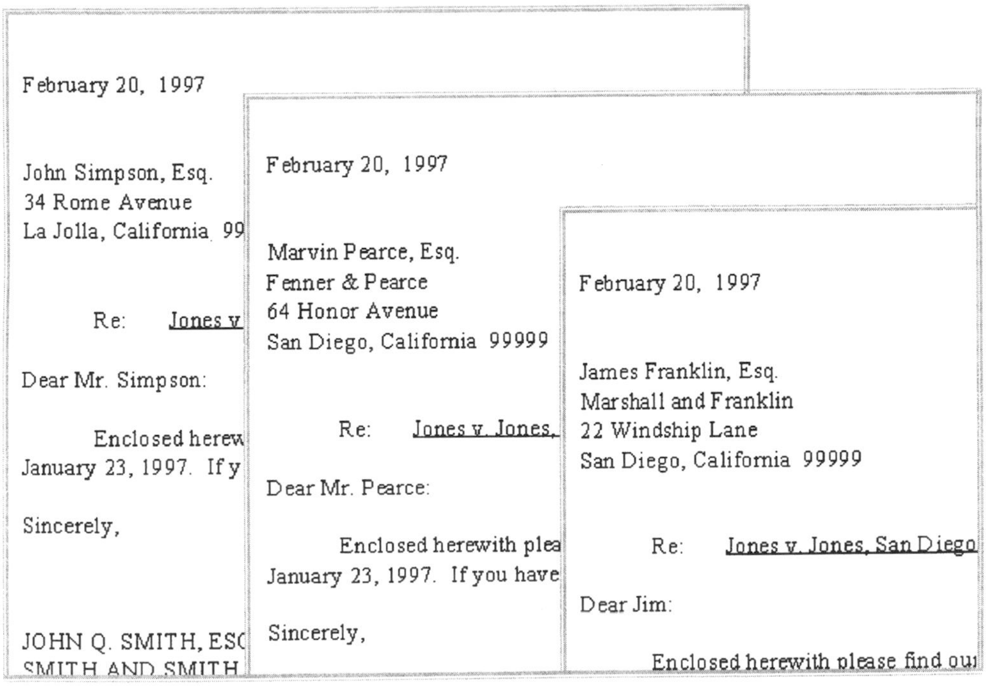

February 20, 1997

John Simpson, Esq.
34 Rome Avenue
La Jolla, California 99

Re: Jones v

Dear Mr. Simpson:

Enclosed herew
January 23, 1997. If y

Sincerely,

JOHN Q. SMITH, ESC
SMITH AND SMITH

February 20, 1997

Marvin Pearce, Esq.
Fenner & Pearce
64 Honor Avenue
San Diego, California 99999

Re: Jones v. Jones,

Dear Mr. Pearce:

Enclosed herewith plea
January 23, 1997. If you have

Sincerely,

February 20, 1997

James Franklin, Esq.
Marshall and Franklin
22 Windship Lane
San Diego, California 99999

Re: Jones v. Jones, San Diego

Dear Jim:

Enclosed herewith please find ou

ARTICLES OF INCORPORATION

OF

{INPUT}Input NAME OF CORPORATION, PRESS [F9]~

I.

The name of this corporation is {INPUT}Input name of corporation, press [F9]~.

II.

The purpose of this corporation is to engage in any lawful act or activity for which a corporation may be organized under the General Corporation Law of California other than the banking business, the trust company business, or the practice of a profession permitted to be incorporated under the California Corporations Code.

III.

The name and address of this corporation's initial agent for service of process is {INPUT}Agent's name and address (CA), press [F9]~.

IV.

The corporation is only authorized to issue one class of stock; and the total number of shares which this corporation is authorized to issue is {INPUT}Input number of shares, then press [F9]~ shares of {INPUT}Type of shares (e.g. common, preferred), press [F9]~ stock.

DATED: {INPUT}Input date or leave blank, press [F9]~

{INPUT}Type incorporator's name, press [F9]~
Incorporator

FIGURE 7.8 Document assembly using merge.

To create a macro to type the above closing, you would select a key combination or name for the macro and then record the keystrokes of the macro. This macro could be identified as [Alt]+[C] for "closing" or could be given the name "closing." After all of the keystrokes are entered, pressing a certain key or selecting a menu option will end the recording of the macro. The macro is stored with your word processing files for use in any subsequent documents you create. When you reach a place in a letter where you would normally type your closing, pressing [Alt] + [C] or selecting the macro "closing" will cause the closing to be typed automatically.

I. PRINTING

Printing is the creation of a hard copy of a document drafted on your computer. To print a document, you need a printer. Having a printer, however, does not always guarantee that it will print your document. The word processing software must be set up to print to your make and model of printer.

If your word processing documents will not print on your printer or have a strange appearance, check the software and printer reference manuals or call their respective customer service numbers. You may need to add a printer driver to your word processing program or change the printer identified in the print section of the program. A printer driver is a software program that interprets word processing instructions so that the printer will understand them. These printer drivers are available from the word processing program manufacturers.

When you print your document, you can print the entire document, specific pages of the document, or a block of text that you have highlighted. You can also set up your document to print in a portrait or landscape format. The portrait option orients the long edge of the page vertically. The landscape option orients the long edge of the page horizontally. The print options will vary between word processing programs. The appearance of the pages of the printed document can be changed with document format options.

J. SUMMARY

Word processing is the use of a computer to generate electronic or printed text. Word processing is a valuable tool for the legal professional. It provides a way to view a document's appearance as it is being created and bypasses secretarial turn-around time. The legal professional, however, is not a typist and should not type documents that have been drafted on paper or dictated.

There are two typing modes within a word processing program, insert and typeover. The insert mode inserts new text at the point of the cursor, pushing existing text to the right. The typeover mode types over the existing text.

Highlighting text is the marking of a group of characters or words using one of the word processor's functions or a mouse. The highlighted text may be deleted, copied, moved, printed, boldfaced, underlined, italicized, or acted upon in a number of other ways. Individual characters may be deleted with the [Delete] or [Backspace] keys.

Many word processors offer special features such as spell checkers, thesauruses, back-up options, columns, tables, merge functions, and macros. As you work with a word processing software program, you will learn about more features with each new document you create.

KEY TERMS

backup, 144
boldface type, 139
centering, 139
columns, 144
cursor, 137
dedicated word processor, 136
document, 135
fonts, 142
highlighting text, 137
insert, 137
italicizing, 139
justification, 139
macro, 147
merging, 146
page break, 140
printing, 150
secondary file, 146
shell document, 146
spell checking, 142
table, 145
thesaurus, 142
typeover, 137
underlining, 139
word processing, 135
word wrap, 136

QUESTIONS

1. What is word processing?
2. What is the difference between a dedicated word processor and a word processing software program?
3. Explain the difference between insert and typeover.
4. What is a block of text?
5. What is a thesaurus?
6. The fonts that you can print from your word processing program are limited by what piece of computer hardware?
7. How would you identify the document, SMITH.MOT, to be retrieved from its location shown below?

```
                  ┌─ \SMITH ──┐┌─ \DISSO
C:\ ──────────────┘           └┘    SMITH.MOT
```

8. What are the two types of columns and how do they differ?
9. Give an example of how a merge feature could be used.
10. What is a macro?

DISCUSSION QUESTIONS

1. The use of computers and word processing programs by legal professionals has reduced much of the workload of legal secretaries. There are times, however, when a legal secretary, because of typing speed and word processing

skills, should be utilized to complete a document. Discuss instances when a legal secretary should input, revise, and finalize a document for the legal professional.

2. Parallel columns, tables, merge functions, and macros are valuable tools used in creating legal documents. Discuss the ways, other than those mentioned in this chapter, that these tools could be used in drafting legal documents.

EXERCISE

Prepare a one- or two-page memorandum to your instructor, using any available word processing software, summarizing a magazine article regarding the use of computers in the law. Legal computing articles can be found in the state bar magazines, The A.B.A. Journal, and legal computing periodicals.

The memorandum should be in the following form:

M E M O R A N D U M

TO:

FROM:

DATE:

RE:

[The text of your memo will go here.]

Instructions

The headings should be boldfaced, and the text of the memorandum should be in normal type.

When you have finished the memorandum, please do the following:

- number the pages of the document
- check the spelling within the document
- print the entire document

CHAPTER

8

Electronic Spreadsheets

An electronic spreadsheet is a computerized version of an accountant's pad. The electronic spreadsheet has similar columns and rows, but it allows you to adjust and tailor the spreadsheet to fit your needs. You place formulas in an electronic spreadsheet where you would normally place manually calculated totals. Then, when information is changed in the spreadsheet, the formulas are automatically recalculated based on the new data, and the new totals appear in each cell.

You will find in working with various electronic spreadsheet programs that they are all very similar. (In fact, they are so similar that there have been several copyright infringement lawsuits filed by software manufacturers against one another.) Therefore, once you have learned about one electronic spreadsheet, you should be able to run just about any other spreadsheet program with a minimum of training time.

This chapter covers:

- common terms used in electronic spreadsheets
- common features found in electronic spreadsheets
- "what if" scenarios
- how electronic spreadsheets are used in the practice of law

A. WHAT ARE ELECTRONIC SPREADSHEETS?

As explained above, **electronic spreadsheets** are a computerized version of an accountant's spreadsheet pad with its preprinted columns and rows. The first electronic spreadsheet, VisiCalc, was developed in the mid-1970s by Dan Bricklin, a Harvard Business School student frustrated with the limits of a paper spreadsheet. Today, the three most popular spreadsheet programs are Lotus 1-2-3, Quattro Pro, and Microsoft®Excel®. Lotus 1-2-3 and Quattro Pro operate in a virtually identical manner. Excel looks similar to the other two programs but performs some tasks in a slightly different manner.

In an electronic spreadsheet, functions and/or formulas are entered into the spreadsheet in place of computed totals. When information within a spreadsheet is changed, each function or formula will respond and automatically display the new total. Some electronic spreadsheets have multiple spreadsheet pages available in a single spreadsheet document. These pages can each be used for different spreadsheets, and a spreadsheet can reference data from another page in a formula or function.

Legal professionals use electronic spreadsheets for some in-house accounting and management functions and for performing "what if" scenarios. "What if" scenarios involve the creation of a spreadsheet with formulas and functions in the totals columns. The information within the spreadsheet is then altered in order to observe and analyze the effect of the changes on the spreadsheet's totals.

Before we go on to examples of the law office uses of electronic spreadsheets, we should cover the terminology common to all electronic spreadsheets.

B. COMMON ELECTRONIC SPREADSHEET TERMS

1. Columns and Rows

Every electronic spreadsheet is made up of **columns** and **rows,** examples of which are shown in Figure 8.1. The columns are labeled with letters and the rows are

FIGURE 8.1 The columns and rows of an electronic spreadsheet.

	A	B	C	D	E
1					
2					
3					
4					
5					
6					
7					

labeled with numbers. Electronic spreadsheets have a large number of columns, so after column Z, the columns continue with AA through AZ, then BA through BZ, and so on.

2. Cells

A **cell** is the intersection of a column and a row. Data entered into the spreadsheet is entered into a cell.

3. Cell Addresses

A cell is identified by its cell address. The **cell address** is the column letter followed by the row number of the cell, such as B2 (column B, row 2) or CF120 (column CF, row 120). Cell B2 is highlighted in Figure 8.2.

4. Cell Pointer

The **cell pointer** is the dark rectangle that appears in one cell in the spreadsheet. Some programs call the cell pointer the "selector" or the "selected cell." Data is entered in the cell containing the cell pointer. The cell pointer can be moved using the keys on the keyboard or with the mouse.

FIGURE 8.2 Cell B2 is highlighted.

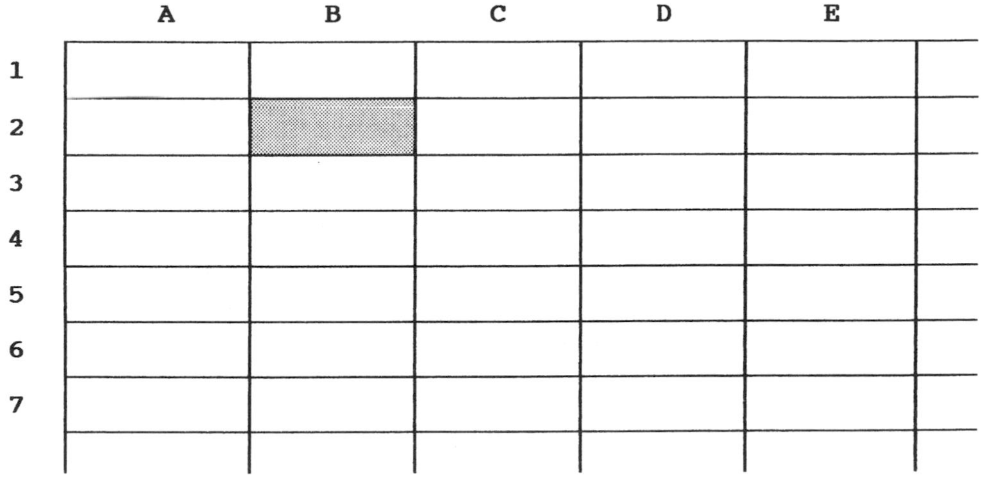

	A	B	C	D	E
1					
2					
3					
4					
5					
6					
7					

5. Ranges of Cells

A group of one or more cells is called a **range.** Many electronic spreadsheet commands and functions allow you to act on a range of cells instead of having to act on each cell individually. A range of cells is identified by the cell addresses of the cell in the upper left-hand corner of the range and of the cell in the lower right-hand corner of the range. The range highlighted in Figure 8.3 is A1..C3. Many programs use ".." to indicate A1 "through" C3. Others use a colon ":" to indicate "through."

6. Cell Entries

There are two types of **cell entries** used in electronic spreadsheets, text and values. A cell entry is the data that is placed inside a cell.

Text Text entries include titles, headings, and other labels.

TITLE ______________ Total

Values Value entries include numbers, formulas, and functions.

Numbers are generally entered without using commas, dollar signs, or other number formats. Only the newest versions of electronic spreadsheets will accept such formats when you are entering your numbers. To place commas, dollar signs, percentages, and other number formats within the number entries, you must select a format option. Formatting cells involves selecting the cells to contain, or

FIGURE 8.3 Range A1..C3 is highlighted.

	A	B	C	D	E
1					
2					
3					
4					
5					
6					
7					

containing, the numbers to be formatted, and then selecting the desired format option.

25 $194.50

Formulas are computations of one or more cells in which the individual cells are identified. For example, placing the formula +A1+A2 in cell A3 will add A1 and A2 and place the total in A3. Excel will begin its formulas with the "=" symbol.

(1-2-3 and Quattro Pro)	+A1+A2	+B6−B7+B12	+A25
(Excel)	=A1+A2	=B6−B7+B12	=A25

Functions are preprogrammed calculating formulas that come with the electronic spreadsheet package. Functions can perform addition, calculate averages, determine principle and interest payments, and perform a number of other tasks. An example of a function that would add cells A1 through A25 would be @SUM(A1..A25). In Excel, the same function would be written as =SUM (A1:A25). The SUM function is common to almost all electronic spreadsheets. Within the parentheses is the range of cells to be acted on.

(1-2-3 and Quattro Pro)	@SUM(A1..A25)	@AVG(B1..B35)
(Excel)	=SUM(A1:A25)	=AVERAGE(B1:B35)

7. Input Line

The **input line** is located above the spreadsheet. This is where data appears as it is being entered. When the [Enter] key is pressed, the data from the input line is placed in the cell containing the cell pointer. Some electronic spreadsheets display the data on the input line and in the cell as it is being entered. In the case of a formula or function, the formula or function will appear on the input line and when the [Enter] key is pressed, the calculated total will appear in the cell. To edit the contents of a cell you can type in a new entry, press the [F2] key to move the cursor to the input line, or click within the input line with the mouse. Pressing the [Enter] key will complete the edit.

C. ELECTRONIC SPREADSHEET FEATURES

1. Adjustment of Columns and Rows

With a paper spreadsheet, you are limited to the columns and rows printed on the paper. An electronic spreadsheet gives you the flexibility to increase or decrease the size of one or all of the columns. Some programs also allow changes in the sizes of the rows. In addition to changing the size of columns and rows, you can insert or delete columns and rows wherever necessary.

2. Automatic Recalculation

Electronic spreadsheets will automatically recalculate formulas and functions when a cell identified in the formula or function is changed in the spreadsheet. Figure 8.4 shows a sample spreadsheet as it will appear on the screen, and Figure 8.5 shows the actual entries within the cells. In the examples shown in Figures 8.4 and 8.5, if a change were made in MDL's rate from $250 to $300, the cell in the TOTAL column, and the cell totaling the TOTAL column, would automatically display new totals.

FIGURE 8.4 A spreadsheet as it appears on the screen.

	A	B	C	D
1		JANUARY BILLABLE HOURS		
2				
3	BILLER	RATE/Hr.	HOURS	TOTAL
4				
5	Partners			
6	MDL	$250	152	$38,000
7	JKK	$200	187	$37,400
8	TLM	$180	165	$29,700
9	Associates			
10	WBB	$180	198	$35,640
11	DLS	$150	187	$28,050
12	JMG	$150	202	$30,300
13	DGA	$140	169	$23,660
14	Paralegals			
15	James	$80	156	$12,480
16	Susan	$80	164	$13,120
17				
18	TOTALS		1580	$248,350

	A	B	C	D
1		JANUARY BILLABLE HOURS		
2				
3	BILLER	RATE/Hr.	HOURS	TOTAL
4				
5	Partners			
6	MDL	$250	152	+B6*C6
7	JKK	$200	187	+B7*C7
8	TLM	$180	165	+B8*C8
9	Associates			
10	WBB	$180	198	+B10*C10
11	DLS	$150	187	+B11*C11
12	JMG	$150	202	+B12*C12
13	DGA	$140	169	+B13*C13
14	Paralegals			
15	James	$80	156	+B15*C15
16	Susan	$80	164	+B16*C16
17				
18	TOTALS		@SUM(C6..C16)	@SUM(D6..D16)

FIGURE 8.5 The actual entries in the spreadsheet cells.

3. Relative and Absolute Cell Addresses

When a cell address is placed within a formula, the electronic spreadsheet finds the cell by its position relative to the cell containing the formula, not by its address. For example, in Figure 8.5 the formula in cell D6 contains relative cell addresses. In reading the formula +B6*C6, the electronic spreadsheet does not look at the actual cell addresses. It reads the formula as: "Take the cell that is two cells to the left of the formula, and multiply it by the cell that is one cell to the left of the formula." Relative cell addresses give you the ability to copy the formula in cell D6 to cells D7 through D16. When you perform the copy, the electronic spreadsheet places the appropriate relative addresses within the other formulas.

In some instances you want the formula to always use a figure found in one particular column, row, or cell, even when you copy the cell. In these instances, you can use the dollar sign "$" to "absolute" part or all of the cell address. If you place the dollar sign in front of the column letter, the column letter becomes absolute and the row number remains relative. In our example, if we used the formula +$B6*$C6, we could copy the formula to cell E6 and still receive the correct answer. Had we not absoluted the column letters, the formula in cell E6 would read +C6*D6. The row number within the formula can be absoluted by placing the dollar sign in front of the row number in the cell address. The formula +B$6*C$6 would allow the columns to adjust when copied but not the rows. If we used this formula in cell D6, and then copied it down to the other cells, they would all contain the same answer because they would always access the numbers from row 6. To completely absolute a cell address within a formula, you place a dollar sign before the column letter and the row number. This will make the formula always reference the same cell. For example, if we wanted column E of our spreadsheet to reflect the number of hours each person billed relative to the senior partner, MDL, we could place the following formula in cell E6: +C6−C6. When we copy the formula to cells E7 through E16, the first part of the formula will adjust and the second part will remain fixed and always access the number from cell C6. The new spreadsheet is shown in Figure 8.6.

4. Moving and Copying Cells

When moving or copying a range of cells, you must identify the range of cells to be moved or copied, and then identify where they will be moved or copied to.

FIGURE 8.6 Column E of the spreadsheet uses a formula that takes each person's hours in column C and subtracts from them the hours billed by the senior partner MDL. The formula in column E (+Cn−C6 where n is the row number) includes an absolute address so that the latter half of the formula will not adjust when copied to other cells in the column.

	A	B	C	D	E
1		JANUARY BILLABLE HOURS			
2					
3	BILLER	RATE/Hr.	HOURS	TOTAL	HOURS +/- MDL
4					
5	Partners				
6	MDL	$250	152	$38,000	0
7	JKK	$200	187	$37,400	35
8	TLM	$180	165	$29,700	13
9	Associates				
10	WBB	$180	198	$35,640	46
11	DLS	$150	187	$28,050	35
12	JMG	$150	202	$30,300	50
13	DGA	$140	169	$23,660	17
14	Paralegals				
15	James	$80	156	$12,480	4
16	Susan	$80	164	$13,120	12
17					
18	TOTALS		1580	$248,350	

You must be careful not to move or copy a range onto cells that already contain information. You may need to insert new columns or rows prior to the Move or Copy command. In Windows-based electronic spreadsheets, you can move or copy using cut and paste or copy and paste. You can also use the mouse to drag the highlighted range of cells. Dragging the range to the new location will perform a move. Dragging the range while holding down the [Ctrl] key will perform a copy.

Copying is frequently used when entering formulas and functions into an electronic spreadsheet. Since the formulas and functions contain relative addresses, you need only enter the formula or function once. You can then copy the formula or function to cells that need a similar formula or function, and the spreadsheet will adjust the cell addresses relative to their placement. To prevent a cell address in a formula or function from adjusting, you would make the address absolute using the dollar sign "$".

5. Printing

To print a spreadsheet, you need to identify the range of cells that you wish to print. You can do this by typing in the range when you access the Print command or by highlighting the range prior to selecting the Print command. Some spreadsheets can select the range themselves when you select the Print command, but they are not always accurate. In the print menu, you can adjust the page margins, add headers or footers, and add page numbers. To see what the spreadsheet will look like prior to printing it, you may want to use the print preview feature available in many electronic spreadsheet programs. If your spreadsheet is wider than the page width, you can adjust the margins, print parts of the spreadsheet separately, have the program wrap the remaining columns below the existing columns on the page, or print in the landscape mode. The landscape mode will print with the long edge of the paper horizontal to the spreadsheet data.

D. SPREADSHEET ANALYSIS AND THE "WHAT IF" SCENARIO

An electronic spreadsheet is an analytical tool. Although at first glance it seems well suited for accounting purposes, there are accounting software packages that perform these tasks more efficiently. Electronic spreadsheets *are* well suited, however, to run "what if" scenarios. **"What if" scenarios** are analyses of several different assumptions to find the best results.

The creation of a "what if" scenario first involves the creation of the form to be used for the analyses. Figure 8.7 is a good example of such a form. This is a typical analysis of a law firm's income and expenses.

The spreadsheet is set up with columns for an item description and the months January through September. Rows are set up for income, expenses, partner draws, and totals. To fill in the spreadsheet's projected numbers, the firm looks at past history and estimates values for each item. Formulas or functions are placed in the totals rows. The spreadsheet is then ready to be manipulated through "what if" scenarios.

We will create a "what if" scenario to determine what effect the June hiring of an additional associate and a paralegal will have on firm income. The costs of the proposed employees (wages, overhead, etc.) are added to the firm's expenses, and the expected income from the employees is added to the firm's income. The firm's income forecast after the proposed hirings is shown in Figure 8.8.

As you can see, the addition of the two employees will increase the firm's projected income by $22,500 per month. More important to the firm's partners, however, is the additional $7,500 they could take home each month. The firm will need to determine whether they have enough work for the two new employees before they follow through with this hiring.

FIGURE 8.7 An income forecast for a law firm prior to adding new employees.

INCOME FORECAST - 1/1/96 through 9/30/96

ITEM	JAN	FEB	MAR	APR	MAY	JUN	JUL	AUG	SEP
INCOME									
Partners									
MDL	40,000	40,000	40,000	40,000	40,000	40,000	40,000	40,000	40,000
JKK	32,000	32,000	32,000	32,000	32,000	32,000	32,000	32,000	32,000
TLM	28,800	28,800	28,800	28,800	28,800	28,800	28,800	28,800	28,800
Associates									
WBB	28,800	28,800	28,800	28,800	28,800	28,800	28,800	28,800	28,800
DLS	24,000	24,000	24,000	24,000	24,000	24,000	24,000	24,000	24,000
JMG	24,000	24,000	24,000	24,000	24,000	24,000	24,000	24,000	24,000
DGA	22,400	22,400	22,400	22,400	22,400	22,400	22,400	22,400	22,400
Paralegals									
James	12,800	12,800	12,800	12,800	12,800	12,800	12,800	12,800	12,800
Susan	12,800	12,800	12,800	12,800	12,800	12,800	12,800	12,800	12,800
TOTAL INCOME	$225,600	$225,600	$225,600	$225,600	$225,600	$225,600	$225,600	$225,600	$225,600
TOTAL EXPENSES	$63,950	$63,950	$63,950	$63,950	$63,950	$63,950	$63,950	$63,950	$63,950
NET INCOME	$161,650	$161,650	$161,650	$161,650	$161,650	$161,650	$161,650	$161,650	$161,650
PARTNER DRAWS									
MDL	40,000	40,000	40,000	40,000	40,000	40,000	40,000	40,000	40,000
JKK	40,000	40,000	40,000	40,000	40,000	40,000	40,000	40,000	40,000
TLM	40,000	40,000	40,000	40,000	40,000	40,000	40,000	40,000	40,000
TOTAL DRAWS	$120,000	$120,000	$120,000	$120,000	$120,000	$120,000	$120,000	$120,000	$120,000
RETAINED EARN.	$41,650	$41,650	$41,650	$41,650	$41,650	$41,650	$41,650	$41,650	$41,650

INCOME FORECAST - 1/1/96 through 9/30/96									
ITEM	JAN	FEB	MAR	APR	MAY	JUN	JUL	AUG	SEP
INCOME									
Partners									
MDL	40,000	40,000	40,000	40,000	40,000	40,000	40,000	40,000	40,000
JKK	32,000	32,000	32,000	32,000	32,000	32,000	32,000	32,000	32,000
TLM	28,800	28,800	28,800	28,800	28,800	28,800	28,800	28,800	28,800
Associates									
WBB	28,800	28,800	28,800	28,800	28,800	28,800	28,800	28,800	28,800
DLS	24,000	24,000	24,000	24,000	24,000	24,000	24,000	24,000	24,000
JMG	24,000	24,000	24,000	24,000	24,000	24,000	24,000	24,000	24,000
DGA	22,400	22,400	22,400	22,400	22,400	22,400	22,400	22,400	22,400
New Associate	0	0	0	0	0	19,200	19,200	19,200	19,200
Paralegals									
James	12,800	12,800	12,800	12,800	12,800	12,800	12,800	12,800	12,800
Susan	12,800	12,800	12,800	12,800	12,800	12,800	12,800	12,800	12,800
New Paralegal	0	0	0	0	0	12,800	12,800	12,800	12,800
TOTAL INCOME	$225,600	$225,600	$225,600	$225,600	$225,600	$257,600	$257,600	$257,600	$257,600
TOTAL EXPENSES	$63,950	$63,950	$63,950	$63,950	$63,950	$73,450	$73,450	$73,450	$73,450
NET INCOME	$161,650	$161,650	$161,650	$161,650	$161,650	$184,150	$184,150	$184,150	$184,150
PARTNER DRAWS									
MDL	40,000	40,000	40,000	40,000	40,000	47,500	47,500	47,500	47,500
JKK	40,000	40,000	40,000	40,000	40,000	47,500	47,500	47,500	47,500
TLM	40,000	40,000	40,000	40,000	40,000	47,500	47,500	47,500	47,500
TOTAL DRAWS	$120,000	$120,000	$120,000	$120,000	$120,000	$142,500	$142,500	$142,500	$142,500
RETAINED EARN.	$41,650	$41,650	$41,650	$41,650	$41,650	$41,650	$41,650	$41,650	$41,650

FIGURE 8.8 An income forecast for a law firm, figuring in additional employees.

E. THE "WHAT IF" SCENARIO AND PARTICULAR AREAS OF THE LAW

In addition to in-house analyses, the "what if" scenario can be a valuable tool in certain areas of law, particularly estate and tax planning and family law.

1. Estate Planning

Estate planners can use a spreadsheet to observe what effect the death of a family's primary wage earner will have on the income and expenses of the family. Figures 8.9 and 8.10 show the family's income and expenses before and after the death of the primary wage earner. Perhaps a larger life insurance policy is needed to compensate for the projected loss in income. This scenario is laid out in Figure 8.11.

FIGURE 8.9 A family's income and expenses.

INCOME AND EXPENSES - THE SMITH FAMILY

ITEM	JAN	FEB	MAR	APR	MAY	JUN	JUL	AUG	SEP
INCOME									
Mr. Smith	3,300	3,300	3,300	3,300	3,300	3,300	3,300	3,300	3,300
Mrs. Smith	2,500	2,500	2,500	2,500	2,500	2,500	2,500	2,500	2,500
Stock Dividends						185			
Savings Interest	10	10	10	10	10	10	10	10	10
State Tax Refund				250					
Fed. Tax Refund				500					
TOTAL INCOME	5,810	5,810	5,810	6,560	5,810	5,995	5,810	5,810	5,810
EXPENSES									
Cable	21	21	21	21	21	21	21	21	21
Car Payments	700	700	700	700	700	700	700	700	700
Car Registration						275		150	
Car Repairs						500			
Child Care	240	240	240	240	240	240	240	240	240
City Fees	33	33	33	33	33	33	33	33	33
Clothing	200	200	200	200	200	200	200	200	200
Club Dues	360	360	360	360	360	360	360	360	360
Entertainment	400	400	400	400	400	400	400	400	400
Food	400	400	400	400	400	400	400	400	400
Gardener	38	38	38	38	38	38	38	38	38
Gasoline	175	175	175	175	175	175	175	175	175
Homeowners	35	35	35	35	35	35	35	35	35
Insurance			433			264			433
Medical	100	100	100	100	100	100	100	100	100
Mortgage	1,124	1,124	1,124	1,124	1,124	1,124	1,124	1,124	1,124
Newspaper	12		12		12		12		12
Property Taxes			795						
Telephone	35	35	35	35	35	35	35	35	35
Utilities	45	45	45	45	45	45	45	45	45
Other	100	100	100	100	100	100	100	100	100
TOTAL EXPENSES	4,018	4,006	5,246	4,006	4,018	5,045	4,018	4,156	4,451
NET INCOME	1,792	1,804	564	2,554	1,792	950	1,792	1,654	1,359

FIGURE 8.10 The effect of the husband's death on the family's income and expenses.

INCOME AND EXPENSES - THE SMITH FAMILY

ITEM	JAN	FEB	MAR	APR	MAY	JUN	JUL	AUG	SEP
INCOME									
Mr. Smith	3,300	0	0	0	0	0	0	0	0
Mrs. Smith	2,500	2,500	2,500	2,500	2,500	2,500	2,500	2,500	2,500
Stock Dividends						185			
Savings Interest	10	10	10	10	10	10	10	10	10
State Tax Refund				250					
Fed. Tax Refund				500					
Insurance Income		333	333	333	333	333	333	333	333
Social Security		300	300	300	300	300	300	300	300
TOTAL INCOME	5,810	3,143	3,143	3,893	3,143	3,328	3,143	3,143	3,143
EXPENSES									
Cable	21	21	21	21	21	21	21	21	21
Car Payments	700	700	700	700	700	700	700	700	700
Car Registration						275		150	
Car Repairs						500			
Child Care	240	240	240	240	240	240	240	240	240
City Fees	33	33	33	33	33	33	33	33	33
Clothing	200	200	200	200	200	200	200	200	200
Club Dues	360	360	360	360	360	360	360	360	360
Entertainment	400	200	200	200	200	200	200	200	200
Food	400	275	275	275	275	275	275	275	275
Gardener	38	38	38	38	38	38	38	38	38
Gasoline	175	75	75	75	75	75	75	75	75
Homeowners	35	35	35	35	35	35	35	35	35
Insurance			433			264			433
Medical	100	100	100	100	100	100	100	100	100
Mortgage	1,124	1,124	1,124	1,124	1,124	1,124	1,124	1,124	1,124
Newspaper	12		12		12		12		12
Property Taxes			795						
Telephone	35	35	35	35	35	35	35	35	35
Utilities	45	45	45	45	45	45	45	45	45
Other	100	100	100	100	100	100	100	100	100
TOTAL EXPENSES	4,018	3,581	4,821	3,581	3,593	4,620	3,593	3,731	4,026
NET INCOME	1,792	(438)	(1,678)	312	(450)	(1,292)	(450)	(588)	(883)

INCOME AND EXPENSES - THE SMITH FAMILY

ITEM	JAN	FEB	MAR	APR	MAY	JUN	JUL	AUG	SEP
INCOME									
Mr. Smith	3,300	0	0	0	0	0	0	0	0
Mrs. Smith	2,500	2,500	2,500	2,500	2,500	2,500	2,500	2,500	2,500
Stock Dividends						185			
Savings Interest	10	10	10	10	10	10	10	10	10
State Tax Refund				250					
Fed. Tax Refund				500					
Insurance Income		1,665	1,665	1,665	1,665	1,665	1,665	1,665	1,665
Social Security		300	300	300	300	300	300	300	300
TOTAL INCOME	5,810	4,475	4,475	5,225	4,475	4,660	4,475	4,475	4,475
EXPENSES									
Cable	21	21	21	21	21	21	21	21	21
Car Payments	700	700	700	700	700	700	700	700	700
Car Registration						275		150	
Car Repairs						500			
Child Care	240	240	240	240	240	240	240	240	240
City Fees	33	33	33	33	33	33	33	33	33
Clothing	200	200	200	200	200	200	200	200	200
Club Dues	360	360	360	360	360	360	360	360	360
Entertainment	400	200	200	200	200	200	200	200	200
Food	400	275	275	275	275	275	275	275	275
Gardener	38	38	38	38	38	38	38	38	38
Gasoline	175	75	75	75	75	75	75	75	75
Homeowners	35	35	35	35	35	35	35	35	35
Insurance			433			600			433
Medical	100	100	100	100	100	100	100	100	100
Mortgage	1,124	1,124	1,124	1,124	1,124	1,124	1,124	1,124	1,124
Newspaper	12		12		12		12		12
Property Taxes			795						
Telephone	35	35	35	35	35	35	35	35	35
Utilities	45	45	45	45	45	45	45	45	45
Other	100	100	100	100	100	100	100	100	100
TOTAL EXPENSES	4,018	3,581	4,821	3,581	3,593	4,956	3,593	3,731	4,026
NET INCOME	1,792	894	(346)	1,644	882	(296)	882	744	449

FIGURE 8.11 Increasing the husband's insurance coverage will enable the family to maintain its income.

2. Tax Planning

Tax planners can create a spreadsheet showing a family's income, deductions, and the computed taxes based on this information. The tax planner can then add a deduction and observe the effect on the family's tax liability. See Figures 8.12 and 8.13.

3. Family Law

Family law practitioners use electronic spreadsheets to assist with, among other things, the division of assets in a marital dissolution action, as is shown in Figure 8.14. Columns are created for the asset names and for the value of assets assigned to the husband and to the wife. The distribution of assets may then be altered to observe the effect on the total value attributed to each person, as is shown in Figure 8.15.

TAX COMPUTATION (Fed.) - THE JONES FAMILY

DESCRIPTION	AMOUNT
INCOME	
Wages, Salaries, Tips, Etc.	38,116
Taxable Interest Income	642
Dividend Income	151
Tax Refunds	523
Other Gains (Losses)	500
TOTAL INCOME	39,932
Adjustments	0
ADJUSTED GROSS INCOME	39,932
DEDUCTIONS	
State and Local Taxes	980
Other Taxes	135
Total Paid Taxes	1,115
Personal Interest	38
Total Paid Interest	38
Total Misc. Contributions	450
TOTAL ITEMIZED DEDUCTIONS	1,603
EXEMPTIONS	6,000
TAXABLE INCOME	32,329
TAXES OWED BEFORE CREDITS	4,849

FIGURE 8.12 A family's tax spreadsheet.

TAX COMPUTATION (Fed.) - THE JONES FAMILY

DESCRIPTION	AMOUNT
INCOME	
Wages, Salaries, Tips, Etc.	38,116
Taxable Interest Income	642
Dividend Income	151
Tax Refunds	523
Other Gains (Losses)	500
TOTAL INCOME	39,932
Adjustments	0
ADJUSTED GROSS INCOME	39,932
DEDUCTIONS	
State and Local Taxes	980
*Real Estate Taxes	1,444
Other Taxes	135
Total Paid Taxes	2,559
*Mortgage Interest	9,831
Personal Interest	38
Total Paid Interest	9,869
Total Misc. Contributions	450
TOTAL ITEMIZED DEDUCTIONS	12,878
EXEMPTIONS	6,000
TAXABLE INCOME	21,054
TAXES OWED BEFORE CREDITS	3,158

FIGURE 8.13 The effect of buying a home on the family's tax liability.

DISSOLUTION OF SIMPSON

ITEM	PETER	SUSAN	NOTES
Residence		$125,000	$325,000 value less mortgage
Cabin	$142,000		$300,000 value less morgage
Investments:			
Savings	$18,500	$18,500	Total value $37,000
Stock	$6,000	$6,000	Total value $12,000
Personal Property:			
Peter's Car	$12,200		Blue Book value
Susan's Car		$10,300	Blue Book value
Recreation Equipment	$1,250	$1,250	Total value $2,500
Computer Equipment	$2,700		
Household Furnishings:			
Television		$300	
VCR		$250	
Stereo	$750		
Living Room		$2,400	
Dining Room		$3,500	
Bedrooms		$2,600	
Family Room		$900	
Cabin Furniture	$4,200		
Refrigerator		$500	
Microwave		$100	
TOTALS	$187,600	$171,600	

FIGURE 8.14 A spreadsheet to assist in the division of marital assets.

F. SUMMARY

Electronic spreadsheets are made up of columns and rows. The intersection of a column and row forms a cell. In the cell may be placed text, a number, a formula, or a function. An electronic spreadsheet is faster than using a paper spreadsheet because the user is able to change a value in the spreadsheet and immediately view the change in the totals.

DISSOLUTION OF SIMPSON

ITEM	PETER	SUSAN	NOTES
Residence		$125,000	$325,000 value less mortgage
Cabin	$142,000		$300,000 value less morgage
Investments:			
Savings	$10,500	$26,500	Total value $37,000
Stock	$6,000	$6,000	Total value $12,000
Personal Property:			
Peter's Car	$12,200		Blue Book value
Susan's Car		$10,300	Blue Book value
Recreation Equipment	$1,250	$1,250	Total value $2,500
Computer Equipment	$2,700		
Household Furnishings:			
Television		$300	
VCR		$250	
Stereo	$750		
Living Room		$2,400	
Dining Room		$3,500	
Bedrooms		$2,600	
Family Room		$900	
Cabin Furniture	$4,200		
Refrigerator		$500	
Microwave		$100	
TOTALS	$179,600	$179,600	

FIGURE 8.15 The allocation of the money from the savings account is changed to create an equal division of assets.

Legal professionals use electronic spreadsheets to perform "what if" scenarios. A "what if" scenario is the creation of a spreadsheet and then the alteration of items within the spreadsheet to analyze the results. Estate and tax planners use "what if" scenarios to analyze possible future events. Family law attorneys use "what if" scenarios to analyze asset divisions in marital dissolution actions.

Electronic spreadsheet programs are all very similar. Learning a single program, such as Lotus 1-2-3, will make it easy for you to learn just about every other spreadsheet program.

KEY TERMS

cell, 155
cell address, 155
cell entry, 156
cell pointer, 155
column, 154
electronic spreadsheet, 153
formula, 157
function, 157
input line, 157
range, 156
row, 154
text, 156
values, 156
"what if" scenario, 161

QUESTIONS

1. What is a cell?
2. What is a cell address?
3. List the two types of cell entries and give examples of them.
4. What *formula* could you enter in cell C9, below, that would add cells C5 through C7?

	A	B	C	D
1		JANUARY INCOME		
2				
3	BILLER	RATE	HOURS	TOTAL
4				
5	EDL	200	158	31,600
6	SRT	180	220	39,600
7	RGM	155	210	32,550
8				
9	TOTALS			

5. Identify the range of cells highlighted below.

	A	B	C	D
1		JANUARY INCOME		
2				
3	BILLER	RATE	HOURS	TOTAL
4				
5	EDL	**200**	**158**	**31,600**
6	SRT	**180**	**220**	**39,600**
7	RGM	**155**	**210**	**32,550**
8				
9	TOTALS			

6. Using the example in Question 4 above, what @SUM function [@SUM(cell address .. cell address)] could you place in cell D9 that would total cells D5 through D7?

DISCUSSION QUESTIONS

1. Discuss other areas of legal practice that can benefit from the use of an electronic spreadsheet.
2. The similarity between electronic spreadsheet programs has given rise to several lawsuits. Read and discuss Lotus Development Corporation v. Paperback Software International, 740 F. Supp. 37 (D. Mass. 1990). For another decision pertaining to this issue, see Lotus Development Corporation v. Borland International, Inc., 788 F. Supp. 78 (D. Mass. 1992).

EXERCISE

Joe and Mary have filed for divorce. They both have established careers. They do not have children. They have agreed that there will not be spousal support for either party. They have also agreed that the parties shall retain their own clothing, jewelry, company retirement benefits, life insurance policies, and books.

You have been asked to prepare a proposal for the division of the remainder of the parties' assets. The residence is to be sold and the proceeds divided. This division is not required to be equal.

Assuming that this is a community property state, use the List of Assets given for Joe and Mary to prepare a worksheet to assist you in distributing the community assets to the parties. All assets on the List of Assets are community property. Any asset may be sold with the proceeds split evenly or unevenly between the parties.

Turn in a printed copy of your worksheet.

Joe and Mary's List of Assets

Residence valued at $250,000 with an outstanding mortgage of $120,000 that will be repaid to the bank upon the sale of the property.

Boat valued at $4,500. Joe uses the boat, Mary despises it.

Time-share in Lake Tahoe valued at $30,000.

Furniture and furnishings:

Dining room set: $5,000
China cabinet: $1,500
Living room furniture: $5,500
Piano: $1,000
Lamps (5): $40 each
Family room furniture: $650
Entertainment unit: $150
Panasonic television: $50
Mitsubishi television: $350
Mitsubishi VCR: $250

Philco VCR: $100
Artwork: $600
Microwave: $255
Refrigerator: $650
Master bedroom furniture: $1,100
Guest bedroom furniture: $600
Plants: $150
Stereo with CD player: $700
CDs: $125
Sewing machine: $200

Computer equipment:

Computer (IBM compatible 486 with color monitor, mouse, and modem): $2,500
Computer software: $1,500

Sporting goods:

Joe's mountain bike: $500
Mary's mountain bike: $500
Joe's racing bike: $300
Rowing machine: $900
Stationary bicycle: $500
Weight set: $250

Automobiles:

Joe's truck: $4,500
Mary's car: $10,000

Other assets:

Checking account: $3,400
Savings account: $800
Money market: $18,000
Stock fund: $6,000

INSTRUCTIONS

Columns

Please create your worksheet with the following 4 columns:

ITEM JOE MARY NOTES

The name of each asset will go in the Item column. A value for that asset will go in Joe or Mary's column, or both if divided. The Notes column will be for any notation you want to insert.

Increasing the Width of a Column

To enter the asset Items and the Notes, you will need to make their respective columns wider. Follow the instructions for your specific spreadsheet software to widen these columns.

Underlines

Under the headings, and above the Totals row of your spreadsheet, put lines across all four columns. Some electronic spreadsheets have a character that will repeat an entry throughout a cell. If your spreadsheet does, please use this character instead of typing multiple underline characters. With Windows-based electronic spreadsheets you can create lines on the border of a cell with a menu option or by clicking your right mouse button in the cell or highlighted range of cells.

The Totals

Enter the Totals functions under the last item in the spreadsheet. Use a Sum function.

Your Name

To ensure you are given the proper credit, place your name in the row just below the bottom of your spreadsheet in column A.

Save the File

Save your spreadsheet to a disk. Remember to specify the disk drive letter before you type the file name. Do not use an extension on your file name. Most spreadsheet software packages will add a special extension to identify the spreadsheet.

Printing Your Spreadsheet

Print your spreadsheet by highlighting the entire spreadsheet (make sure you include your name) and selecting the print option, or by specifying the range after selecting the print option.

CHAPTER

9

Databases

A **database** is an organized collection of related information. Databases can be anything from a recipe file to a telephone book to a library. All of these databases contain related information: recipes, telephone numbers, and reference materials. They are organized respectively by the type of recipe; the name of an individual or business; and the title, author, or subject of a book or periodical.

As a legal professional you will use computerized databases containing reference materials to perform legal research. You will also use database software programs to create your own databases for client information, case information, document forms, conflict of interest checks, office and case calendars, and litigation support.

This chapter covers

- how legal professionals use databases
- summary and full-text databases
- searching within the summary database
- setting up a summary database
- using full-text databases for litigation support and legal research
- searching within the full-text database

A. DATABASES IN THE LAW OFFICE

There are two main uses for databases within a law office—the management of information and legal research. Database management systems (DBMSs) are software programs that manage information databases. The data within these databases is stored in computer files. Legal research databases are accessed with a modem or from CD-ROM disks. There are two types of computerized databases: summary and full-text. **Summary databases** contain selected bits of information about each document or item within the database. This type of database would be similar to a library card catalog, with the name of the material, its catalog number, author, subject, and location within the library. This type of database does not require a large amount of storage space, but it does require that a person review each item of information to enter it into the database.

Full-text databases contain the entire text or image of documents or pieces of information. An image is a picture of a document or photograph. To search within these databases, you can tell the computer to search for a particular document or to search for words that would be found in the document.

Legal professionals use summary and full-text databases to organize

1. *client information*—client names, addresses, and telephone numbers
2. *case information*—case name, client, responsible attorney, opposing party, and opposing counsel
3. *document forms*—document title, area of law, drafting attorney, date, file location, and other information regarding all documents created by the firm; this type of database assists you in locating a document to reference when you are drafting another document of the same type
4. *conflict of interest checks*—client names and opposing parties—for example, when a new client comes in with a case, the names of the opposing parties as well as the client's name can be searched for within the database to see if a conflict exists
5. *calendaring*—event, date, time, case, and attorney—for example, to keep track of an individual, or the firm's, calendar
6. *litigation support*—a summary or the full text of pleadings or evidence for a particular litigation

Legal professionals use legal research databases to find cases and statutes and to check citations. Case law and statutory authority to support or rebut an argument can be located by searching for words that are pertinent to the legal question involved. For example, cases to support an argument for punitive damages in a breach of contract action could be found by searching a database containing cases for the words *breach, contract,* and *punitive damages.* All cases within the database that contain these words would be retrieved.

B. SUMMARY DATABASES

Summary databases, also called "flat file," "relational," "bibliographic," "abstract," and "index" databases, store a summary of each document or item of information. Summary databases are made up of files, fields, and records.

A database **file** is the entire database. For example, the entire card catalog of a library is a file.

Database **fields** are the pieces of information that will be abstracted from each item to be entered into the database file. In a card catalog there are fields for the title of the book, its catalog number, its author, its subject, and miscellaneous other information.

A database **record** is the group of field entries for each item of the database. In a card catalog a record is each individual card with its fields of information about a single book.

Another example of a summary database is a telephone book. The database file is the telephone book itself. The fields within the telephone book are name, address, and telephone number. A record within the telephone book is the group of fields that corresponds to a single person or entity.

TELEPHONE BOOK DATABASE FILE

Name	Address	Number	
			← Fields
Smith, Mary	44 Singer Road	555-1212	
Smith, Melvin	12455 Main Street	555-8945	← Record
Smith, Nelson	82 Ridge Road	555-1546	
Smithe, Alison	123 Fairfield Place	555-7667	

1. Relational Operators

To conduct a search of a summary database, you choose one or more fields and search for information within them. **Relational operators** (also referred to as "comparative operators") allow you to identify the type of data you would like the database to search for within a field. For example, a Name field could be searched to find all records that equal "Smith, Mary." A Date field could be searched for all records with a date "less than or equal to 12/31/93." The relational operators used in most summary databases are:

Symbol	*Definition*
=	Equals
>	Greater than
<	Less than
>=	Greater than or equal to
<=	Less than or equal to
<>	Not equal to

The Name field search would use the equals (=) operator:

Name = Smith, Mary

The Date field search would use the less than or equal to (<=) operator:

Date <= 12/31/93

Relational operators are used throughout database software programs. The actual symbols that represent the operators may vary. Using the telephone book example, a search of the Name field could be conducted looking for the telephone number of John Smith. The search would look as follows:

NAME = Smith, John

The results of the search could be several listings, as shown below.

Name	Address	Number
Smith, John	77 Story Avenue, Orange	555-0904
Smith, John	12225 MacArthur Blvd., Irvine	555-9845
Smith, John	3342 Brook Place, Irvine	555-2546
Smith, John	354 Stonehenge Court, Irvine	555-3667

Although it would be very easy to determine the telephone number of our John Smith in a telephone book with only four John Smiths, in all likelihood a normal telephone book would contain many more. In such a case, connectors could be used to help narrow the search.

2. Connectors

Connectors are used to connect two or more relational operator search conditions. In a telephone book database with 100 John Smiths, we would need to add another condition to our search. To find John Smith who lives at 3342 Brook Place, Irvine, we would combine the initial search of the Name field with a search of the Address field. A connector would connect the two searches.

The three most common connectors are:

NOT
AND
OR

The telephone book database example, with its four records for Smith, John, will be used to illustrate the use of connectors.

a. NOT

The NOT connector excludes the conditions after the NOT from the results of the search conditions before the NOT. In this example, the search would look as follows:

Name = Smith, John NOT Address = 3342 Brook Place, Irvine

This search would find:

Name	Address	Number
Smith, John	77 Story Avenue, Orange	555-0904
Smith, John	12225 MacArthur Blvd., Irvine	555-9845
Smith, John	354 Stonehenge Court, Irvine	555-3667

The record that had 3342 Brook Place, Irvine, within the Address field was excluded from the search results.

b. AND

The AND connector takes the results of the condition before the AND and finds those records that also meet the conditions set forth after the AND. In this instance, the search would look as follows:

Name = Smith, John AND Address = 3342
Brook Place, Irvine

This search would find:

Name	Address	Number
Smith, John	3342 Brook Place, Irvine	555-2546

Only the record with Smith, John, in the Name field, and 3342 Brook Place, Irvine, in the Address field is included in the search result.

c. OR

The OR connector includes the results of the condition before the OR with the results of the condition after the OR. In this instance, the search would look as follows:

Name = Smith, John OR Address = 3342
Brook Place, Irvine

This search would find:

Name	Address	Number
Smith, John	77 Story Avenue, Orange	555-0904
Smith, John	12225 MacArthur Blvd., Irvine	555-9845
Smith, John	354 Stonehenge Court, Irvine	555-3667
Smith, John	3342 Brook Place, Irvine	555-2546
Smith, Mary	3342 Brook Place, Irvine	555-2546

The records in which Smith, John, is found in the Name field or records with 3342 Brook Place, Irvine, in the Address field comprise these search results.

3. Setting Up a Summary Database

Setting up a summary database involves looking at the data to be contained within the database and then deciding on the fields to be created.

One possible in-house use for a database is the maintaining of a record for each contract, pleading, or other substantive document created by the firm. Legal professionals use these old documents as forms for the creation of new documents. A database that contains information regarding these documents is called a Forms File database. The name of our database file will be FORMS.

To decide on the fields that will make up the database, imagine that we will be creating an index card for each document drafted by the firm. We need to decide what headings we would place on that index card. The following fields could be created for this database:

Fields: Document No.
Area of Law
Document Type
Document Name
Date
Drafting Atty
Case Name
File Number
WP Doc. Name
Summary

The contents of each of the fields will be explained below.

Document No.: Documents are often given numbers as they are created in law firms. We will assume that our firm numbers its documents.

Area of Law: This category lets us classify the documents by the area of law for which they are created. For our firm, the areas of law will be

Contracts
Corporations
Tax
Family Law
Personal Injury
Bankruptcy
Civil Litigation

Document Type: This category is a subcategory of each of the areas of law. For example, in the Contracts area of law, possible document types will be employment contract, real estate contract, and the like. In the Civil Litigation area of law, the possible document types will be complaint, demurrer, answer, interrogatories, appellate brief, and the like.

Document Name: The Document Name field will contain the actual name of the document as it is displayed within the text. For example, a contract may have the name Employment Contract of Thomas Jenkins. A pleading may have the name Complaint for Personal Injuries and Property Damage.

Date: The Date field will contain the date the document was filed, entered into, or signed.

Drafting Atty: This field lets you see who drafted the document (you can see if it was drafted by the senior partner or an associate), and will allow you to search for all documents drafted by a certain attorney or paralegal. Most legal professionals are referred to in the firm by their initials. Therefore, our entries will be in capitalized initials: e.g., RAF.

Case Name: This field will have the formal case name used by the accounting department. A sample case name is:

Minton Corp./Smith vs.

File Number: The File Number field will contain the number of the case file where the document is located. Many case files contain the client number, matter number, and file number separated by periods. For example:

8024.9.5

This file number would represent client number 8024, the ninth matter for which we have represented this client, and the fifth file created for the ninth matter.

WP Doc. Name: This field will contain the word processing document name for this document (for example, MINTON.ANS for Minton's Answer to the Smith Complaint). Not all of the documents we enter into our forms file database will have a word processing document name.

PRACTICE TIP

Not all documents that we enter into this database will have been created on the computer or even by our firm. It may be that the Smith complaint against our client, Minton Corp., is an excellent example of a complaint for wrongful termination. We will want to keep a record of this form in our database so we can use it to create future complaints of our own.

Summary: This field will contain a summary of the document. Summary or memo fields in databases often allow the entry of large amounts of text. In this field you would describe the document and its significance.

The records for this database will be the documents submitted into the forms file. Usually, when a document is finalized, the original is filed with the court or sent to another party. A copy of the document is then filed in the case file. The person in charge of the Forms File database either receives the document copy prior to its being placed in the file, or gets a separate copy from which to enter the information into the database.

We have received the following three documents to be entered into our database.

1. A corporate merger agreement, entitled "Merger of Keel Industries," for Keel Industries/Corporate dated January 15, 1996, document number 10023, drafted by James S. Douglas. The word processing name for this document is KEEL.MRG, and it is located in file 4405.3.2.
2. An answer to a complaint for personal injuries in the McNeil/Hoffman case, entitled "Answer to Complaint for Personal Injuries and Property Damage," dated January 25, 1996. It does not have a document number. This pleading is from the opposing party and is signed by Joan F. Perkins. There is no word processing name for this document because it was not drafted by our firm. The document is located in file 5478.1.1.
3. A marital settlement agreement in the Marston/Marital Dissolution matter, titled "Marston Marital Settlement Agreement," dated January 26, 1996. Document number 10045, drafted by Randolf Alton Fax. The word processing name for this document is MARSTON.MSA, and it is located in file 4536.5.2.

The records for these documents would appear as follows:

#1	Document No.	*10023*
	Area of Law	*Corporations*
	Document Type	*Merger Agreement*
	Document Name	*Merger of Keel Industries*
	Date	*01/15/96*
	Drafting Atty	*JSD*
	Case Name	*Keel Industries/Corporate*
	File Number	*4405.3.2*
	WP Doc. Name	*KEEL.MRG*
	Summary	*You would enter a summary here based on your review of the document—i.e., "Merger agreement between Keel and Rudder Corporation specifying that Keel Industries remain the name of the merged corporation and that Rudder Corporation shareholders receive a price of $4.50 per share."*
#2	Document No.	
	Area of Law	*Personal Injury*
	Document Type	*Answer*
	Document Name	*Answer to Complaint for Personal Injuries and Property Damage*
	Date	*01/25/96*
	Drafting Atty	*JFP*
	Case Name	*McNeil/Hoffman*
	File Number	*5478.1.1*
	WP Doc. Name	
	Summary	*General denial and boilerplate affirmative defenses. Creative affirmative defense for driving while intoxicated.*
#3	Document No.	*10045*
	Area of Law	*Family Law*
	Document Type	*Marital Settlement Agreement*
	Document Name	*Marston Marital Settlement Agreement*
	Date	*01/26/96*
	Drafting Atty	*RAF*
	Case Name	*Marston/Marital Dissolution*
	File Number	*4536.5.2*
	WP Doc. Name	*MARSTON.MSA*
	Summary	*Standard MSA providing for sale of home, equal division of assets, spousal support for wife, and joint custody of the minor children.*

4. Searching a Summary Database

To search our Forms File database, we will use relational operators along with connectors. Some sample searches are shown below.

Search 1. Randolf Alton Fax would like to see a list of all of the documents that he has created during his tenure with the firm. To accomplish this task, we will search the Drafting Atty field for Mr. Fax's documents as follows:

Drafting Atty = RAF

Search 2. You are drafting a demurrer to a complaint. The subject of the demurrer will be the complaint's failure to state whether the contract claimed to have been breached was written or oral. Specifically, you would like to see the points and authorities for this demurrer so that you will not have to reinvent the wheel. Your colleague, James S. Douglas, tells you that he drafted a demurrer on this subject back in 1995. A search for Mr. Douglas's demurrer could be constructed as follows:

Drafting Atty = JSD AND Document Type = Demurrer AND
(Date >= 01/01/95 AND Date < 01/01/96)

Note in the above example that you may use parentheses in your searches just as you would in mathematical operations.

Search 3. Someone in the firm is looking to carve off of a complaint for wrongful termination. She does not want one that was created before December 31, 1989, when the California Supreme Court changed the rules regarding the damages that could be claimed in such an action. This search could be constructed as follows:

Document Type = Complaint AND Date > 12/31/89

This search will yield a list of several complaints. Reviewing the Document Name fields of the records on the list will show which complaints involved wrongful termination. Many summary databases allow you to search for words contained within a field using a special relational operator. If the containing operator is $, our search could look as follows:

Document Type = Complaint AND Document Name $ wrongful
termination AND Date > 12/31/89

Search 4. You are looking for an employment contract and a stock buy-sell agreement to use to prepare documents for a new client who is buying into a corporation. You do not, however, want to use any contracts drafted by John W. Miser, who was recently fired by the firm for incompetence. The search could be constructed as follows:

(Document Type = Employment Contract OR Document Type = Buy-
Sell Agreement) NOT Drafting Atty = JWM

This search could also be written:

(Document Type = Employment Contract OR Document Type = Buy-Sell Agreement) AND Drafting Atty <> JWM

Search 5. You would like a list of every document that has been created by the firm in the Contracts and Corporations areas of law. This search would be constructed as follows:

Area of Law = Contracts OR Area of Law = Corporations

C. FULL-TEXT DATABASES

Full-text databases hold the full text or image of a document. A database containing the full text of a document holds each printed character found in the document but not necessarily in the same format (margins, spacing) as the original. A database containing the image of a document stores a picture of each document or photograph on an optical disk.

1. Full-Text Research Databases

Full-text research databases are available through the telephone lines and on CD-ROM disks. LEXIS and WESTLAW are the primary legal research databases. Other research databases provide a wide range of news and business reference materials. Some are available through LEXIS and WESTLAW. Others must be subscribed to separately.

a. Computer-Assisted Legal Research (LEXIS and WESTLAW)

Computer-assisted legal research (CALR) is the use of a computer to perform legal research. **LEXIS** and **WESTLAW,** the two largest CALR databases, contain the contents of the perfect law library and combine it with material found in nonlegal libraries. Each publication contained within LEXIS and WESTLAW is an individual database. These databases may be searched singly or in conjunction with other databases.

LEXIS and WESTLAW are searched by selecting the desired database and then selecting key words, which are the words you would expect to find in the materials for which you are searching.

LEXIS and WESTLAW also provide access to other independent databases such as DIALOG. DIALOG provides a large selection of business, medical, science, technology, and news databases. Databases like DIALOG can be beneficial when researching the nonlegal aspects of a case. For example, you may want to review the financial history of the company that is the opposing party in a litigation. You can do this type of research in DIALOG.

b. CD-ROM

CD-ROM disks are offered by a variety of legal publishers as an alternative, or in addition, to the bound volumes of their books. (To use a CD-ROM disk, your computer needs a CD disk drive.) Each 4¾-inch disk can hold hundreds of thousands of text pages—for example, an entire collection of state case reporters can be put on a few CD-ROM disks. Figure 9.1 shows West Publishing Company's California Reporter® on CD-ROM. The approximately 200 volumes of this reporter are stored on only three CD-ROM disks. A new set of current CDs is shipped periodically to the owners of law books on CD-ROM disks. The old CDs are sent back to the publisher. Between CD updates, the owner receives paper updates similar to those used with the bound volumes.

CD-ROM databases contain an index of the materials on the disks similar

FIGURE 9.1 West Publishing Company's California Reporter® on CD-ROM.

to the index in the bound volumes. The advantage the CD-ROM disks have over the bound volumes, besides storage space and portability, is that they can be searched with key words similar to the method used with LEXIS and WESTLAW. With some CD-ROM disks, references to other cases or code sections contained within a case or statute can be brought up on the screen by simply highlighting the reference and pressing a key.

2. Full-Text Litigation Support Databases

Full-text litigation support databases are primarily used to manage evidence. A scanner is used to enter each piece of evidence into the database. Scanning involves taking each page and passing it through the scanner, much like operating a copy machine. Court reporters supply magnetic diskettes containing the full text of depositions, hearings, and trial transcripts for entry into this type of database.

Databases that utilize **optical character recognition** scanning read the text of a document onto a magnetic disk or tape. The format of the document (margins, spacing, etc.) is not always the same as the original document. A large amount of storage space on a hard disk or magnetic tape is necessary to store the database.

Full-text **imaging** databases use a scanner to scan a document onto an optical disk. This is useful because what is placed on the disk is not simply the text of the document but an exact copy with handwriting and graphics. The document image may be printed to a laser printer when a copy is needed. This allows the paper evidence files to be put into storage until the originals are needed.

Full-text databases can be searched using key words, although some also allow you to set up summary database fields when you are entering the documents. Imaging databases cannot be searched full-text unless they have a feature that stores the actual text of the document on a separate disk. The reason is that an imaging database stores a picture of the document on the optical disk. It does not recognize the individual words of the document. Imaging databases that do not store a full-text version of the imaged document on another disk operate like a summary database, with the user entering information into fields as each document is scanned into the database.

3. Searching the Full-Text Database

Searches within a full-text database involve the use of

- key words
- connectors
- proximity operators
- root expanders and wild card characters

For full-text databases that also contain fields, you may use searches similar to those used with a summary database. For an example of how you would search within a full-text database, assume your firm represents the widow of a man who died as a result of injuries suffered in an automobile crash in California. The case is established as being under the jurisdiction of the California courts. The man did not die in the crash and incurred tens of thousands of dollars in medical bills prior to his death.

The widow would like to bring a lawsuit for wrongful death against the company that owns the 18-wheel truck that caused the accident. She would also like to recover the cost of the medical bills. The question lies in how to file a complaint that may claim the wrongful death damages and the personal injury damages. In California the damages that can be claimed by a surviving spouse in a wrongful death action are only those that accrued after the death. This would exclude the medical bills that occurred prior to the husband's death. The heirs under the deceased's estate, however, may recover the costs of the medical bills. The task at hand is to search for statutory authority to see if we can join the two actions.

The database we will select is California Statutes. To search the statutes, we will develop what is called a **query** from the legal question at issue.

Our question is: Can we join the widow's wrongful death action within an action by the heirs of the estate?

To formulate the query we must look at the question we wish to have answered and analyze its parts. Our query will search within the database of California statutes and show us each statute that contains the words or phrases that we include in the query. The words or phrases we include in the query are called key words.

a. Key Words

Key words are words that will likely be found in the materials for which you are searching. The key words for the question regarding joining the wrongful death action with another action could be:

join
joinder
heirs
party
parties
action
wrongful death

The key words will be connected within the query with connectors.

b. Connectors

Connectors are used to connect the key words in the search. The primary connectors are the same as with summary database searches: **NOT, AND,** and **OR.**

c. *Proximity Operators*

Proximity operators differ from database to database, but generally they tell the database to search for a key word within a certain proximity of another word. For instance, LEXIS will allow you to use an operator that will look for a certain word within so many words of another word:

"wrongful death" w/5 action

This search would find all materials where the phrase *wrongful death* is found within five words of the word *action.*

WESTLAW uses the w/n operator (where n = number of words) and operators that look for words in the same sentence or paragraph:

"wrongful death" /s action

This search would find all materials where the phrase *wrongful death* is found in the same sentence as the word *action.*

d. *Root Expanders and Wild Card Characters*

A **root expander** is used to find words with a common root. For example, *join* and *joinder* have the common root "join." *Party* and *parties* have the common root "part." The root expander cuts down on the number of search terms needed in the query. Using a root expander following the root will locate all words with that root, no matter the length of the word. The root expander used by LEXIS and WESTLAW is "!".

A **wild card character** is used to replace a *single character* anywhere in a word. For example, "dr*nk" will find *drink, drunk,* and *drank.* The wild card character "*" is used by both LEXIS and WESTLAW.

e. *The Search Query*

Using the elements discussed above, our query could look as follows:

("wrongful death" w/5 action) AND part! AND heir AND join!

Note that the singular version of a word will pick up most plurals. We will search for the phrase *wrongful death* within five words of *action* because we are searching for statutes regarding wrongful death actions. The root expander, !, will pick up *join* and *joinder, party* and *parties.*

The statute that answers our question was found by this query. The statute as displayed in LEXIS and WESTLAW is shown in Figures 9.2 and 9.3, respectively.

D. SUMMARY

A database is an organized collection of related information. The two main uses of databases in the law office are to manage information and perform legal research. There are two types of databases: summary and full-text.

Summary databases contain pieces of information about each document or item to be referenced by the database. Summary databases are made up of files, fields, and records. The database file is the entire database. The fields within the database are the pieces of information to be abstracted from the documents or items. The records are the group of fields that pertain to each individual document

FIGURE 9.2 The WESTLAW query results.

```
Citation              Rank(R)     Page(P)      Database   Mode
CA CIV PRO s 377      R 2 OF 8    P 1 OF 10    CA-ST      T
West's Ann.Cal.C.C.P. s 377

                  WEST'S ANNOTATED CALIFORNIA CODES
        CORP. (c) WEST 1991 No Claim to Orig. Govt. Works
                     CODE OF CIVIL PROCEDURE
                     PART 2. OF CIVIL ACTIONS
             TITLE 3. OF THE PARTIES TO CIVIL ACTIONS

s 377. Wrongful death; right of action; damages;
consolidation of actions

(a) When the death of a person is caused by the wrongful act or
neglect of another, his or her heirs or personal representatives
on their behalf may maintain an action for damages against the
person causing the death, or in case of the death of such
wrongdoer, against the personal representative of such wrongdoer,
whether the wrongdoer dies before or after the death of the person
injured. If any other person is responsible for any such wrongful
act or neglect, the action may also be maintained against such
other person, or in case of his or her death, his or her personal
representatives. In every action under this section, such damages
may be given as under all the circumstances of the case, may be
just, but shall not include damages recoverable under Section 573
of the Probate Code. The respective rights of the heirs in any
award shall be determined by the court. Any action brought by the
personal representatives of the decedent pursuant to the
provisions of Section 573 of the Probate Code may be joined with
an action arising out of the same wrongful act or neglect brought
pursuant to the provisions of this section. If an action be
brought pursuant to the provisions of this section and a separate
action arising out of the same wrongful act or neglect be brought
pursuant to the provisions of Section 573 of the Probate Code,
such actions shall be consolidated for trial on the motion of any
interested PARTY.
```

```
Cal Code Civ Proc @ 377 (1991) Deering's Cal Codes (c) 1991

TITLE 3.  Parties  to Civil Actions

                    Cal Code Civ Proc @ 377 (1991)

@ 377.  [Wrongful death]

(a) When the death of a person is caused by the wrongful act or
neglect of another, his or her heirs or personal representatives
on their behalf may maintain an action for damages against the
person causing the death, or in case of the death of such
wrongdoer, against the personal representative of such wrongdoer,
whether the wrongdoer dies before or after the death of the person
injured. If any other person is responsible for any such wrongful
act or neglect, the action may also be maintained against such
other person, or in case of his or her death, his or her personal
representatives. In every action under this section, such damages
may be given as under all the circumstances of the case, may be
just, but shall not include damages recoverable under Section 573
of the Probate Code. The respective rights of the heirs in any
award shall be determined by the court. Any action brought by the
personal representatives of the decedent pursuant to the
provisions of Section 573 of the Probate Code may be joined with
an action arising out of the same wrongful act or neglect brought
pursuant to the provisions of this section. If an action be
brought pursuant to the provisions of this section and a separate
action arising out of the same
```

FIGURE 9.3 The LEXIS® query results.

or item. Summary databases are searched by identifying the field to be searched and then specifying the information for which you are searching within the field.

Full-text databases contain the full text or image of a document. An image is a picture of the document. Full-text databases containing text are searched by looking for key words within the text of the database records. Image databases cannot be searched with full-text methods unless the text is stored on a separate disk. Full-text databases that contain fields can be searched using the search concepts of a summary database.

Databases are useful tools for the legal professional. Whether performing research or keeping a record of each piece of evidence in a case, you will find that databases save a great amount of time, which would otherwise be spent looking through books or case files.

KEY TERMS

CD-ROM, 186
computer-assisted legal research (CALR), 185
connectors (full-text databases), 188
connectors (summary databases), 178
database, 175
field, 176

file, 176
full-text database, 176
imaging, 187
key words, 188
LEXIS, 185
optical character recognition, 187
proximity operators, 189
query, 188
record, 177
relational operators, 177
root expanders, 189
summary database, 175
WESTLAW, 185
wild card character, 189

QUESTIONS

1. Explain what a database is, and give an example of one.
2. Explain the difference between summary and full-text databases.
3. What are the three components of a summary database?
4. What are the three most common connectors used in database searches?
5. Using key words, connectors, proximity operators, root expanders, and wild card characters (if warranted), draft a query for the following question:

Can a witness to an accident file an action for damages for emotional distress?

DISCUSSION QUESTIONS

1. Summary databases contain a summary of information about a document. Full-text databases contain the full text or image of a document. What are the advantages and disadvantages of the two types of databases in terms of hardware requirements and information availability?
2. Many publishers of state codes and case reporters are putting their volumes on CD-ROM disks. What do you think a law firm's library will consist of in five years? What about the local law library?

EXERCISE

Using a summary database software program, create a database to manage the evidence for our client Lisa Smith's personal injury action. Develop the fields for your database by reviewing the information contained in the documents listed below. Then, enter a record for each of the documents listed. Save the database file to a magnetic disk and print a list of the records.

Documents

1. A police report from the Philadelphia Police Department, dated May 12, 1996, regarding the accident between the car driven by our client, Lisa Smith, and the Wilson Catering van driven by Mike Lancaster. This document is located in file number 7110.1.5.
2. A written statement from Lisa Smith, dated May 15, 1996, regarding the accident. This document is located in file number 7110.1.5.
3. An ambulance bill for $150 to Lisa Smith from Faster Ambulance Company, dated May 12, 1996, for transporting Lisa Smith to the hospital. This document is located in file number 7110.1.6.
4. A medical bill to Lisa Smith from Valley Hospital for $355, dated May 13, 1996, for Lisa Smith's emergency room treatment on May 12, 1996. This document is located in file number 7110.1.6.
5. A letter to our firm, Johnson and Kline, from Wealthy Insurance Company, dated July 2, 1996, offering to settle the matter for $3,500. This document is located in file number 7110.1.2.
6. The statement of witness, Alan Simpson, dated June 15, 1996, stating that the Wilson Catering van was being driven erratically prior to the accident. This document is located in file number 7110.1.5.

CHAPTER

10

Office Automation

This chapter addresses the purchase and organization of a computer or computer system. A computer purchase is not as simple as going into a store and buying the latest and greatest computer, printer, and software. Purchasing a computer requires an understanding of what you need from the computer and an understanding of the computers available to meet those needs. For inexperienced computer users or firms, this may necessitate the hiring of a computer consultant to assist in the purchase decision.

The organization of a computer or computer system involves formulating a system of directories or folders on the main storage disk, developing uniform file names, and setting up a system of archiving and backing up files. A poorly organized computer is like a messy desk—it becomes very hard to find things. A well-organized computer is like a well maintained office—desks are clear, documents are in the proper files, and old files are put into storage or discarded.

This chapter covers:

- purchasing a computer system
- disk organization
- naming files
- backing up the computer system
- archiving files
- developing contingency plans
- choosing a password

A. THE COMPUTER PURCHASE

A legal professional or firm should not rush into the purchase of a computer. This is a decision that requires the consideration of current needs and the evaluation of plans for future growth.

The decision to purchase a computer involves the following six steps:

- assessing the individual's or the firm's needs
- weighing the costs
- projecting future growth
- shopping for the computer system
- making the purchase
- signing the contract

1. Assessing the Individual's or the Firm's Needs

It is very important to begin any computer purchase by considering what the individual's or the firm's needs are that led to the decision to purchase a computer.

What do we need to automate?

Most legal professionals begin with a need to automate their accounting systems and word processing. Are there litigation support software packages that the firm wants to use? Will the firm be using CD-ROM disks? If so, will a single CD-ROM drive be sufficient, or does the firm need a drive that holds multiple CDs?

Do we need to share information?

Do the people in the firm need to share a common bank of information, or will exchanging files on diskettes be sufficient? A need to share information may necessitate the purchase of a local area network (LAN), a minicomputer, or a mainframe. Does our firm need a wide area network (WAN) to connect offices in different cities?

How many people in the firm will be using the computers?

The size of the firm will help to determine whether individual microcomputers, a local area network, a minicomputer, or a mainframe should be purchased.

Small Firms: A firm with a secretary, a paralegal, and two attorneys may do fine with four individual microcomputers. When files need to be exchanged, they can do so with diskettes.

Small to Medium Firms: If the firm later grows to four secretaries, two paralegals, and five attorneys, exchanging diskettes becomes more cumbersome. This firm may wish to consider cabling microcomputers together in a network. The network will allow everyone in the firm to share information and peripheral devices.

Medium Firms: In a firm of ten or more attorneys, a paralegal staff, and secretarial and accounting support, a microcomputer network with a microcomputer or minicomputer file server is warranted.

Medium to Large and Large Firms: Big law firms will want to consider one or more local area networks in the office. Many large firms have existing mainframe computer systems. These computers traditionally use terminals cabled to a main computer. You can, however, configure them with microcomputer workstations, attach microcomputer networks to the computer system, and use the telephone lines to form wide area networks with other offices.

2. Weighing the Costs

The next step is to accurately determine the current costs of the tasks that the legal professional wants to automate. These costs should then be compared to the cost of the equipment and training needed to automate those same functions.

What is the current cost to perform a given function?

For example, maybe the accounting department currently requires one person to collect and post the time of the firm's legal professionals to the proper clients. Another person is required to prepare the billing statements and accounts receivable and other accounting reports. A hypothetical cost of these two employees is shown below:

Employees (2)	Salary		$45,000/yr.
	Insurance		2,400/yr.
	Other		1,000/yr.
Office space, furniture, materials, etc.			2,400/yr.
		TOTAL	$50,800/yr.

What is the cost to automate the same function?

Assuming that automating the accounting function will reduce the number of necessary employees to one, the costs of automation are shown below:

Employee (1)	Salary	$22,500/yr.
	Insurance	1,200/yr.
	Other	500/yr.

Office space, furniture, materials, etc.		1,200/yr.
Computer		1,500
Accounting software		500
Printer (laser)		1,000
Training (included)		0
Maintenance contract		600/yr.
	TOTAL	$29,000/yr.

This is only the cost for the first year, however. The next year's cost will be:

Employee (1)	Salary		$22,500/yr.
	Insurance		1,200/yr.
	Other		500/yr.
Office space, furniture, materials, etc.			1,200/yr.
Computer			0
Accounting software			0
Printer (laser)			0
Training (included)			0
Maintenance contract			600/yr.
		TOTAL	$26,000/yr.

Comparing the costs of personnel and materials necessary to manually perform these tasks with the costs to automate the same functions will help the legal professional decide which tasks should be automated.

Nearly every task performed in the law office can be automated in one way or another. Computers are commonly used to automate:

- time and billing
- document creation (word processing)
- accounting reports (sometimes included in time and billing software packages)
- case information
- document control
- calendars
- spreadsheet creation
- demonstrative evidence creation
- legal research
- evidence management
- conflict of interest checks
- form preparation

3. Projecting Future Growth

After determining which tasks are profitable to automate, the firm needs to consider its future and determine what its needs will be in the next two to five years.

What will our needs be in the next two to five years?
A firm with plans for six computers in its offices should not purchase a microcomputer network with software permitting up to eight workstations if its plans for growth show that in the next year or two the firm will grow to ten computers. If this is the case, the firm should consider a microcomputer network with software that permits at least 15 to 25 workstations.

4. Shopping for the Computer System

If the prospective computer purchaser has reviewed needs, compared costs, and considered future growth, the actual purchase becomes a well-informed decision.

What are other firms like ours using?
Before deciding on specific manufacturers of hardware and software, ask other firms in the area what they are using.
Can we see a demonstration of the product?
Insist on demonstrations from the vendors of the equipment and software. Make sure that you have the person who will be using the hardware or software attend the demonstration. The bookkeeper, for example, will be the best person in the firm to evaluate the advantages and disadvantages of time and billing software packages.

NOTE

It is very important when you are selecting a new software package for your office that you research it thoroughly. These programs can be very expensive, so it pays to ask the vendor a lot of questions. Make sure that the program will do what you want it to do without the vendor having to make major adjustments to the software, and make sure that the software has been around for a while and is not new and full of "bugs." The seller will usually provide you with names of other law firms currently using the software so you can call them and gauge their satisfaction with the product.

What type of microcomputers do we need for the LAN?
If the decision has been made to purchase microcomputers and networking software, the purchaser needs to decide on the

type of microcomputer to buy and from whom to buy it. It pays to check computer magazines to determine which microprocessor is currently being used in new computers, how much RAM these new computers have, and which manufacturers are rated the highest. Microcomputers have about a five-year life before they become outdated and need to be replaced in order to run new software. The computer running the network should be equipped with the newest technology. By considering the newest technology in terms of the microprocessor, amount of RAM, and the hard disk capacity, the purchaser will maximize the life of the computer system. The individual workstations of the network do not need to be as sophisticated because they depend on the computer running the network for network processing and file storage.

5. Making the Purchase

When a decision has been made as to the hardware and software that will be purchased, it is time to consider the provisions of the purchase contract.

How much?

There is a very large markup on hardware and software. The price is usually negotiable.

How much are the installation charges?

Installation charges will vary depending on the type of computers you purchase. With a network, you will need to run cable throughout the office to connect each computer, so the installation cost will be higher.

Is training offered?

Training for the computers and software is usually available through the retailer. Check to see if there is a charge for training.

Is there a service contract?

With a service contract, the purchaser pays a fee to have service available for the computers and other hardware. Check to see who supplies the service and whether there is a charge for service calls and/or replacement parts. Also, see if a loaner computer or printer is available while your system is being repaired.

Is there a telephone number I can call for support?

Many software and hardware manufacturers provide a support line, which you can call with questions regarding your equipment. Check to see if the manufacturer you are purchasing from has such a number and whether there is a charge for the support service.

What warranties apply to the hardware and software?

For each of the items being purchased, find out what the warranty period is, what is covered by the warranty, and who supplies the warranty service.

6. Signing the Contract

Before signing the contract, consider and agree on each of the items enumerated above. Check the contract to make sure that the exact name of each piece of hardware and software and all guarantees and warranties made by the vendor are included in the contract.

An informed and well-researched decision results in a computer system that fulfills the needs of the computer's users.

B. COMPUTER ORGANIZATION

When the purchase is complete and the computer system is in your office, you must organize the way you will store files on the computer, how you will name the files, how you will back up the files to prevent losing them, and how you will remove old files from the computer. You will also need to develop an emergency plan for generating documents if the computer breaks down ("crashes"). Finally, in the event that your computer system requires passwords, there are certain rules that should be followed when creating the passwords.

1. Disk Organization

In most cases, the computer you will be using will have a hard disk for the storage of files. If you were to save all of the computer's files in the root of the hard disk, the disk would become cluttered and disorganized. The best way to prevent this clutter is to create directories. Directories are represented by folders in Windows and Windows 95.

The first directories or folders that should be created are for the operating system files and the application program files that will be installed on the hard disk.

DOS. For a DOS system, the directory structure could look like the one pictured below. The hard drive has been labeled D:. The directories are made using the MD command.

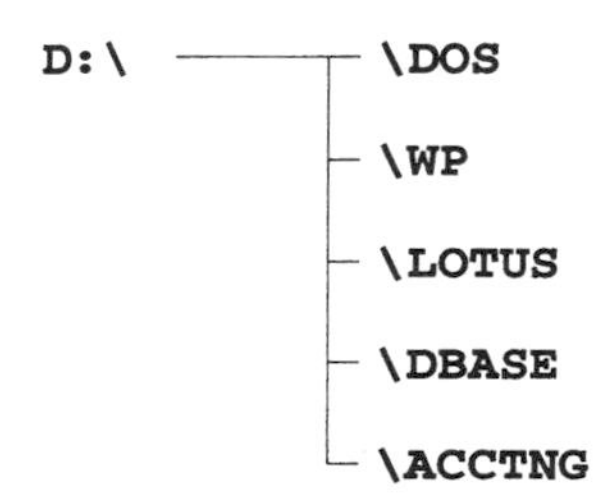

Windows. The DOS directory structure, in the form of folder icons, is shown in Figure 10.1. To create the directories, the File Manager window is accessed. The Create Directory option is then selected in the File menu.

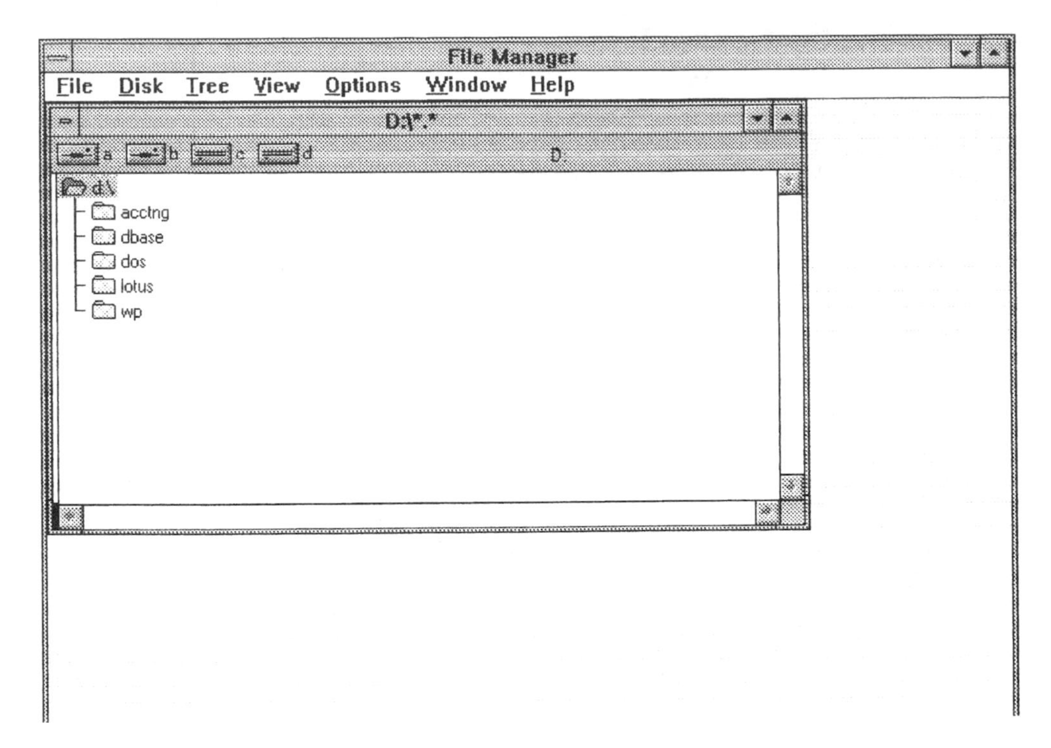

FIGURE 10.1 The Windows directory folder icons.

Windows 95. To create the directory folders, open the Windows Explorer from the Programs option of the Start menu. Click on the icon for the correct drive, open the File menu, point to New, and click on Folder. When the new folder icon appears, give it a name and press the [Enter] key.

The next step in organizing the disk is to decide how the client directories will be set up. Firms that want to organize their disk by client and matter will use the clients' names in the first level of directories off of the root. Subdirectories off of the client name directories will be created for each matter opened for that client. In our example the firm has different departments that practice different areas of law. The first level of directories off of the root will be directories for each department. Subdirectories of the department directories will be created for each client handled by the department.

DOS. The firm in our example handles primarily personal injury actions (PI), marital dissolutions (DISSO), and criminal matters (CRIMINAL). In the event that a bankruptcy case comes in or some other case comes in that does not fit into these three categories, a new directory will need to be created for miscellaneous cases or for that category of cases.

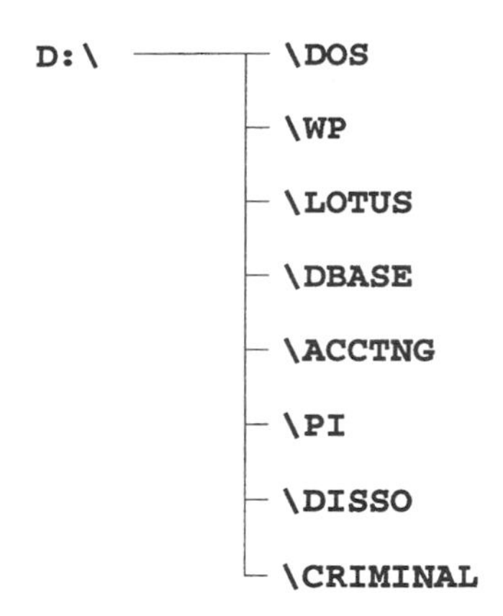

Windows. The Create Directory option in the File menu can be used to create the directories PI, DISSO, and CRIMINAL, as shown in Figure 10.2.

Windows 95. In the Windows Explorer, the PI, DISSO, and CRIMINAL directory folders would be created in the same manner as that used for the program directories.

The third set of directories or folders that should be created are the second-level directories for the individual cases within the areas of law. For example,

FIGURE 10.2 New directories added to Windows.

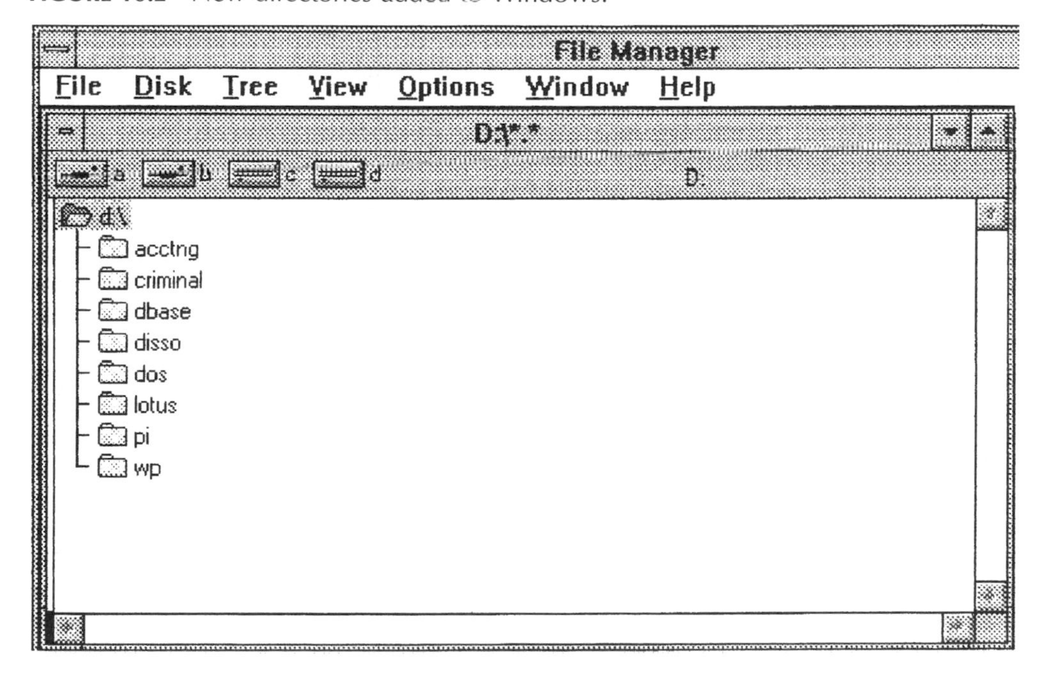

assume five new cases have come into the firm. There are two personal injury cases, one marital dissolution, and two criminal matters. The case titles are as follows:

Personal Injury Cases
Smith v. Singer (the firm represents Singer)
Newberry v. Hampton (the firm represents Newberry)

Marital Dissolution
Weskovic v. Weskovic

Criminal Matters
Mason DUI
Harrington Assault and Battery

The directories and folders for these cases are shown below and in Figure 10.3.

DOS. New directories for clients are added as subdirectories of the area of law directories using the MD command.

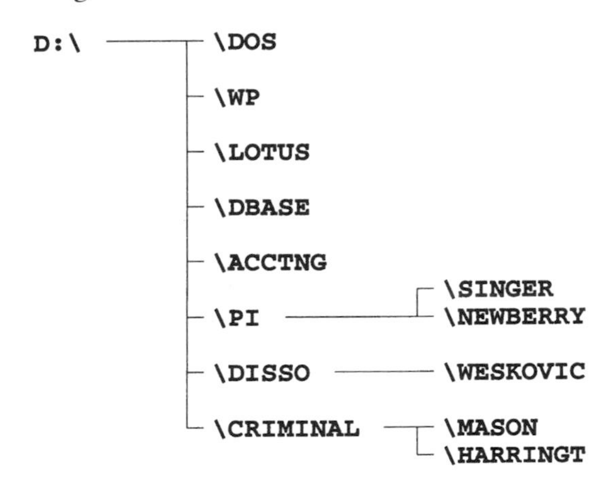

Windows. Figure 10.3 shows the folders as they would appear in Windows.

Windows 95. To create the client folders, you would click on the department folder in the Windows Explorer and create a new folder using File, New, Folder.

This disk organization scheme makes it very simple for anyone in the office to locate a file. It is important that everyone store his files in the proper directories in order to make this organization efficient. Many times new users will save their files to the root directory or within the directory (or folder) of the applications file that they are using. A short explanation to each person in the office regarding

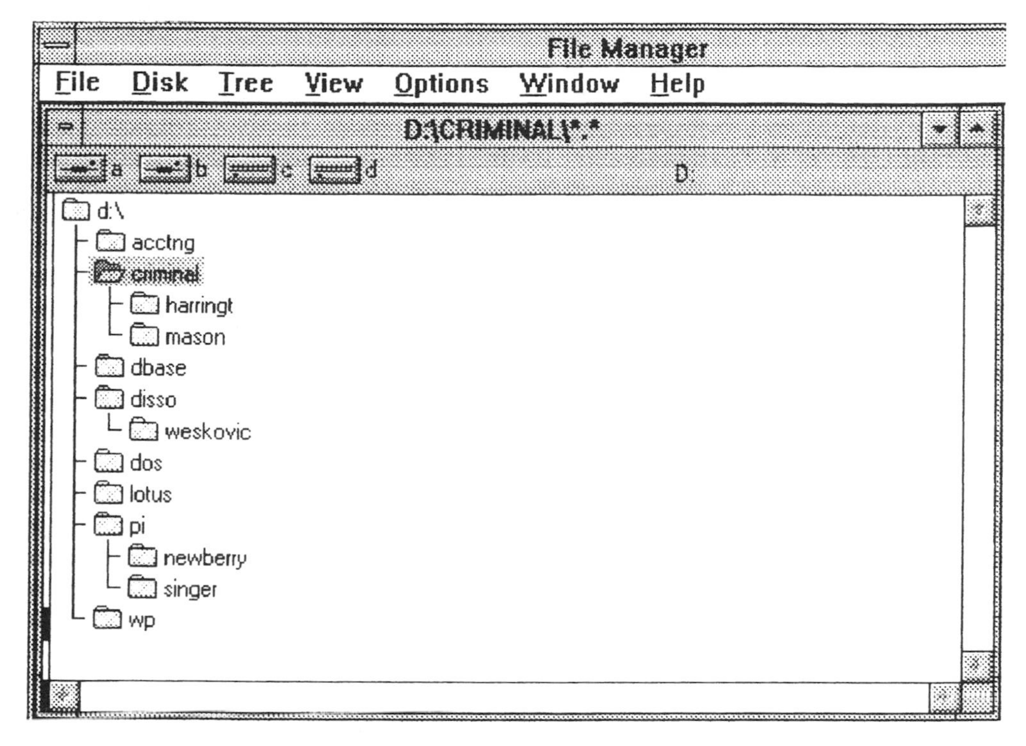

FIGURE 10.3 Windows directory icons.

how the disk organization works and how to save files will help to remedy this problem.

2. Naming Files

File names on a computer system should follow a set of guidelines.

DOS and Windows. The best file name format, from the standpoint of a computer systems manager, is to set up a uniform set of file name extensions. Remember that file names saved from any program on a computer using DOS must be eight characters or less, followed by an optional period and a one- to three-character extension. Samples of commonly used file extensions are shown below. The extensions .EXE and .COM should not be used when naming files. These are the extensions used by DOS-based software for executable and command program files.

ANS	Answer
ART	Articles of Incorporation
BRF	Brief

BYL	Corporate Bylaws
CON	Contract
CPL	Complaint
DEM	Demurrer
DEP	Deposition
JI	Jury Instructions
LTR	Letter
MEM	Memorandum
MIN	Corporate Minutes
MJP	Motion for Judgment on the Pleadings
MOT	Miscellaneous Motions
MSA	Marital Settlement Agreement
MSJ	Motion for Summary Judgment
PNA	Points and Authorities
RFA	Requests for Admissions
ROG	Interrogatories
RPD	Requests for Production of Documents
STR	Motion to Strike
SUM	Deposition Summary
WIL	Will
WRT	Writ

The first eight characters of the file name should relate to the case name in some way. For example, in the Smith v. Singer case, the answer filed by our firm could be named Singer.ans. This document would be stored in the \SINGER subdirectory of the \PI directory along with all the other files created in this case.

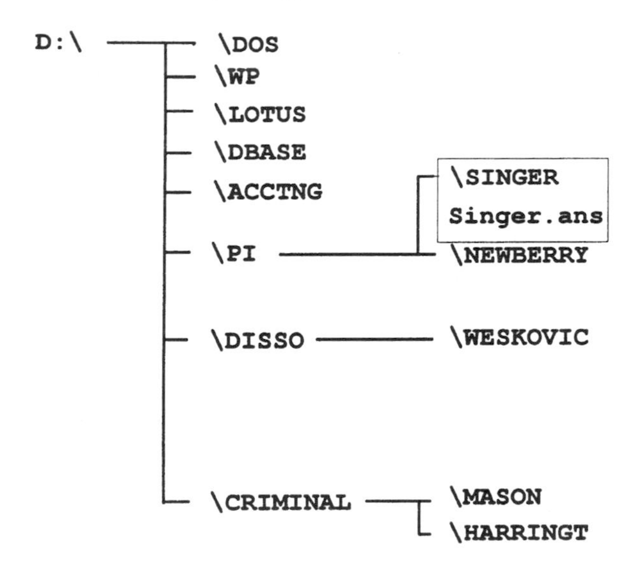

Windows. The Windows file icons are shown in Figure 10.4.

Windows 95. Windows 95 is not as restrictive on file names as DOS and Windows. The file names in Windows 95 can contain 255 characters, including

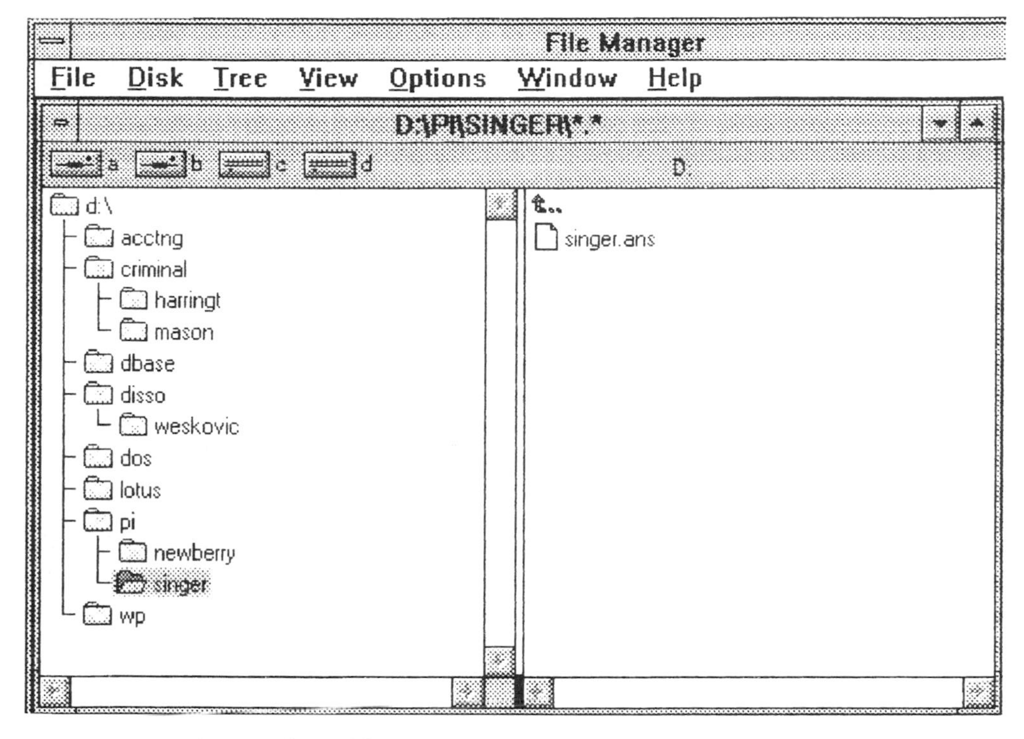

FIGURE 10.4 The Windows file icons.

spaces. This allows you to be very descriptive when naming your files. For example, the file that we named Singer.ans in DOS and Windows could be named "Singer Answer to Complaint" in Windows 95.

A well-organized disk and good file naming parameters make it almost impossible to lose a file on the system.

3. System Backup

System backup is the copying of some or all of the files on the computer's hard disk onto diskettes or magnetic tape. Then, in the event that the hard disk is erased or somehow damaged, the files may be copied back onto the old, or a new, hard disk.

For a small computer, diskette backup may be all that is needed to keep copies of the files. For computers with large hard disks, however, backup to magnetic tape is more efficient. The average diskette will hold only one to two megabytes of data. A magnetic tape can hold from under ten megabytes to several gigabytes of data. Magnetic tape requires a special tape drive that normally fits into the space in the system unit for a diskette drive.

A firm should back up its computer system at least once a day. There are software programs available that will handle the backup for you. You may even set the program to back up the computer at a certain time each day.

Some files, like the WordPerfect program files, do not need to be backed up every day because they are rarely changed. Backup programs with full and incremental backup formats can be used to save time and space. A full backup copies every file on the hard disk; an incremental backup copies only those files that have been changed since the previous backup was performed. With this type of system, you can perform a full backup weekly and an incremental backup daily.

4. Archiving

Archiving is the process of removing files from the hard disk and storing them on tape or diskette, or in some instances just deleting them from the hard disk. Archiving is necessary because as more and more files are added to a hard disk the computer slows down. When the hard disk gets to 70 percent or 80 percent full, it is time to archive some files off of the system.

The files that should be archived are those files that are no longer being used by anyone in the firm. Cases that have been settled or concluded, or that the firm no longer handles, should be archived off the system.

Using the Singer case as an example, let's say that the case has been settled, and the settlement agreement has been signed. There will probably not be any more documents created for this case. It is a good practice to wait 30 days before archiving documents off of the system to ensure that everyone is finished with the documents related to the case. If you are archiving to diskette, a separate disk should be labeled for this client. All files from the case directory should then be copied onto the diskette and erased from the hard disk. If you are archiving to magnetic tape, an archive tape should be set up and the entire case directory copied to it. The files should then be erased from the hard disk and the directory or folder removed.

5. The Contingency Plan

A **contingency plan** should be developed to continue the firm's work in the event of a computer or printer failure. Computers have an incredible knack for failing on the day that you have a pleading that must be typed and filed by 5 P.M. A good contingency plan will enable you to continue working with a minimum of downtime.

For each piece of hardware in the computer system (computers, printers, etc.) the manufacturer, model number, identification number, service provider, warranty agreement, and service agreement should be kept in the computer contingency file. Also, keep the telephone number of a local computer rental company in the file. For each piece of computer software, you should also have on file a telephone number where you can receive answers to questions about the software.

Additionally, spare parts should be available for the printers. Extra toner, ribbons, ink cartridges, printer drums, developers, paper, and parallel and serial printer cables should all be kept in a location known to everyone in the firm. An extra printer is also good to have around in the event of a failure. If you do have an extra printer, include in the contingency file an explanation of where and how to connect it to the computer system and what changes will need to be made to the software to work with the new printer. A sample contingency plan is shown in Figure 10.5.

6. Passwords

Computers are often set up with **passwords** to prevent unauthorized users from getting into the computer files. There are some rules, however, that should be followed when creating passwords:

1. Avoid names, initials, birth dates, favorite animals, hobbies, and the like. These are the first passwords attempted by someone trying to break into your system.
2. Make the password at least five characters in length.
3. Use letters *and* numbers in the password.

Some sample passwords are shown below.

J824LK
MPKD431
P3W6D3T5

C. SUMMARY

A computer purchase is not a simple task. There are a number of factors to consider before the purchase. The firm's or individual's needs, costs, and future growth should all be considered prior to the purchase. Before signing the contract, all items and their respective warranties should be discussed and agreed upon. Each item should be listed in the contract.

After the computer system is in the office, the information stored on the computer requires some method of organization. Creating directories or folders on the computer's hard disk will organize the files. All files created on the system should be named so that they are easily identified. The files should be routinely backed up onto a diskette or magnetic tape, and old files should be archived off the system when they are no longer being used. Finally, a contingency plan should be developed so that the firm can continue to generate documents in the event of a system failure.

O'KEEFE AND O'NEAL

COMPUTER CONTINGENCY PLAN

System Hardware

Pentium 120 MHZ, 20 gigabyte hard drive, 32 MB RAM, 3 ½ inch diskette drive. Identification number 643576.

486 30 MHZ, 80 megabyte hard drive, 8 MB RAM, 3 ½ inch diskette drive, tape drive. Identification number 78235.

2 Monitors. Identification numbers 37544 and 65754

Laser printer. Identification number 9809-01

Service and Rentals

Service: Pinkman's Computers, 555-1212
Rental: Computer Rental Company, 555-2234

Spare Printer and Parts

Inkjet printer. Identification number 8764-22

Printer spare parts are located on the third shelf in the file room. Extra parts may be obtained from John's Printer Repairs, 555-4565.

The inkjet printer is located in the northwest corner of the file room. A parallel printer cable is attached to the printer and may be connected to the parallel printer port currently housing the laser printer cable. When printing in WordPerfect, the printer selection will need to be changed from the laser to the inkjet. This can be done in the print dialog box. Spare ink cartridges for this printer are on the third shelf in the file room.

FIGURE 10.5 A sample contingency plan.

KEY TERMS

archiving, 208
contingency plan, 208
passwords, 209
system backup, 207

QUESTIONS

1. What are the three elements to consider prior to shopping for a computer system?
2. What should you make sure is included in the computer purchase contract?
3. How could you organize DOS directories for the following categories of files? Draw a directory tree.

    WordPerfect files
    DOS files
    Lotus files
    Johnson v. Miller case files (we represent Johnson)
    Johnson, corporate matters files
    Hamilton v. Smith case files (we represent Hamilton)

4. Create file names for the following files using DOS parameters:

    a demand letter in the Johnson v. Miller case
    a complaint in the Johnson v. Miller case
    a motion for summary judgment in the Johnson v. Miller case
    a trial brief in the Hamilton v. Smith case

5. Create a sample password that you could use on a computer system.

DISCUSSION QUESTIONS

1. Does your school or office have a contingency plan in the event of a failure of the computer system?
2. How often does your school or office back up the computer system? Do they use tape, diskettes, or, possibly, removable disks? Where are the backups stored? (If the office burns down, the backups are not effective if they were also stored in the office.)

CHAPTER

11

On-Line Services and the Internet

Traditionally, legal professionals have used LEXIS and WESTLAW to obtain legal information on line. With the growing popularity of commercial on-line services and the Internet, many legal professionals are turning to these services to obtain legal and nonlegal information, post and read messages on message boards, send and receive electronic mail, and participate in on-line chats. The information available through on-line services and the Internet grows daily. To assist you in finding your way around on-line, this chapter will cover

- on-line etiquette
- bulletin board systems
- commercial on-line services
- the Internet
- UNIX
- mailing lists
- Usenet
- Telnet
- FTP
- Gopher and WAIS
- the World Wide Web

A. ON-LINE ETIQUETTE

Before you go on-line, you need to understand some of the rules of etiquette (often referred to as "netiquette") involved. When you violate the rules of etiquette, other users will not hesitate to let you know. Gross violations can result in action by the on-line service to suspend, restrict, or cancel your account. An understanding of these rules will prevent this embarrassment.

1. Message Boards and Newsgroups

Message boards and newsgroups are where you post and read messages on specific topics. The rules of etiquette apply mainly to the posting of messages. Typing in all capital letters is referred to as **shouting.** If you do intend to shout, you can type a sentence or phrase in all capitals to get your point across. However, typing the entire message in all capitals will result in replies telling you to stop shouting. **Flaming** is the posting of a message that is violently argumentative or a personal attack on someone. It is fine to post a message that disagrees with another's point of view but stick to the issues and avoid attacks on the individual. **Spamming** is the posting of a message that does not relate to the topic of the message board or newsgroup—for example, posting a message regarding paralegal certification exams on a message board devoted to intellectual property law. **Cross-posting** is the posting of the same message to several message boards or newsgroups. It is frowned on because the multiple messages take up space and are a nuisance to readers who find the same message under several different topics.

In addition to the above-mentioned errors in manners, avoid posting personal messages to another user on a message board or newsgroup. Other people reading the message will not be interested, and it may result in your being flamed. Also, do not post an e-mail message you have received on a message board or newsgroup unless you have the permission of the person who sent you the e-mail.

2. E-Mail

When sending e-mail to another person, you want to avoid shouting and flaming. You also want to avoid sending, or responding to, chain letters. A chain letter is an e-mail that is forwarded to you by another person with the request that you forward it on to others. You will recognize an e-mail chain letter by the listings at the bottom of the message of the addresses of each person who has been sent the e-mail. This creates a message that takes up a lot of space and is therefore discouraged by on-line services. If you are receiving unwanted e-mail or chain letters, you can report them to the postmaster of your on-line service.

3. FTP Sites

FTP (File Transfer Protocol) sites are computers that you can contact to download files. These sites are usually busy networks that are conducting normal business activities during business hours. When people contact the FTP site during business hours, it slows down their computer system. Therefore, it is proper netiquette to avoid contacting FTP sites from 6:00 A.M. to 6:00 P.M., when their computers are busy.

4. Chats

A **chat** is an on-line multi-user discussion of a general or specific topic. Messages are sent into the chat room for all to see. Do not shout, unless shouting is warranted, or send flaming messages into the chat. Also, in chats on a specific topic, do not send messages that do not relate to the topic of the discussion. You will be asked to leave.

5. Tone of Message

When you are typing a message, you must think about how you are wording it in order to avoid misunderstandings. The written word does not necessarily reflect a sarcastic tone or humor, so what you say may be taken literally unless you add the inflection with a word enclosed in < > symbols or with a graphic created using keyboard characters. An example would be a humorous sentence followed by the indication <grin>. Popular keyboard graphics inserted at the end of sentences are shown below:

:) :-) :(:-(;-) |:(:~) :-O :-{

B. BULLETIN BOARD SYSTEMS

A **bulletin board system** (BBS) is a message board computer system that is accessed through a modem and allows users to post and retrieve messages or programs. A BBS can be a single microcomputer with a modem and software that allows the computer to be used as a message and program posting board. Other BBSs are networked together to share information with other BBS systems on the network. Among the BBS networks are FIDOnet, WWIVnet, and Usenet. Some BBSs have only one phone line, so only one person can access the BBS at a time. Others have multiple phone lines and can allow the users to chat with one another. Many hardware and software manufacturers have BBSs that a user can call to post a question, read answers to frequently asked questions (FAQs), and download new hardware drivers, macros, or software patches. The BBS is run by the System Operator, who is referred to as the SYSOP. The SYSOP monitors the messages and programs that are uploaded onto the BBS and determines who may access the BBS and how much time they are allowed on the system.

1. Accessing a BBS

To access a BBS, you need a communications software package that will allow you to connect to remote computers through your modem. Some BBSs have software that you load onto your computer to access them, but most do not. When you enter the communications software package, you will need to set up the profile for accessing a specific BBS. The information necessary for the profile is as follows:

- **The telephone number of the BBS.** The telephone call to the BBS is billed to you. Most people who use BBSs try to find those within their area code to avoid the long-distance charges.
- **The type of terminal that you should have your computer emulate.** The newest communications programs have an auto-detect mode that will detect the terminal emulation necessary and adjust the computer accordingly. With other software packages, you will need to select a terminal emulation such as ANSI, Minitel, TTY, VT100, or VT52. If you do not know what type of terminal emulation to select, try ANSI or VT100. If one does not work when you dial in to the BBS, try another.
- **The baud rate used by the BBS.** The baud rate is measured in bits per second (bps). Some modems will automatically adjust to the baud rate accepted by the BBS, but usually you will have to determine the rate from literature about the BBS or by trial and error. Most BBSs support 2400 baud. Faster baud rates are 4800, 9600, 14400, 28800, 38400, 57600, and 115200.
- **Your data bits, parity, and stop bits.** This setting sets the size of your data bits, sets the parity error checking mechanism to odd, even, or none (O, E, or N), and sets the number of stop bits that will be sent at the end of a data cluster and before text. The most common setting is eight data bits, no parity, and one stop bit. You will see this abbreviated as "8,N,1."

Once you have set up the profile of the BBS, you are ready to select the option to dial the telephone number. When the computer dials in to the BBS, you will hear the sounds of your modem trying to connect with the other modem. If it does connect, you will get a message that a connection has occurred, and text will begin to appear on your screen. If text does not appear, try pressing the [Enter] or the [Esc] key a couple of times. Most BBSs operate in a text mode. You will not see graphics unless your communication package and the BBS have graphical user interfaces. The welcome screen of the Law MUG BBS is shown in Figure 11.1.

When the connection has been established, you will be prompted to enter your user name or select a new-user option. If you are a new user, you will be asked to register with a user name, password, and responses to some questions. If you have visited before, type your user name and you will be prompted for your password. After you have signed on, you will be notified about any new information on the bulletin board and given a menu of options such as reading bulletins or posted mail, sending mail, uploading files and downloading files. Some BBSs charge

```
* Network Address 1:115/661.0 Using FrontDoor Version 2.00

╔══════════════════════════════════════════════════════════════╗
║                  WELCOME TO THE LAW MUG RBBS                 ║
║                      Chicago, Illinois                       ║
╠══════════════════════════════════════════════════════════════╣
║            Dedicated to the Legal Profession and             ║
║              Electronic Information Transfer                 ║
║                                                              ║
║                 On-Line Since Sept. of 1983                  ║
║                 Member of the SDS and SDN                    ║
║                                                              ║
║                     FIDO : 1:115/661                         ║
║   Reshet 36:711/200 KesherNet 18:711/200 LawNet 7:70/6       ║
║                                                              ║
║             Mail Processing : 04:00AM-5:00AM                 ║
║                 Using a USR HST 9600 Baud                    ║
╚══════════════════════════════════════════════════════════════╝

Loading BBS.......
```

FIGURE 11.1 The welcome screen of the Law MUG bulletin board system.

a fee to people who want to access certain parts of the BBS. If there is a fee involved, you will be notified on the screen. Usually you will be given a limited amount of time for each session on the BBS, and your time remaining will be displayed. Your call will automatically be disconnected when the time runs out.

2. Downloading Files

Offering files available for downloading is one of the primary features of a BBS. Menus of the categories of files available will be displayed for your selection. After you have selected a category, the files will be listed on the screen. In some BBSs you can select the files that you want to download with a keystroke; in others you have to make note of the name of the file for when you are ready to download.

When you begin the download process, you will be prompted with or for the file name(s) that you wish to download. You will also be prompted for a download protocol. Common protocols are Xmodem, Ymodem, Ymodem-G, Zmodem, and Kermit. Ymodem-G and Zmodem seem to send files the fastest. After the selections have been made, you will be prompted to begin the download. Once you begin the download, you will need to select the download or receive file option from your communication package. You will be prompted for the download protocol and the directory in which to place the file(s). When the download is complete, you will be returned to the BBS screen.

3. Leaving the BBS

To leave the BBS, select the quit or goodbye option from one of the BBS menus. If the BBS is not responding or you cannot find the quit or goodbye option, select the hang up or disconnect option on your communication package.

4. Law-Related BBSs

There are several law-related BBSs located within the United States. To find them, you have to locate a list of BBSs or read about one in a periodical and note its telephone number. A popular law-related BBS is the Law MUG BBS, which contains messages and information about legal topics and software and has files available for downloading. The telephone number for the Law MUG BBS is (312) 661-1740. Use 9600 baud or less and 8 bits, no parity, and one stop bit.

C. COMMERCIAL ON-LINE SERVICES

Commercial on-line services are information services that provide their users with e-mail capabilities, access to business services, information sources and exchanges, and gateways to access some or all of the Internet. The most popular commercial on-line services are America Online, CompuServe, and the Microsoft Network. Without even traveling through their gateways to Internet information, these services offer a great deal of information to the legal professional. Information on law-related topics can be found in legal forums that are accessed using the key word "legal" or by selecting "Go legal."

In the legal forums you will find reference materials, files available for downloading, message boards, chats, and information from software companies regarding their legal software packages. The reference materials available on each service vary. Many contain U.S. Supreme Court opinions and some federal and state codes. Within the files available for downloading are legal software demonstration packages, legal word processing macros, legal newsletters, and the texts of interesting cases. On the message boards, which are similar to bulletin board systems, you can read messages posted by others and reply or post new messages. Chats are live discussions where you can send instant messages to the others in the chat room. Often the legal forum will have a scheduled chat time and room for paralegals.

1. Accessing the Commercial On-Line Service

To access a commercial on-line service, you must have a modem and the communications software package supplied by the service. To register for the service, the software package dials into the service and goes through a setup process where you choose, or are given, a user name and password, asked for your address and telephone number, and asked for a credit card number. The service will then select, or allow you to select, a local telephone number to use to access the service. You should select the one with the highest baud rate supported by your modem. Normally, these services offer the first month or ten hours free. You will be charged at the beginning of the second month or at the end of your free hours. Each month, the fee for the service will be charged to your credit card.

After you have gone through the initial installation, you can sign on to the service by double clicking on its icon or by selecting the option from a menu. To sign off, open the File menu and select Exit. The main screen of America Online is shown in Figure 11.2.

2. Sending E-Mail

Through commercial on-line services you can send e-mail to anyone at another Internet site. All you need to know is their user name and the address of their site, called the domain name. Most e-mail is addressed in the following form:

username@site.address

FIGURE 11.2 The America Online main screen.

America Online's Internet domain name (site address) is *aol.com*. CompuServe's site address is *compuserve.com*. The Microsoft Network's site address is *msn.com*. To send e-mail to a person with the user name *onelegal* at America Online or the Microsoft Network, the address would be:

onelegal@aol.com

or

onelegal@msn.com

User names on CompuServe are primarily made up of numbers. An example would be 104150,1660. When you address e-mail to someone at CompuServe, you will need to replace the comma in their user name with a period. To send e-mail to this person, the address would be

104150.1660@compuserve.com

To save time and connect charges, you can compose your mail off-line before you enter the service. Then, when you sign on to the service, you select the send mail option.

On most services, you have the ability to attach software files to your e-mail message. To do this, you select the attach file option at the e-mail screen and give the location of the file on your computer and the file name. When the person receives the e-mail message, they also receive the file. If it is a text file, it may be displayed as another e-mail message. If it is not, the file can be downloaded to the user's own computer and viewed in the appropriate application.

3. Downloading Files

Downloading files involves selecting the file to be downloaded, clicking on the download option, and indicating the directory to place it in on your computer. You will find many areas within the on-line service that contain software files for downloading. When you look at the list of available files, you can select a file and see a description of its contents and the amount of time that it will take to download. Many large files are in a *.zip*—that is, compressed—format. The on-line service may unzip (uncompress) them when you sign off, but you usually need an unzipping program like *pkunzip*. To get the *pkunzip* file, you will need to locate it on your on-line service and download it. Then, when you download zipped files, you can unzip them at the DOS prompt by typing *pkunzip filename*. Make sure that you have placed the zipped file in a new directory, because when you unzip it you may find that it contains many files. You may also want to use a virus scanner to determine whether the files contain any known computer viruses.

4. Internet Gateways

Commercial on-line services have Internet gateways to allow you to access many parts of the Internet, including the World Wide Web, Usenet newsgroups, FTP sites, Gopher and WAIS sites, and Telnet sites. The most popular part of the Internet is the World Wide Web. Most commercial on-line services provide a graphical Web browser to view the graphics of the various Web pages. They also will have a search engine, or will connect you to a search engine, that will enable you to search through the World Wide Web for sites that are of interest to you. All of these Internet terms are explained in the Internet portion of this chapter.

5. Posting and Reading Messages on Message Boards

Message boards regarding a wide range of topics are available on the commercial on-line services. As noted earlier, legal message boards can often be found by selecting the key word "legal" or selecting "Go legal." When you enter a message board, you will see a number of topics related to the general category you have selected. When you locate a topic you are interested in, such as Employment Opportunities for Paralegals, you can choose to read through all of the messages or only the new messages that you have not yet read. To add a new message, select the new message option, enter a short title in the subject line such as "Paralegal salaries in Texas," and then type your message. When you are reading through the messages, if you see one you would like to respond to, select a respond option and type in a message. The subject line will indicate that you are responding to the subject of the message you have read. For example, if you are reading a message with the subject line "Is it necessary to take a certification exam?" your responding message will have the subject line "Re: Is it necessary to take a certification exam?" When you post a message, should you prefer a personal reply instead of a responsive message on the board, ask to have any responses sent to your e-mail address and give the address.

6. Chats

On commercial on-line services, there are chat rooms or conference rooms that are always open, and chats that are scheduled on different subjects such as various areas of legal practice, paralegals, law students, and lawyers. When you enter a chat room, you can see a list of who is there, and the other participants can see that you are there. You can just sit and listen or you can participate in the discussion by typing a message in the message box and sending it in. When you are finished listening or participating, simply exit the room.

D. THE INTERNET

The **Internet** is the largest computer network in the world. Actually, it is a network of networks. It began as a research project by the Defense Department to utilize packet-switching to get information from one computer to another in the event that part of the network was destroyed by a nuclear weapon. As the project developed, NASA and the NSF (National Science Foundation) added their packet-switching networks to the Internet to exchange research information. Funding from the federal government also encouraged universities to add their computers to the Internet. Today, there are millions of host computers on the Internet, each of which has an address that you can access to find the information that they are distributing. These host computers consist of universities, government agencies, businesses, and organizations that connect their networks to the Internet to provide reference materials, information, products and services, and communications with other Internet users.

1. Accessing the Internet

To access the Internet, you need a modem and an account with an Internet provider. If your school or law firm is an Internet site, you can usually obtain an Internet account at no cost. If you cannot obtain a free account, you will need to subscribe to a commercial on-line service or a commercial Internet access provider. Commercial Internet access providers such as Netcom or Delphi provide direct access to the Internet. Of the hundreds of Internet access providers in the United States, some operate nationwide while others are local. They offer a number of fee packages for the use of their services.

The software required to access the Internet varies. With commercial on-line services you only need their communication software for most Internet access. For more extensive access into areas like Telnet, you may need to download additional software. With direct Internet access providers, you may need to install TCP/IP and other software tools. TCP/IP (Transmission Control Protocol/Internet Protocol) is a communications protocol that allows all different types of computers, with their varying operating systems, to communicate and exchange files and data.

2. Internet Domains

Each network server connected to the Internet is a **domain.** Each domain has a name, often called a site address. For example, the domain name or site address for America Online is *aol.com*. The site address of the White House is *whitehouse.gov*. The suffix of the site address identifies the type of organization associated with the server. The most common suffixes are

.edu college or university
.com commercial site
.org nonprofit organization
.gov government agency
.mil military agency
.net large company or organization networks

3. UNIX

UNIX is an operating system used by many of the networks that are connected to the Internet. If your connection to the Internet does not provide you with a user interface, you will need to know the network's operating system commands in order to get around. UNIX is similar to DOS in that it uses directories and files. Directory names are separated with a forward slash, as opposed to the backslash used by DOS. Commands in UNIX are case-sensitive. Using the wrong case (lowercase or capital letters) will result in an error message. Some of the basic commands used in UNIX are explained below:

cd The change directory command. This command is used to move from one directory to another. The command is written:

cd [name of directory]

For example, to change to the "legal" directory you would type:

cd /legal

To move backwards up the directory tree you can use the command:

cd ..

Note: There must be a space after the cd.

ls List files. This command lists the files in the current directory. To have the listing pause at every 24 lines, use the command:

ls | more

The | character is found to the left of your backspace key. To see the size of each file and the date when it was created or last modified, use the command:

ls -l

cp Copy file. This command copies a file from one location to another. The form of the command is:

cp [file name] [new file name]

Be careful that the new file name is not an existing file or it will be overwritten.

cat Read a file. This command is similar to the DOS "type" command. To write the command so that it will pause at each screen, type:

cat [file name] | more

You could also write this command as:

more [file name]

Pressing [Ctrl] + C will stop the reading of the file.

mv Move or rename a file. To move a file to a new directory, the command form is:

mv [file name] [directory]

For example, to move a file named legal.lst to the Legal directory, the command would be:

mv legal.lst Legal

To rename a file, use the following command form:

mv [file name] [new file name]

rm Deletes a file. The command form is:

rm [file name]

man The help command. This command will provide help pertaining to a specific topic or command verb. The man command can be written in either of the following forms:

man [topic]

man [command verb]

pwd Displays the current directory name. Your prompt in UNIX does not always reveal where you are in the directory tree. This command will show you where you are.

On UNIX systems, you will also use UNIX commands to enter various areas on the Internet. These commands are discussed in the section regarding these areas.

PRACTICE TIP

If you find that your [Backspace] key is not working on a UNIX system, try the command below. In most cases this corrects the problem.

stty erase [press the Backspace key]

---

4. E-Mail

To send electronic mail (e-mail) on the Internet, you need to know the addressee's user name and the name of the Internet site. Most e-mail can be sent using the following form:

username@site.address

For example, you can send e-mail to the President with the following address:

president@whitehouse.gov

To find a person's e-mail address, you will need to ask her or look it up in an Internet white pages or yellow pages. These directories are available at some sites, but keep in mind that many services do not publish a list of their users.

To send e-mail on a service that provides a user interface, you simply select the mail option and enter your message. On UNIX systems, e-mail is sent and received using *elm* or *pine*. Elm is an e-mail program that uses menus to help you read and send mail. Pine is like Elm but has additional features such as an address book, word wrapping, and spell checking. Most of the commands are used in conjunction with the [Ctrl] key. For example, the command for "page down" is ^V. The caret symbol represents the [Ctrl] key.

5. Mailing Lists

Many special interest groups on the Internet exchange information through mailing lists. Messages are e-mailed to the list and handled by a central moderator who then either sends the message out to all of the subscribers to the list or compiles them into a digest. You can find a list of the available mailing lists and their topics in the Usenet newsgroup:

news.announce.newusers

You can subscribe to a mailing list by sending an e-mail message to the list using one of the following two forms:

listserv@site.address

majordomo@site.address

In the message portion of your e-mail, type *subscribe listname username@site.address*. The "listname" will be the actual name of the list. The user name and site address are your e-mail address. Once you are a subscriber, you can send a message to the mailing list by addressing your e-mail message to

listname@site.address

To unsubscribe to a mailing list, prepare an e-mail message in the same manner as you did to subscribe, but in the message portion type *unsubscribe listname.*

Law-related mailing lists can be found in legal resource sites on the World Wide Web. One job listing mailing list is shown below with its e-mail address and the format for subscribing to the list.

Lawjobs-L@lawlib.wuacc.edu listserv@lawlib.wuacc.edu
subscribe lawjobs-L your e-mail address

6. Usenet

When a mailing list grows large enough, it becomes a newsgroup. Newsgroups are similar to bulletin board systems and on-line message boards. **Usenet** is a network separate from the Internet that handles these newsgroups. Internet sites and other systems such as bulletin boards can choose to carry Usenet. When you subscribe to a newsgroup, you do not receive e-mail as you would with a mailing list. Instead, you post messages within the newsgroup or read the messages found there. On systems with a user interface, there will be a menu item or icon to click on to access Usenet newsgroups. You will then select menu options until you reach the newsgroups that you want.

On UNIX systems you will need to use a special software program called a "newsreader" to access Usenet newsgroups. The most common newsreaders are:

nn

nr and

trn

To access a specific newsgroup, you will type the newsreader's command name followed by the name of the newsgroup in the form shown below:

nn newsgroup or

nr newsgroup or

trn newsgroup

A good place to start is in the newsgroup *news.announce.newusers.* To reach that newsgroup in your newsreader, you would type:

nn news.announce.newusers or

nr news.announce.newusers or

trn news.announce.newusers

If you enter the newsreader simply by typing its command name, you will be bombarded with all of the newsgroups on your computer system and asked if you would like to subscribe. You will need to go through these once, saying "no" to virtually every listing. Thereafter when you enter the newsreader, you will only see those groups to which you are subscribed and the listings of new groups available to you. Each newsreader uses different commands to read and post messages. These commands can be reviewed by pressing the [help] key, which is usually the letter *h*. To find newsgroups regarding a particular topic such as "legal," do not enter the newsreader. At the UNIX prompt, type your newsreader's command to locate newsgroups on a specific topic. For the *nn* newsreader, you would type:

nngrep legal

For the *trn* newsreader, you would type:

trn legal

Usenet can be difficult to navigate at first. However, once you have subscribed to newsgroups that interest you, you will find that you are able to exchange information with people from many states and countries. Read your messages often; you will find that they build up very quickly. Some law-related newsgroups that you can subscribe to are listed below:

courts.usa.config
courts.usa.federal.supreme
law.library.future
law.listserv.net-lawyers
misc.legal
misc.legal.computing
misc.legal.moderated

7. Telnet

Telnet is a program that allows you to log into and execute commands on a remote computer. You can use Telnet to access library catalogs, databases, and information resources throughout the world. Like Usenet, access to Telnet is provided by many Internet sites. In systems with a user interface, you will select the Telnet option from a menu or icon. You can then type the name of the site that you wish to travel to or search for sites on a specific topic.

On UNIX systems you can enter Telnet by typing *telnet*. To Telnet to a specific site you will use the Open command to enter the name of the site. When you have finished with the site, you will use the Close command to close the connection. You can also Telnet directly to a specific site by using the following command form at the UNIX prompt:

telnet sitename

Each Telnet site has two addresses, one that is similar to normal domain names and one that consists of numbers. You may need to know both to enter some sites.

When you enter a Telnet site, your computer becomes a remote terminal of another computer. Since your computer is not a terminal, the communications package you are using will emulate a terminal. The Telnet site will ask you what type of terminal you are emulating. The most common terminal emulation is VT100. Also watch when you enter the site for the escape code used by the site and note it. The escape code will allow you to exit the site if you have a problem. The most common escape code is the [Ctrl] key in combination with the right square bracket key "]." You can also try the ~ key. At a Telnet site, you will either find a friendly menu system or a UNIX command line. Here you may need to know the UNIX commands that were previously discussed.

Many Telnet sites require that you provide a login name or register as a user in order to access the information available there. An interesting Telnet site that contains Supreme Court decisions and Ohio decisions can be found at *freenet-in-c.cwru.edu*. To find other law-related sites, you can look at Telnet listings on the World Wide Web. The sites for LEXIS/NEXIS and some law libraries that are available through Telnet are listed below. Any login and exit instructions are also given.

LEXIS/NEXIS	nex.lexis-nexis.com	Login: Must know the terminal emulation beginning with a period (.vt100) Exit: Sign Off (.so) or Ctrl +]
Columbia University	pegasus.law.columbia.edu	Login: pegasus Exit: J on the main menu
Georgia State University	library.gsu.edu	Login: none required Exit: Type "quit"
New York University	mclib0.med.nyu.edu	Login: library Exit: D on the main menu
UC Berkeley, Boalt Hall	lawcat.law.berkeley.edu	Login: library Exit: D on the main menu
University of Nebraska	iris.unl.edu	Login: library Exit: D on the main menu
Washburn University	lib.wuacc.edu	Login: LIB Pick a terminal emulation (VT100) Exit: D on the main menu

8. FTP

FTP (File Transfer Protocol) is a program that is used to copy files from an Internet site to your account or computer. FTP is accessed from a menu or icon on services with a user interface. Once in the FTP area, you can FTP to a site by typing in the site name or search for sites or files. On UNIX systems, FTP is accessed by typing *ftp*. Once in the FTP program, an FTP site can be accessed with the Open command. To close the FTP program, you will type *close*. From the UNIX prompt you can travel directly to an FTP site by typing *ftp sitename*.

Once you reach an FTP site, you will login as *anonymous* unless you have an ID at that site. If you are admitted, you will then be given a prompt, such as *ftp*>, at which you can use UNIX commands such as *ls* to list files, *cd* to move between directories, and *pwd* to find where you are in the directory tree. When you find a file that you would like to transfer to your account or computer, you will type

get filename

Many of the file names and directory names are case-sensitive so pay attention to the case. If you are transferring a computer program, you will need to use the command *bin* before transferring the file. Transferred files will be placed in your account directory on your Internet service or in a directory on your computer.

If you are trying to find a file on the Internet, but you do not know the site name where the file is located, you can use the Archie search tool to find sites that contain the file. To access Archie, you need to Telnet to an Archie site, such as

archie.unl.edu

Once in Archie, you can search the Internet for a file using the Find or Prog command followed by all or part of the file name. For example, if you are looking for a file that has a name beginning with *legallist,* you could type

find legallist or
prog legallist

The listing will display the name of the FTP site where the file is located. The listing also displays the directory that contains the file. You can exit Archie by typing *quit,* and then FTP to the site containing the file, cd to the proper directory, and get the file.

Remember: You should not enter FTP sites during the business hours of 6:00 A.M. to 6:00 P.M.

9. Gopher and WAIS

Gopher and **WAIS** (Wide-Area Information Servers) are services that allow you to browse through files and documents on the Internet by topic. When you select a topic, the service scans the Internet for files or documents that are pertinent to that topic. Both services offer menus of topics. When you choose a menu topic, you often receive another menu. You continue to choose from menus until you reach a listing of files or documents. The difference between Gopher and WAIS is that Gopher menus are like the table of contents of a book while WAIS menus are like a book's index.

If your Internet provider has a Gopher service and a user interface, you will access it from a menu or an icon. On UNIX systems you will type *gopher.* Once you have entered the Gopher, you will select from menus until you reach the files or documents that you are interested in reading or transferring. In addition to Gopher sites, you will see menu items that will take you to FTP and WAIS sites. If you find a particularly interesting site, you can add it to a bookmark list by typing a capital *A*. Later, to access the bookmark list, type the letter *v*. If you would like to see the site address for a menu item, highlight the menu item and press the equals key "=". The site name will be listed amid other information. Some common Gopher commands are listed below:

a Add a menu line item to your bookmark list.
A Add an entire Gopher menu to your bookmark list.
v View your bookmark list.
d Delete any entry from your bookmark list.
s Save highlighted file to your home directory.
= View the site name of a highlighted menu item.
u Move up in the menu structure.
q Quit or exit the Gopher.

If you know the name of a Gopher site, you can go directly to it from the UNIX prompt by typing *gopher sitename.* On systems with a user interface, there will be a place to enter a specific site name to travel to.

If you would like to search through the Gophers without traveling through endless menus, you can use the Veronica or Jughead search tools. Veronica will search all Gophers for menu items that contain specified words. Jughead searches within a confined area, such as your network system's Gopher menus. You will find the Veronica and Jughead search tools under one of the menu items on your Gopher service. Searches are conducted using key words and connectors such as "and" and "or." For example, to find all menu items with the words "law" or "legal" you would type the search as *law or legal.*

WAIS databases can be found through the Gopher menus or by using a WAIS client program. If your system has a WAIS client program and a user interface, you will select the program from a menu or an icon. On UNIX systems you will type *swais.* When you enter the WAIS client program, you will see a list of databases. Typing a capital *K* will take you to the next page. A capital *J* will move you back a page. To select a database to search, move the cursor bar over the database name and press the [Space Bar]. An asterisk will appear next to the line number. Repeat this until you have selected all of the databases that you wish to search. Once you have selected your databases, pressing the letter *w* will prompt you for key words to use in a search of the databases. Separate each key word with a space. When you press the [Enter] key, the search will begin. The search will be completed in about a minute and a new menu will appear with a list of articles that contain your key words. Highlight the menu item for an article that you want to read and press the [Enter] key.

10. The World Wide Web

The **World Wide Web** ("Web") is part of the Internet that is connected by hypertext links. Hypertext allows you to travel to another document or site by selecting an underlined portion in the document you are currently viewing. A good example of hypertext is found in the help menus in many Windows programs. Web sites contain documents that consist of text, images, sound, and video. Most Internet service providers have a World Wide Web graphical interface, called a Web browser, that allows you to easily access Web sites and other Internet services. On UNIX systems, you will access the Web by typing *www* or the command name of your text interface, such as *lynx*.

Once you have accessed the Web, you will reach your site's home page. America Online's home page is shown in Figure 11.3. As you travel through the Web, clicking on hypertext links that take you to other computers throughout the world, you may get lost. Graphical interfaces have a left arrow button that will take you back to the previous page and a home button that will take you

FIGURE 11.3 America Online's home page on the World Wide Web.

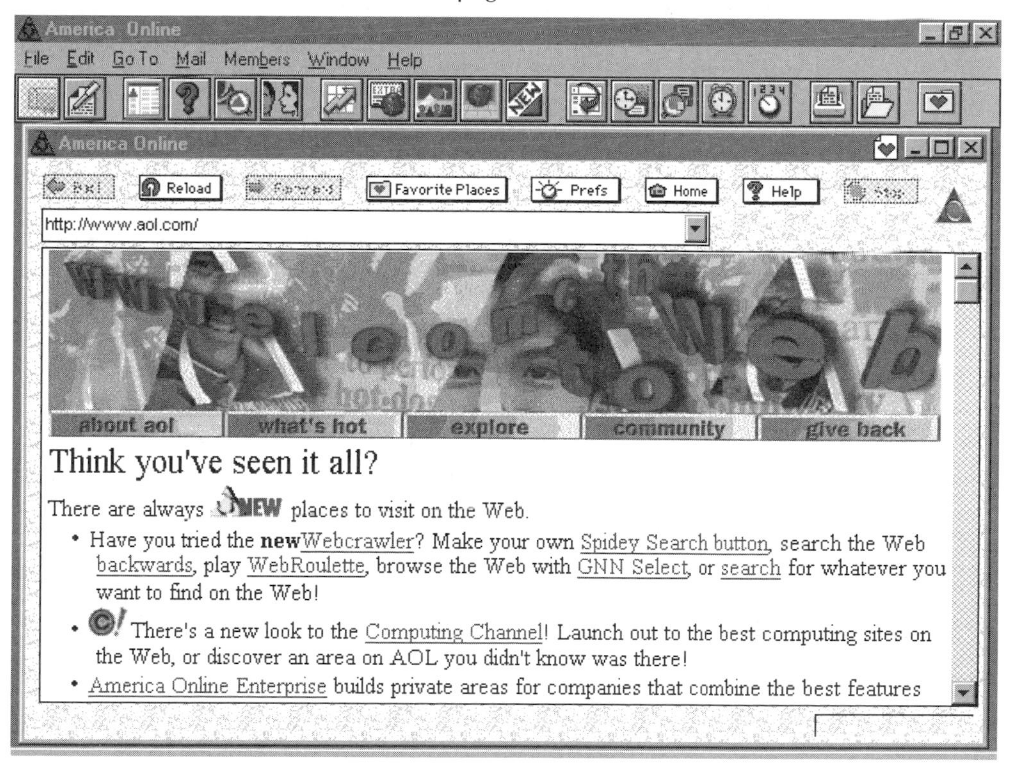

back home. With text interfaces, you use your [Up Arrow] and [Down Arrow] keys to move up and down the page. The [Right Arrow] key will follow a hypertext link to a new site. The [Left Arrow] key will take you back to the previous site. To return home there will be a menu option for "Home" or "Main Screen."

To travel directly to an Internet site you need to know its **URL** (Uniform Resource Locator). The URL is the resource name followed by the site address. Common resource names are

http://

telnet://

ftp://

gopher://

Your Web browser may or may not be able to access Telnet, FTP, or Gopher sites through the Web. HTTP (Hypertext Transport Protocol) sites are Web sites. In graphical Web browsers there will be a line where you can enter the URL. In text Web browsers, you will need to select the menu option for "Go," and then type in the URL.

If you do not know the URL of a site that you want to travel to, you can find sites on a particular subject using a **search engine.** Search engines are Web sites that allow you to type in key words and have the search engine find sites containing those key words. Popular search engines are Yahoo and Lycos. They can be found at the following sites:

http://www.yahoo.com

http://www.lycos.com

Once you find a site that contains information that interests you, you can add the site to your Web browser's bookmark list or favorite places. A list of favorite sites for accessing legal information is given below. Please note that sites change their addresses and may be here one day and gone the next. Also, note that you may not know who has uploaded the legal information. Do not rely on, or quote from, legal information that you find on the Internet. Double-check the information on LEXIS or WESTLAW, CD-ROM, or in the bound volumes.

Legal Information on the Web

Type of Information	*Site Name*
Legal Information Institute—Cornell University	http://www.law.cornell.edu
WWW Virtual Library—Law	http://www.law.indiana.edu/law/lawindex.html

Leflaw's Virtual Law Library—Links to Law Sites	http://leflaw.com/general.html
Internet Law Library—U.S. House of Representatives	http://www.pls.com:8001/
LEXIS/NEXIS	http://www.lexis-nexis.com

E. SUMMARY

There is a wide range of information available to the legal professional on-line. Bulletin board systems are message boards that you can access through a communication software package to send and receive messages and files. Commercial on-line services are accessed through their own software package and provide information, e-mail services, files, and gateways to the Internet. The Internet is a network of networks. It is made up of mailing lists, Usenet newsgroups, Telnet sites, FTP sites, Gopher and WAIS sites, and the World Wide Web. You will access these sites through a user interface or directly from an operating system such as UNIX. Mailing lists are sites where subscribers send e-mail to be distributed to all of the other subscribers. Usenet newsgroups are message boards where you can post and read messages on a particular topic. Telnet sites are remote computers that you can connect to and access library catalogs and services such as LEXIS/NEXIS. FTP sites are sites that make the files on their computers available for downloading. Gopher and WAIS sites search for documents and files on the Internet, and then make the information available through a series of menus. The World Wide Web is a collection of sites that are connected through hypertext links and contain documents that consist of text, images, sound, and video. To find legal information on the Internet, you either need to know the name of the site or you need to use a search tool or search engine to locate sites that contain the information you want. On-line services and the Internet are growing daily, and there is a vast amount of legal information available through all of these services. Your challenge is to find it.

KEY TERMS

bulletin board system, 215
chat, 215
commercial on-line services, 218
cross-posting, 214
domain, 222
flaming, 214
FTP, 228
Gopher, 229
Internet, 221
search engine, 232
shouting, 214
spamming, 214
Telnet, 227
UNIX, 223
URL, 232
Usenet, 226
WAIS, 229
World Wide Web, 231

QUESTIONS

1. What is shouting? What is flaming?
2. What is the person called who monitors a bulletin board system?
3. How would you address an e-mail message to a person with the user name *pop* who has an account with America Online?
4. How can you access the Internet?
5. Which UNIX command will display your current location in the directory tree?
6. How do you subscribe to a mailing list?
7. What is Telnet?
8. How do you find a file on the Internet when you do not know the name of the site where it is located?
9. What is the World Wide Web?
10. What is a URL and what is it used for?

DISCUSSION QUESTIONS

1. If your college or university has an Internet site, how do you obtain an account? What type of interface does it have—graphical, text, or UNIX? Do you have access to a Web browser?
2. What sites have you found on the Internet that are of particular interest to you? Have you found any good paralegal sites?

Glossary

Application program. Software program that assists in the performance of business-related and personal tasks. This category of software includes programs that create documents, spreadsheets, and databases and produce billing statements.

Archiving. The process of removing files from the hard disk and storing them on tape or diskette.

Arithmetic/logic unit. The unit of the CPU that performs calculations and compares data.

Backup. The creation of a duplicate copy of a data file in case the original is lost or corrupted.

Bar code reader. An input device that scans a bar code and transmits the code to the computer. A distinct bar code is stored in the computer for each item in the bar coding system. The computer associates each scanned bar code with the item that it represents.

Bit. An individual unit of computer memory.

Boldface type. A darker than normal type used to add **emphasis** to a document.

Bulletin board system (BBS). A message board on-line computer system that is accessed by modem and allows users to post and retrieve messages or programs.

Byte. A memory storage unit for a single character. Usually made up of eight bits that are charged or not charged in an order that represents a given character.

Calendaring software. Software that is used to maintain the calendar of a firm, case, and/or individual. Similar to a wall calendar but with a variety of features that make calendaring more efficient.

Case management software. Software that is used to manage a firm's client, case, and calendaring information.

CD-ROM (Compact Disk-Read Only Memory). An optical disk that can only be read. Similar to music CDs, these disks require a special disk drive in order to be read by the computer. Many legal reference books are available on CD-ROM.

Cell. The intersection of a column and a row within an electronic spreadsheet in which text or values are placed.

Cell address. The address of a cell indicated by the column letter followed by the row number, such as "A1."

Cell entry. The contents of a cell.

Cell pointer. A dark rectangle that appears in one cell in an electronic spreadsheet. When data is entered, it is placed in the cell containing the cell pointer.

Centering. The positioning of text so that it will print in the center of the printed page or item.

Central processing unit (CPU). The computer's brain. Comprised of an arithmetic/logic unit, a control unit, and main memory.

Chat. An on-line multi-user discussion of a general or specific topic.

Clicking. A mouse action performed by pointing to an object with the mouse pointer and pressing a mouse button.

Column. In an electronic spreadsheet, the vertical divisions in the spreadsheet.

Columns. Used to create columns of text in word processing documents. Can be in parallel or newspaper form. Parallel columns are read from left to right; newspaper columns are read from the top to the bottom of the first column, and then to the top of the next column to the right.

Commercial on-line services. On-line information services that provide their users with e-mail capabilities, access to services and information sources and exchanges, and gateways to access some or all of the Internet.

Communications software. Software that allows a computer to communicate with another computer or machine such as a fax machine.

Computer-assisted legal research (CALR). The use of a computer to perform legal research.

Computer language. Codes used to create computer programs and software.

Connectors. In databases, used to connect two or more search conditions or key words. Common connectors are AND, NOT, and OR.

Contingency plan. The creation of a plan to follow in the event of a breakdown in the computer system.

Control unit. The unit of the CPU that directs the operations of the computer's hardware. It directs data entered from the keyboard to the other two units of the CPU and directs it to an output device when necessary.

Cross-posting. The posting of the same message to several on-line message boards or newsgroups. Considered a breach of on-line etiquette.

Cursor. The flashing line character or box displayed on the computer's screen, which indicates where data will be placed from an input device.

Data processing machine. A simple calculating machine used by companies prior to the use of computer systems. This machine was capable of calculating totals and sorting information.

Database. An organized collection of related data.

Database management systems (DBMSs). Computer software used to manage databases of information such as evidentiary documents, document forms, client information, conflict of interest information, and the like.

Dedicated word processor. A computer that performs word processing exclusively or has some other limited capabilities.

Deposition summarization software. Software that assists in the summarization of depositions by displaying the deposition transcript and preparing the summary from the portions of the transcript highlighted by the user.

Desktop. The main work space in Windows upon which windows are placed.

Dialog box. Boxes displayed in graphical operating environments such as Windows that request information from you or supply you with information that you may need.

Digital video disk (DVD). Optical disks that are similar to compact disks in size and appearance but are capable of storing many gigabytes of data.

Direct access. The data storage and retrieval method utilized by magnetic disks. The read/write head of the disk drive can access data or storage space directly, as opposed to running through the entire disk in order to find it.

Directory. Storage places created on a disk in which to keep related files.

Disk drive. A piece of computer hardware that contains a disk or into which a disk is inserted. Read/write heads within the disk drive read information from, and/or write information to, a disk.

Diskette. A magnetic disk that can be inserted and removed from disk drives at the front of the system unit. Often called a "floppy disk." There are two primary sizes of magnetic disks, 5¼-inch and 3½-inch.

Document. Computer-generated text.

Document codes. The visible or invisible indicators that identify where a word processing feature, such as a tab, underline, or bold, has been placed.

Document generation. The creation of a template document or form and the subsequent integration of the template with case information to create an individualized document.

Document management software. Software that requests information about a document when it is saved, and then allows you to easily find the document again through a document number or name or through a search by drafter's initials, client name, or the like.

Domain. A network server connected to the Internet. Each domain has a name, often called a site address, that identifies it on the Internet.

DOS (Disk Operating System). The primary operating system used by IBM-compatible microcomputers.

Double clicking. A mouse action performed by pointing to an item with the mouse pointer and pressing a mouse button twice in quick succession.

Dragging. A mouse action performed by pointing to an item with the mouse pointer, holding down a mouse button, and dragging an item or a window border to a new location.

Electronic mail. Also known as "e-mail," electronic mail is the use of a computer to send messages or mail to another computer.

Electronic spreadsheet software. Software used in the creation of spreadsheets for accounting and financial purposes or for the analysis of alternatives ("what if" scenarios).

Expansion slots. Openings at the rear of a system unit that enable the user to expand the features of a computer by adding circuit boards for devices such as a mouse or modem.

Field. In a database, a category of information to be abstracted from each item entered into the database file.

File. An information storage unit that stores parts of a software program or a document, spreadsheet, database, or other item created with a software program.

File server. The main computer in some network configurations. A file server contains the programs and data to be accessed by the workstations in the network.

Flaming. The posting of an on-line message that is violently argumentative or a personal attack on someone. Considered a breach of on-line etiquette.

Floppy disk. A magnetic diskette that can be inserted and removed from a disk drive at the front of the system unit. Primarily available in 5¼-inch and 3½-inch sizes.

Folders. Storage places created on a disk in which to keep related files. Similar to directories in DOS.

Fonts. Characters or symbols of a specific size and design that represent a type style.

Formatting. The act of preparing a magnetic disk or tape with sections for the storage of data.

Forms software. Software that contains the preprinted forms used by the court systems. The forms are completed on the computer in much the same manner as they would be with a typewriter.

Formula. In an electronic spreadsheet, performs a calculation on cells identified within the formula, such as "+A1+A2−A3."

FTP (File Transfer Protocol). A program used to copy files from an Internet site to your own computer.

Full-text database. A database that contains the full text or image of documents or other information stored within the database.

Function. A preprogrammed formula that is part of the program files of an electronic spreadsheet—for example, @SUM(A1..A3).

Gigabyte (GB). A byte measurement indicating approximately one billion bytes.

Global (wild card) characters. Special characters that can be used to represent one or more characters in DOS commands or database searches.

Gopher. An on-line service that allows you to browse through files and documents on the Internet by topic.

Handwriting recognition. The ability of a computer to understand and interpret handwritten characters and symbols on its input pad.

Hard disk. Magnetic disks that are rigid and normally fixed within the computer's system unit. Some hard disks are available in cartridge form and are removable from the system unit. Removable hard disks require a special disk drive.

Hardware. The tangible components of a computer system. Examples of hardware include the computer's system unit, monitor, keyboard, mouse, and printer.

Highlighting text. The act of marking or selecting text to perform some action upon it such as copying, moving, or deleting.

Holding. A mouse action performed by pointing to an item with the mouse pointer and holding down the mouse button until a particular effect or result is achieved.

Icon. A graphic that represents a program, disk, or file.

Imaging. The storing of a picture of a document or photograph on an optical disk. Often used to store case evidence in a database.

Input. Data that is entered into the computer with an input device or the act of entering data into the computer.

Input devices. Hardware devices that allow the user to input information into the computer for processing. Examples include a keyboard, mouse, scanner, bar code reader, and touch screen.

Input line. In an electronic spreadsheet, it is located above the spreadsheet and displays the contents of the cell or data as it is being entered.

Insert mode. In a word processing package, the mode in which characters typed at the cursor push existing characters to the right.

Integrated pointing device. A device mounted in some portable computers that resembles an eraser on the end of a pencil. The pointer on the screen moves in the direction that the device is pressed.

Internet. The largest computer network in the world. A network of networks, the Internet began as a Defense Department research project. Today the Internet consists of host computers operated by universities, government agencies, businesses, and organizations that connect their computers to the Internet to provide reference materials, information, products, services, and communications to other Internet users.

Italicizing. A typeface that slants the characters to the right. Italicizing is often used to add *emphasis* within documents.

Justification. The positioning of text in relation to the left and right margins of a page or cell.

Keyboard. The primary input device of a computer, it contains alphanumeric keys and keys that perform other computer functions.

Key words. Words used in searches of some databases. These words are those that are likely to be contained within the cases, statutes, articles, or other materials for which one is searching.

Kilobyte (KB). The measure of computer memory representing approximately one thousand bytes.

LEXIS. The computer-assisted legal research database.

Local area network (LAN). Two or more microcomputers cabled together to share information and peripheral devices such as printers and modems. A local area network can also be a part of a mainframe or minicomputer system of computers.

Macintosh. The microcomputer and operating system manufactured by Apple Computer. The operating system contains a graphical operating environment that uses icons and pull-down menus that can be manipulated using a mouse or the keyboard.

Macro. A group of keystrokes that are recorded, labeled, and then executed with a simple key combination.

Magnetic disk. A round rigid or flexible disk that stores data magnetically on its surface.

Magnetic tape. A tape that stores data magnetically on its surface. Can be stored on reels or within cartridges.

Mainframe. The largest type of computer in terms of size, storage capacity, and speed. A mainframe computer system consists of several terminals or PC workstations cabled to the mainframe.

Main memory. The computer's primary memory stored on chips. Main memory consists of ROM (Read Only Memory) and RAM (Random Access Memory). ROM contains permanent data, which can be used by the computer but cannot be altered; RAM holds programs and data awaiting processing or transfer to a secondary storage device.

Main memory unit. The unit of the CPU that contains the computer's primary memory, ROM and RAM.

Massively parallel processing. An internal processing configuration consisting of multiple microprocessors linked together to divide computing tasks.

Megabyte (MB). The measure of computer memory representing approximately one million bytes.

Merging. In a word processing software program, the act of combining a shell document with input information or the contents of a secondary file.

Microcomputer. The smallest type of computer in terms of size, storage capacity, and processing speed, also known as a personal computer or PC. Microcomputers can be operated by themselves or can be connected to a network, minicomputer system, or mainframe system.

Microprocessor. The CPU of a microcomputer.

Minicomputer. The intermediate type of computer in terms of size, storage capacity, and processing speed. Minicomputer systems contain several terminals or PC workstations cabled to the main computer. Minicomputers can also be networked with other minicomputers or microcomputers.

Modem. A device that allows a computer to contact another computer through the telephone lines. The modem in the sending computer takes the computer's digital signals and translates them into analog signals for transportation on the telephone line. A modem in the receiving computer takes the analog signals and translates them back into digital signals.

Monitor. A hardware device that displays data on a television-like screen. Also known as a CRT (cathode ray tube) or a VDT (video display terminal). A monitor may be monochrome (two-color) or color (three or more colors).

Mouse. An input device that rolls on a ball located on its bottom surface. The movement of the ball corresponds with the movement of a cursor or pointer on the screen. Buttons on the top of the mouse allow items to be selected.

Multimedia. The merging of text, sound, pictures, and motion in games, presentations, and other productions generated by a computer.

Multitasking. The ability to have multiple computer programs open in the operating system simultaneously.

My Computer. A feature found on the desktop in Windows 95 that will display the contents of disk drives and allow for the changing of many of the computer's settings.

Operating environment. The presentation of an operating system to the user. A graphical operating environment will present the operating system through icons and pull-down menus that can be manipulated with a mouse or the keyboard.

Operating system. The collection of programs that manage the operations of the computer and allow the user to use software files and manage disk space.

Optical character recognition. The computer's ability to recognize text from a scanned document.

Optical disk. A data storage device that stores the image of text and pictures.

OS/2. The operating system and graphical operating environment available for IBM-compatible microcomputers.

Output. Processed data, which is sent to an output device for storage, printing, or display.

Output device. A hardware device that stores or displays the results of a computer's processing. Examples of output devices are printers and monitors.

Page break. The place within a word processing document where one page ends and another begins. A hard page break may be placed in a specific place by the user in order to break the page at a location different from the one selected by the computer.

Passwords. Letters, numbers, and characters that identify a user to the computer in order to obtain access to a computer, a disk drive, or a file.

Path. The location of a file consisting of its drive letter and directory or folder location. The path may also contain the file's name. An example of a path would be C:\personal\resume.

Peripheral devices. Hardware devices that are connected to a computer system. Printers, modems, and external hard disk drives or CD-ROM drives are examples of peripheral devices.

Personal computer (PC). A microcomputer.

Plotter. Graphics printers that print using drawing pens selected by a drawing arm.

Pointing. A mouse action performed by moving the mouse pointer with a mouse in order to point to an item to be selected.

Printer. An output device that prints data onto paper or other medium. The two categories of printers are impact and nonimpact. Impact printers impact the paper with some part of the printer hardware; nonimpact printers transfer the characters without striking the paper with the printer hardware.

Printing. The act of sending a hard copy of a file to a printer.

Program. A set of instructions written in a computer language that tells the computer how to perform a specific task. Also known as software.

Proximity operators. Connectors within a database search that tell the database to look for a term or condition within a certain proximity of another term or condition.

Pull-down menus. Menus at the top of a window or screen that pull down from the menu title when selected.

Punched card. Cards upon which holes are punched to represent data or instructions. The card is inserted into a card reader, which detects the holes and translates the position of the holes into data or instructions understood by the computer.

Query. A search within a database.

RAM (Random Access Memory). Temporary memory that is utilized, while the computer is operating, to store data that is being processed or awaiting storage on a secondary storage device. When the computer is turned off, RAM is erased.

Range. A group of cells identified by the address of the cell in the upper left corner of the range and the address of the cell in the lower right corner of the range.

Read/write head. Part of a magnetic disk drive that reads data stored on the disk or writes data to the disk by placing magnetized spots upon the disk.

Record. In a database, the group of field entries for each item contained within the database.

Recycle Bin. A feature found on the desktop in Windows 95 that contains files that have been removed from the computer system but are still available to be restored. Emptying the Recycle Bin deletes the files.

Relational operators. Symbols used in database programs to identify the type of data to be located with a search. The common relational operators are =, <, >, < =, > =, and <>. Relational operators are also referred to as "comparative operators."

ROM (Read Only Memory). The computer's permanent memory, which can be read but not written to or altered during normal computer operations. The computer's manufacturer stores information and instructions within the ROM to make communications possible between the CPU and the computer's hardware.

Root. The main directory on a magnetic disk.

Root expanders. Used in database searches to locate words with a common root. For example, "motor!" will locate *motorboat, motorcycle, motorized,* and the like.

Row. The horizontal divisions in an electronic spreadsheet.

Scanner. An input device that reads printed pages or images into the computer.

Search engine. A World Wide Web site that will search for other sites based on categories that you choose or key words that you enter.

Secondary file. In a merge function, the file that contains the information to be combined into the shell document or primary file.

Secondary memory storage. The type of memory storage where data can be permanently stored until erased. Includes magnetic disks, magnetic tape, and optical disks. Also referred to as "auxiliary memory storage."

Sequential access. The method of data storage and retrieval utilized by magnetic tape. The tape runs sequentially from beginning to end to locate data or a blank spot to store new data.

Service bureaus. Companies that process information on their own computers for others. Clients submit information to the bureau, which then inputs the information into its computers for processing.

Shell document. In a merge function, the form document into which information or the contents of a secondary file are merged. Also called the "primary file."

Shortcut. A feature used in Windows 95 that creates an icon to quickly activate a program or file. Shortcuts can be placed on the desktop, in the Programs menu, or in folders.

Shouting. Typing a message on-line using all capital letters. A breach of on-line etiquette except in cases where you do want to shout.

Software. The coded instructions that direct the operation of a computer. Also known as a program.

Spamming. The posting of a message to an on-line message board or newsgroup that does not relate to the topic of the message board or newsgroup. Considered a breach of on-line etiquette.

Speech recognition. The ability of a computer to interpret speech into data understood by the CPU.

Spell checking. The computer's comparison of the words contained within a document with the words contained within a dictionary file. When a match does not occur, the spell checking feature informs the user and may give alternative spellings.

Subdirectory. A directory created as a subpart of another directory.

Summary database. A database that stores the summary or an abstract of data from a document or item. Also referred to as "relational," "flat file," "bibliographic," "abstract," and "index" databases.

Supercomputer. Computers designed to perform calculations at the maximum speed permitted by existing technology.

System backup. The creation of a duplicate copy of data files in a computer system in case the originals are lost or corrupted. A system backup can be full or incremental.

System unit. The computer's main unit, which houses the central processing unit, circuit boards, main memory, and disk drives.

Table. A word processing feature consisting of columns and rows similar to those found in an electronic spreadsheet. The intersection of a column and a row forms a cell in which data is entered.

Telnet. A program that allows you to log into and execute commands on a remote computer. Access to Telnet is provided by many Internet sites.

Template. A piece of plastic or other material that lies above or around the function keys on a keyboard and describes their functions.

Terabyte. A byte measurement indicating approximately one trillion bytes.

Terminal. A monitor and keyboard (sometimes referred to as a "dumb terminal"). A terminal does not contain a processing unit and is dependent on the computer to which it is connected.

Text. In an electronic spreadsheet, a type of data that consists of alphanumeric characters (letters, special characters, and numbers not intended for mathematical calculations).

Thesaurus. A word processing feature that provides synonyms for words selected by the user.

Time and billing software. Software used to keep track of legal professionals' billable hours, allocate the billed time to the appropriate clients, and produce invoices and accounting statements.

Time sheet. A document, usually prepared daily, that is used to enter the date, client and matter name, work performed, and the time spent performing the work.

Time slip. A billing slip that is prepared for each task, or group of tasks, that is performed on a particular matter during a day. The biller notes the date, client and matter name, work performed, and time spent performing the work.

Time-sharing systems. A computer system in which data storage space and processing time are rented to clients.

Touch pad. A touch-sensitive pad mounted in some portable computers. Moving a finger across the pad moves the screen pointer in the same direction on the screen.

Touch screen. A special monitor that allows a user to input information by touching the computer's screen with a finger or an electronic pen.

Track ball. Similar to an upside-down mouse and either clipped to the side of a portable computer or mounted in the computer's case. As the user spins the ball, the screen pointer moves in the direction of, and with the speed of, the ball's motion.

Tree. The map of a directory structure beginning with the root directory and branching out to the various subdirectories of the root and their individual subdirectories.

Typeover mode. In a word processing package, the mode in which characters typed at the cursor replace existing text.

Underlining. The placing of a line under a word or item.

UNIX. An operating system used by some microcomputers and minicomputers. Used by many of the networks that are connected to the Internet.

URL (Uniform Resource Locator). A location of an Internet site that includes the resource name (e.g., http://) and the site address.

Usenet. A network separate from the Internet that handles newsgroups. Newsgroups are similar to bulletin board systems and on-line message boards, in that you can read and post messages on a subject that interests you.

User. A person using a computer or software program.

Utility program. Programs that help users operate their computers more efficiently. Programs that can undelete files, unformat disks, or back up files to magnetic tape fall into this category.

Values. In an electronic spreadsheet, a type of data that consists of numbers intended for use in mathematical calculations, formulas, and functions.

WAIS (Wide-Area Information Servers). Server sites that can be contacted to locate computer files and documents on the Internet by topic.

WESTLAW. The computer-assisted legal research database operated by West Publishing Company.

"What if" scenario. The analysis of several different assumptions to find the best results. Often used by legal professionals with electronic spreadsheets.

Wide area network (WAN). A network of computers connected through dedicated telephone lines. Often used by law firms with offices in different cities to connect all of their computers together to share information.

Wild card characters. Special characters that can be used to represent one or more characters in DOS commands or database searches.

Window. A rectangular area on the screen in graphical operating environments that contains a software program, software icons, or folders and files. Windows can be moved on the screen, can be made larger or smaller, and can be placed on top of one another.

Windows. The operating environment manufactured by Microsoft that takes the DOS operating system and presents it to the user in a graphical interface with icons and pull-down menus.

Windows Explorer. A feature found in Windows 95 that is similar to the File Manager in the Windows operating environment for DOS. This feature provides a familiar method for Windows users to manage their folders and files.

Windows 95. An operating system developed by Microsoft that enhances the DOS and Windows combination by creating a more user-friendly graphical interface.

Word processing. The use of a computer to create a document.

Word processing software. Software that facilitates the creation of documents using a computer.

Word wrap. A word processing feature that continues the typed text to the next line without the user having to press the [Enter] key.

Workstation. An individual computer, usually a microcomputer (PC), cabled to a local area network, a minicomputer system, or a mainframe system.

World Wide Web (WWW). A part of the Internet connected by hypertext links that allows a user to travel to other sites and documents by selecting underlined text or graphics in a Web page on the screen.

WORM (Write Once Read Many). The storage method of some optical disks. Data is stored on the disk and then cannot be altered.

Write protect tab. A piece of tape, usually supplied by a diskette manufacturer, that is placed over the write protect notch on a 5¼-inch diskette to prevent the data on the diskette from being altered.

Index

ABA Electronic Data Retrieval Committee, 7
Accounting, computer use in, 47-51
American Bar Association (ABA), 7
Application programs, 47
Archiving files, 208
Arithmetic/logic unit, 18
Assembly programming language, 42
Auxiliary memory storage. *See* Secondary memory storage

Bar code reader, 34
BASIC programming language, 42, 43
Bits, 20
Bulletin board systems
  accessing, 216, 217
  defined, 215
  downloading files, 217
  exiting, 218
  explained, 215-218
  FIDOnet, 215
  law-related, 218
  Sysop, 215
  Usenet, 215, 226, 227
  WWIVnet, 215
Bytes, 20, 21

Calendaring software, 57, 58
CALR. *See* Computer-assisted legal research
Case management software, 56, 57
CD-ROM
  databases, 186, 187
  defined, 12, 27-28
  drives, 70, 99
  legal research and, 14, 63, 175
Central processing unit (CPU)
  defined, 18
  supercomputers, 5
Clock speed, 21
COBOL programming language, 42
Communications
  defined, 37-39
  electronic mail (e-mail), 38, 39, 64, 214, 219, 220, 225
  fax boards, 64
  fax modems, 64
  local area networks (LAN), 38
  modems, 37, 38, 63, 64
  network software, 64
  software, 63, 64
  wide area networks (WAN), 38
Compact disks. *See* CD-ROM
Computer-assisted legal research (CALR)
  ABA demonstration (1960), 7
  CD-ROM. *See* CD-ROM
  connectors, 187, 188
  defined, 13, 185
  DIALOG, 185, 186
  first use of, 7, 14
  key words, 187, 188
  legislative drafting, use in, 9
  LEXIS. *See* LEXIS
  proximity operators, 187, 189
  root expanders, 187, 189
  WESTLAW. *See* WESTLAW
  wild card characters, 189
Computer languages, 42, 43
Computers
  categories of, 4, 5
  communications, 37-39

defined, 3
first uses in the law, 6-11, 14
law office uses, 3, 4, 10, 12-14, 135, 136, 154, 175, 176
modern uses in the law, 12-14
paralegal use of, 12
processing, 4, 5
service bureaus, 10, 11, 14
time-sharing systems, 10, 11, 14
Contingency plans, 208, 209
Control unit, 18
Court automation, 10, 11, 13, 14
C++ programming language, 42
CPU. *See* Central processing unit

Damage calculation software, 53-55
Databases
CD-ROM, 63, 186, 187
database management systems, 60-63, 175
defined, 60-63, 175
explained, 175-191
full-text databases
CD-ROM, 63
connectors, 187, 188
defined, 61, 63, 176
explained, 185-190
key words, 187, 188
litigation support, 187
optical disks, 186, 187. *See also* Imaging
proximity operators, 187, 189
queries, 188-190
root expanders, 187, 189
searching in, 61, 187-190
wild card characters, 189
imaging, 59, 187
law office uses, 175, 176
legal research. *See* Computer-assisted legal research
LEXIS. *See* LEXIS
relational databases. *See* summary databases, below
summary databases
comparative operators, 177, 178
connectors, 178-180
defined, 60-63, 175, 176
entering records, 61, 182, 183
explained, 176-185
fields, 60, 61, 176, 177
files, 60, 176
records, 60, 177
relational operators, 177, 178
searching in, 61, 183-185
setting up, 180-183
WESTLAW. *See* WESTLAW
Data processing machines, 9-11
Decision prediction, computer use in, 9, 14
Deposition summarization software, 59
DIALOG, 185, 186
Digital video disks (DVD), 28, 29
Direct access data storage and retrieval, 7, 27-28
Directories, DOS, 70, 71
Disk drives
defined, 23
density, 25, 73, 74
DOS drive labels, 70, 99
Diskettes (floppy disks)
care of, 26
defined, 21-26
density, 25, 73, 74
locking, 25-26
write protection, 25-26
write protect tabs, 25-26
Document creation. *See* Word processing
Document generation, 51, 52
Document imaging software, 59
Document management software, 55, 56
DOS (Disk Operating System)
command list, 89-91
commands. *See* DOS commands
defined, 43, 44, 69, 70
directories, 70, 71
disk drive labels, 70
disk drives, moving between, 70
disk organization, 70-72
explained, 69-89
file names, 72, 73
files, 72, 73
global characters, 77, 87, 88, 91

law office disk organization, 201-205
prompt, 70, 72
root directory, 70, 71
running an application, 88, 89
subdirectories, 71
tree, 71
wild card characters. *See* global characters, above
DOS commands
changing directories (CD, CHDIR), 82-84, 90
changing the prompt (PROMPT), 70, 72
checking a disk (CHKDSK), 43, 44
comparing disks (DISKCOMP), 90
copying disks (DISKCOPY), 87, 90
copying files (COPY), 43, 85, 90
deleting files (DEL), 86, 90
DIR, 74-79, 89
DIR/P, 77, 78, 89
DIR/W, 78, 79, 89
erasing files (ERASE), 43, 86, 90
explained, 73-87
FORMAT, 43, 73, 74, 90
listing files and directories. *See* DIR, above
list of, 89-91
making directories (MD, MKDIR), 79-82, 90
PATH, 90
PROMPT, 72
removing directories (RD), 84, 85, 90
renaming files (REN, RENAME), 85, 86, 90
TREE, 90
wild cards, 77, 87, 88, 91

Electronic Data Retrieval Committee (ABA), 7
Electronic mail (e-mail), 38, 64, 214, 219, 220, 225
Electronic spreadsheets
absolute cell addresses, 159, 160
adjustment of columns and rows, 157, 158
automatic recalculation, 158
cell addresses, 155, 159, 160
cell entries, 156, 157
cell pointer, 155
cells, 155
columns, 154, 155
copying cells, 160, 161
defined, 52, 53, 153
estate planning, use in, 53, 163
explained, 153-169
family law, use in, 53, 165
formulas, 156, 157
functions, 156, 157
input line, 157
legal professionals' use of, 154
moving cells, 160, 161
printing, 161
ranges of cells, 156
relative cell addresses, 159, 160
rows, 154, 155
tax planning, use in, 53, 165
text in, 156
values in, 156, 157
"what if" scenarios and, 161-168
Estate planning, electronic spreadsheets and, 53, 163
Evidence management, 12. *See also* Databases
Expansion slots, 17

Family law, electronic spreadsheets and, 53
FAT. *See* File allocation table
Fax boards, 64
Fax modems, 64
File allocation table (FAT), 22
File server, 4, 38
Files, DOS, 72, 73
Floppy disks. *See* Diskettes
Formatting a disk, 22, 73, 74, 90, 104, 127
Forms software, 57-59
FORTRAN programming language, 42
FTP, 214, 215, 228, 229
Full-text database. *See* Databases
Function keys, 30-31

Gigabyte, 20, 21
Gigaflops, 5
Gopher, 229-231

Handwriting recognition, 35
Hard disk, 21-24
Hardware
  defined, 6, 17
  input devices. *See* Input devices
  output devices. *See* Output devices
  system unit. *See* System unit
  types of, 17-39

IBM 650, 7
Icons, 96, 97, 116, 118
Imaging
  databases, 59-61, 187
  software, 59
Input, 4
Input devices
  bar code readers, 34
  defined, 6, 30
  handwriting recognition, 35
  integrated pointing devices, 33
  keyboards, 30, 31
  mouses, 32, 33
  punched cards, 31-32
  scanners, 32
  speech recognition, 35
  touch pads, 33
  touch screens, 34, 35
  track balls, 33
  types of, 30-35
Integrated pointing devices, 33
Intel Corporation, 5, 21, 22
Internet
  accessing, 222
  defined, 221, 222
  domains, 222
  e-mail, 225
  etiquette, 213-215
  FTP, 228, 229
  Gopher, 229-231
  legal research, 13, 14
  mailing lists, 225
  newsgroups, 226, 227
  TCP/IP, 222
  Telnet, 227, 228
  UNIX commands, 223, 224
  Usenet, 226, 227
  WAIS, 229-231
  World Wide Web, 13, 231-233

Juror selection, computer use in, 11

Keyboard
  defined, 30, 31
  function keys, 30-31
  templates, 31
Key words. *See* Databases
Kilobyte, 20

LAN. *See* Local area networks
Legal research. *See* Computer-assisted legal research
Legislative drafting, computer use in, 9, 14
LEXIS
  database contents, 185, 186
  introduction of, 8
  original databases, 8
  searches in, 187-190
Litigation support, computer use in
  databases, 175, 176, 187
  first use, 9, 11
Local area networks (LAN)
  advantages of, 5, 6
  defined, 4, 38, 64
  file servers, 4, 38
  law office use of, 4, 196, 199, 200
  workstations, 4, 38
Lotus 1-2-3, 6, 45, 154

Machine Language programming language, 42
Macintosh, 43, 45, 46
Magnetic disks
  defined, 21-26

direct access data storage method, 7, 26
diskettes. *See* Diskettes
file allocation table (FAT), 22-23
formatting, 22, 73, 74, 90, 104, 127
hard disks. *See* Hard disk
read/write head, 23
Magnetic tape
backup uses, 26
defined, 26
drives, 26
sequential access data storage method, 7, 26-27
Mainframe, 5, 14
Main memory
defined, 19
RAM. *See* Random Access Memory
ROM. *See* Read Only Memory
Massively parallel processing, 5
Megabyte, 20
Megahertz (MHz), 21
Microcomputers (PCS)
defined, 4, 5
local area networks. *See* Local area networks
Microprocessors, 5, 17, 21, 22
Microsoft Windows. *See* Windows operating environment
Minicomputer, 5
Modems, 37, 38, 63, 64
Monitor, 36
Mouses, 32, 33
MS-DOS. *See* DOS
Multimedia, 37
Multitasking, 20, 93

Netiquette, 213-215
Network communications, 64
Nuclear weapons tests, 5

Office automation
archiving files, 208
computer backups, 207, 208
computer organization, 201-209
computer purchasing, 196-201
contingency plans, 208, 209
disk organization, 201-205
explained, 195-209
file naming, 205-207
first uses of computers in, 9, 10, 14
local area networks, 196, 199, 200
passwords, 209
Ohio Bar Automated Research (O.B.A.R.), 8
On-line services
bulletin board systems. *See* Bulletin board systems
commercial services
accessing, 218, 219
America Online, 218
chats, 221
CompuServe, 218
defined, 218
downloading files, 220
e-mail, 219, 220
Internet gateways, 221
message boards, 221
Microsoft Network, 218
e-mail. *See* Electronic mail
etiquette, 213-215
FTP, 228, 229
Gopher, 229-231
Internet. *See* Internet
legal research, 13. *See also* LEXIS; WESTLAW
mailing lists, 225
newsgroups, 226, 227
Telnet, 227, 228
Usenet, 215, 226, 227
WAIS, 229-231
World Wide Web, 231-233
Operating environments
defined, 44, 45
Windows. *See* Windows operating environment
Operating systems
defined, 43-46
DOS, 43, 44. *See also* DOS
Macintosh, 45, 46
OS/2, 46
UNIX, 46
Windows 95, 45
Optical character recognition, 32, 187

Optical disks
  CD-ROM. *See* CD-ROM
  defined, 27-29
  Digital video disks, 28, 29
  evidence management and, 13
  rewritable, 29
  WORM disks, 29
OS/2, 43, 46
Output, 4
Output devices
  defined, 35-37
  monitors, 36
  plotters, 37
  printers, 36, 37
  speakers, 37

PASCAL programming language, 42
Passwords, 209
PC-DOS. *See* DOS
Pentium processor, 22
Pentium Pro processor, 5, 22
Peripheral devices, 4
Personal computer. *See* Microcomputers
Plotters, 37
Primary memory. *See* Main memory
Printers
  daisy wheel, 36
  defined, 36, 37
  dot matrix, 36
  impact, 36
  ink jet, 36, 37
  laser, 36, 37
  nonimpact, 36, 37
Programs, 4
Punched cards, 7, 9, 31-32

RAM. *See* Random Access Memory
Random Access Memory (RAM), 19, 20
Read Only Memory (ROM), 19, 20
Relational databases. *See* Databases
ROM. *See* Read Only Memory
Root directory, DOS, 70, 71
Root expanders, 187, 189

Sandia National Laboratories, 5
Scanners, 32
Secondary memory storage
  defined, 21-29
  magnetic disks, 21-26
  magnetic tape, 26-27
  optical disks, 27-29
Sequential access data storage method, 7, 26-27
Service bureaus, 10, 11, 14
Software
  accounting, 47-51
  application programs, 47
  calendaring, 12, 57, 58
  case management, 12, 56, 57
  categories of, 42-47
  communications, 63, 64
  computer languages, 42, 43
  copying, 64, 65
  copyright rules, 64, 65
  court reporting, 13
  damage calculating, 53-55
  database management systems, 12, 60-63
  defined, 6, 41
  deposition summarization, 59
  document generation, 51, 52
  document imaging, 59
  document management, 55, 56
  electronic spreadsheets, 52, 53
  ethical considerations, 64, 65
  forms, 57-59
  freeware, 65
  law office uses, 47-64
  operating systems, 43-46
  public domain software, 65
  shareware, 65
  time and billing, 47-50
  utility programs, 47
  word processing, 51
Speakers, 37
Speech recognition, 35
Spreadsheets. *See* Electronic spreadsheets
Subdirectories
  DOS, 71
  Windows, 106, 107
Summary databases. *See* Databases

System unit, 6, 17-21

Tax planning, electronic spreadsheets and, 53, 165
Telnet, 227, 228
Templates, keyboard, 31
Terabyte, 20
Teraflops, 5
Terminal, 5, 10, 136
Time and billing, computer use for, 12, 47-50
Time-sharing computer systems, 10, 11, 14
Time sheet, 47, 48
Time slip, 47-49
Touch pads, 33
Touch screens, 34, 35
Track balls, 33
Traffic courts, computer use in, 11

UNIX, 43, 46, 223, 224
Usenet, 215, 226, 227
User, 4
Utility programs, 47

WAIS, 229-231
WAN. *See* Wide area network
WESTLAW
  contents of, 185, 186
  introduction of, 8, 9
  key numbering system, 8
  searches in, 187-190
West Publishing Company, 8
Wide area network (WAN), 38, 64
Window, 94
Windows 95
  Control Menu, 117
  Control Panel, 117, 118, 120, 125
  defined, 45, 115
  desktop, 116
  dialog boxes, 117, 118
  diskettes, formatting, 127
  drive icons, 125
  entering from DOS, 129
  exiting a program, 124
  exiting Windows 95, 121, 129
  explained, 115-130
  file names, 123
  file paths, 123, 124
  files
    acting on several at once, 127
    copying, 127
    copying to diskette, 127
    deleting, 127
    managing, 125-127
    moving, 126, 127
    opening, 124
    renaming, 126
    saving, 124
  finding a folder or file, 121
  folders
    acting on several at once, 127
    copying, 127
    copying to diskette, 127
    deleting, 127
    managing, 125-127
    moving, 126, 127
    new, 126
    renaming, 126
  formatting, 127
  help, 121
  icons, 116, 118
  Menu Bar, 117
  mouse
    clicking, 116
    double clicking, 116
    dragging, 116
    holding, 116
    pointing, 116
    using, 115, 116
  MouseKeys option, 115
  My Computer, 116, 119, 121, 124-128
  printers, 120, 125
  program folders, 121, 122
  properties, 119
  pull-down menus, 123
  Recycle Bin, 116, 127
  running a program, 118, 121-124
  scroll bars, 117
  settings, changing, 120

shortcuts, 118, 119, 122, 128, 129
shut down, 121
sizing buttons, 116
Start button, 116, 119
Start menu, 119-122
starting a program, 122, 123
taskbar, 116, 120
title bar, 116
tree, 129
Windows Explorer, 119, 121, 128, 129
windows in, 116, 117
Windows operating environment
applications, running, 96, 98
Control Menu, 94, 95
defined, 44, 45, 93
desktop, 94
dialog boxes, 95, 98
directories
acting upon, 103, 104
copying, 103, 108
creating, 103, 105-107
defined, 100
deleting, 103, 104, 109, 110
moving, 103
disk drive labels, 99
disk drives, viewing contents of, 99
disks
acting upon, 104, 105
copying, 104, 105
formatting, 104
DOS prompt
returning to windows from, 111, 112
transferring to, 110, 111
entering a program, 96, 98, 105
exiting, 111, 112
exiting a program in, 106
explained, 93-112
File Manager, 99-105
file names, 101, 102
files
acting upon, 102
copying, 102, 103, 108
defined, 101, 102
deleting, 102, 109
moving, 102, 103, 107
opening, 102
saving, 105, 106
folders, 100, 103-105, 108. *See also* directories, above
Help, 99
icons, 96
adding, 97
deleting, 97
Main group window, 94
menu bar, 94
mouse
clicking, 94
double clicking, 94
dragging, 94
holding, 94
pointing, 94
using, 93, 94
multitasking, 20, 93, 110
program groups, 96, 97
Program Manager, 94
pull-down menus, 97, 98
screen settings, 98
scroll bars, 95
subdirectories, 106, 107
switching applications, 110
title bar, 94
windows in, 94, 95
window sizing buttons, 95
Word processing
backup options, 144
boldfacing, 138, 139
centering, 139, 140
columns, 144, 145
copying text, 138
cursor, 137
cutting and pasting text, 138
dedicated word processors, 136
defined, 51, 135
deleting text, 138
documents, 135
opening, 144
saving, 143
explained, 135-150
file names, 143
fonts, 142-143
highlighting text, 137, 138
indenting, 140

insert mode, 137
italicizing, 138, 139
justification, 139
law office uses, 135, 136
macros, 147, 149
merging, 146, 147
moving text, 138
opening a document, 144
page breaks, 140
primary file, 146. *See also* shell document, below
printing, 150
saving, 143
secondary file, 146
selecting text, 137, 138
shell document, 146
spell checking, 142
tabbing, 140
tables, 145, 146
thesauruses, 142
type styles, 142-143
typeover mode, 137
underlining, 138, 139
word wrapping, 136, 137
Workstations, 4, 38
World Wide Web, 13, 231-233
WORM disks, 59
Write protection of diskettes, 25
Write protect tab, 25